The Retirement Maze

The Retirement Maze

What You Should Know
Before and After You Retire

Rob Pascale,
Louis H. Primavera, and
Rip Roach

Based on a survey conducted in partnership with Marketing Analysts, Inc.

ROWMAN & LITTLEFIELD
Lanham • Boulder • New York • Toronto • Plymouth, UK

Published by Rowman & Littlefield
4501 Forbes Boulevard, Suite 200, Lanham, Maryland 20706
www.rowman.com

10 Thornbury Road, Plymouth PL6 7PP, United Kingdom

Distributed by National Book Network

British Library Cataloguing in Publication Information Available

Library of Congress Cataloging-in-Publication Data

The hardback edition of this book was previously cataloged by the Library of Congress
as follows:

Pascale, Rob, 1954–
  The retirement maze : what you should know before and after you retire / Rob
Pascale, Louis H. Primavera, and Rip Roach.
    p. cm.
  Includes bibliographical references and index.
  1. Retirement. 2. Retirement—Planning. I. Primavera, Louis H., 1943– II. Roach,
Walter (Rip), 1953– III. Title.
  HQ1062.P37 2012
  332.024'014—dc23   2011047875

ISBN: 978-1-4422-1618-1 (cloth : alk. paper)
ISBN: 978-1-4422-1619-8 (pbk. : alk. paper)
ISBN: 978-1-4422-1620-4 (electonic)

∞™ The paper used in this publication meets the minimum requirements of
American National Standard for Information Sciences—Permanence of Paper
for Printed Library Materials, ANSI/NISO Z39.48-1992.

Printed in the United States of America

Contents

Acknowledgments

$\mathcal{W}$e would like to thank the partners and staff at Marketing Analysts, Inc. Without their unswerving dedication, assistance, and generosity, this work would not have been possible. In particular, we are greatly indebted to Montey White for making sure our research was conducted at the highest quality and to Laura Simmons for her incredible patience and responsiveness in enduring our never-ending data processing requests. We would also like to thank Dr. Anne Primavera for her invaluable assistance in editing and fine-tuning our manuscript.

We owe a huge debt of gratitude to all of our respondents but particularly to those who had to tolerate the in-person interviews. While many eventually found the experience to be therapeutic, still our constant badgering with questions and then more questions required a great deal of commitment and soul-searching, sometimes painfully so, on their part. In the end, we are certain they will take pride in the fact that their efforts may come to help others who are experiencing the same issues in their retirement.

Finally, to all the social scientists researching this and other topics, we applaud you. These professionals work tirelessly to find ways to improve the human condition, often doing so with limited funds, for little compensation, and without the recognition they deserve. Theirs is truly a labor of love, and their efforts and insights were invaluable in directing many aspects of our own research on this subject.

I

A FRAME OF REFERENCE

· 1 ·

Motivations and Objectives

The trouble with retirement is that you never get a day off.

—Abe Lemons, basketball coach

If you were to ask our opinion about retirement, the answer might surprise you: "Be careful what you ask for. Retirement is a full-time job: it demands constant attention and a great deal of effort to do it well. If you're not up to the challenge, stay at work."

Most people will have to retire at some point, whether they want to or not; they'll start to sense that day approaching as they get to their early or mid-fifties, and as they get older it becomes more and more inevitable. Nevertheless, despite the fact that retirement looms for everyone, surprisingly few are truly prepared for it.

Our lack of preparedness may be a result of holding on to antiquated views of what retirement is all about. In the past, retirement was basically the few remaining years left to us after capping off a life of toil. But retirement has evolved. You can now spend as many years in retirement as you did in your career, and today those added years have led psychologists and sociologists to see it as a separate life stage. It has its own set of issues, problems, and phases of adjustment.

Unfortunately, it is a life stage often characterized by the loss of one's identity, sense of purpose, and, above all, structure to one's days—the things that many people derive from their work. From its onset, it entails the adoption of new roles, alternative ways of thinking, and new behavioral and attitudinal patterns. Retirement is very much about building a new life, mostly from the ground up and usually without much help. That's what makes it such a challenge.

We know—it sounds a bit scary, perhaps even daunting. Frankly, we hope it does, because armed with that knowledge, you may approach retirement with a little more vigilance. Now it's not necessarily a disaster for all. Many anticipate their retirement with enthusiasm, and a few even enjoy it when they get there. It can offer the freedom to pursue new interests and passions and the promise of relaxation and stress-free living. However, for some retirees-in-waiting, there can be worries, and sometimes these can be overwhelming. There are questions as to what their life will be like without the sense of meaningfulness—and often perceived financial security—that work provides. And for some who have already entered this phase, things may never be quite right. Even those who claim to love retirement will feel occasional discomfort after they give up their jobs. In walking into this shapeless void, almost all retirees may at some point ask themselves whether leaving the workforce was the right decision.

So it is for all retirees—the mostly adjusted and the not-yet adjusted—that we conducted the survey that underlies this book: a full-scale examination of the retirement adjustment process. By talking to retirees from all walks of life, we seek to understand how retirees go about creating their new lives, the difficulties they encounter along the way, and the tactics and strategies that led some to a successful transition.

From the insights of other retirees, we aim to chart a path through the maze, pointing out the blind alleys, dead ends, pitfalls, and other obstacles that lurk in the uncharted territory of retirement. With some light shed on the process, we hope to manage expectations for those about to retire so they won't be bushwhacked by events or situations they could not have anticipated. And we hope to offer assistance to those already retired so that they may come to understand that others share their difficulties adjusting and that there are ways around many problems.

We're not going to pull any punches here. Our goal from the onset has been to provide an honest assessment of retirement, starting from the not-always-acknowledged fact that it is a serious undertaking with lots of difficulties along the way. We will of course cover the many positive aspects of retirement, but we have not tried to present the negative elements as simple problems with simple solutions. In fact, we have devoted more of our attention to retirement's difficulties not out of a wish to be negative but rather from a belief that the positives of this life stage are their own rewards. So as you read on, we are going to take you on a journey through the various aspects of day-to-day living in retirement, one that may at times make you a little uncomfortable. But it's all for the good because in the end, you may see there is a light at the end of the tunnel.

We've done more than study retirement as just an intellectual exercise. One of us has lived it, and this book is a direct result of his experiences and his desire to help others going through the same process. Dr. Rob Pascale, research psychologist and founder of Marketing Analysts, Inc., a market research firm, decided to retire in 2005 at the age of 51. At that point in his life, he had planned his retirement for well over three years, first making sure his finances were in order and then exploring the ways he could build a new life. He thought he was doing everything right. He was well aware that he was entering an unknown world, but at that point—little did he know—the process still seemed to him simple enough. Rob had a number of outside interests that he expected would fill his time and let him feel productive and useful. At first, he enjoyed the lack of structure and freedom from daily responsibilities:

> Throughout my career, I lived by the clock, arriving at the office at 7 A.M. and heading home about 7 P.M. After a quick dinner, I often worked for a couple of hours. My life was very structured, and I defined myself as a person almost entirely based on what I did for a living. When I retired, the first few weeks of retirement were great. My days were completely stress free, and I felt liberated from all pressures. I didn't care what time I went to bed or woke up because to me every day was a holiday and every night Saturday night. I thought at the time that my life could not get any easier.

Gradually, however, the lack of structure and reduced sense of purpose caught up with him. Within a few months, with no need to be or go anywhere, he began to loosen his grooming habits, shaving less frequently and paying less attention to his wardrobe. Furthermore, despite his planning efforts and variety of interests, it became harder and harder to fill the hours of each day with things that were personally meaningful. One example in particular caught him by surprise. During his career, Rob had always thought he loved to paint, but soon after retiring, he realized that for him painting had actually been mostly a diversion, a way of breaking away from job-related pressures. When he retired and those pressures were eliminated, his interest in painting waned along with them.

A few months deeper into Rob's retirement, his initial joy eroded still further. He began experiencing frequent emotional ups and downs. At times he was happy about the freedom and lack of stress, but at other times he felt the loss of his personal identity and prestige, a sense of just drifting along aimlessly, feeling useless and unproductive. He felt his difficulties might have been compounded by the fact that, as an entrepreneur and business owner, his job had provided some level of prestige and a feeling of personal control over his life. As his retirement proceeded, he came to feel that both of those important aspects of his life had been radically diminished if not surrendered completely:

> At some point, I realized I had to come to terms with the fact that I am nobody. I was no longer an important contributor to the company I founded. My partners were focused on maintaining the business and no longer had much time for me, and my advice and opinions were no longer sought after. Whatever I accomplished before had no relevance to my life going forward.

Over time, it became increasingly clear to Rob that he had to break the emotional connection to his former life and start building something new. He realized that he had to approach his retirement as a full-time job, requiring the same effort and attention to detail as required from his career. Much to his surprise, Rob's acceptance of the idea that he was "a nobody" actually turned out to be a psychological breakthrough: he stopped bucking the tide, trying to hold on to his old role. From that point, he was able to open his mind to new ventures and had the freedom to begin looking for new fields to conquer. As he explored his options, he eventually adopted the idea of returning to his roots as a social scientist, but not without lots of hiccups along the way. That path he ultimately chose led to this book.

Of course, one person's problems are hardly the reason for a book. Rather, Rob saw it, much more importantly, as an opportunity to help others as he was helping himself: he figured that in all likelihood, he was not alone in experiencing difficulties and that other retirees were very likely running into similar problems.

And so he found himself with a unique opportunity to bring the experience of his former career to bear on a topic important to him and many others. Through a broad-based survey, he knew he could explore all the issues facing retirees. Certainly, there were a few he was aware of, but he also knew that there were probably others—perhaps many—that he had yet to face. He also believed that there could be ways of thinking and acting, unknown to him, that had helped some retirees to adjust effectively. A well-targeted survey might be able to point out the full range of challenges, both the obvious and the not so obvious. From there, it would be possible to come up with sound advice, based on actual retiree experiences, that with any luck might help recent and future retirees enjoy the most fruitful and rewarding retirement they can.

From there, our research project was born. We set out to interview a large number of retirees representing all walks of life. But we also wanted to talk to people still in the workforce. From our viewpoint, the not-yet retired can provide a frame of reference, a way to gauge changes in attitudes and behaviors that might occur in retirement. For example, comparisons between retirees and nonretirees might give us an idea as to whether leaving the workforce affects a retiree's psychological health, such as reduced stress. It's not that we expected to conclude directly that retirement reduces stress since there may be factors other than the job itself (e.g., no longer commuting) that can reduce stress after leaving the workforce. But there is considerable value in establishing the relationship between how one feels living in retirement versus living in the workforce.

But we also wanted to learn what nonretirees expected from retirement. Specifically, are they realistic about what is in store for them? If not, then that could affect how well they adjust when they actually do retire. To address this, we looked at what nonretirees think retirement would be like and compared their views to the actual experiences from real retirees. If, for example, those still working were more likely to consider retirement to be exciting in comparison to retirees' experiences, we'd have an idea that nonretiree expectations about retirement are unrealistic—an important piece of information, to be sure, because there may be ways to manage expectations if that is what is needed.

But first we had to deal with one crucial question: what exactly does it mean to be retired? How would we best define the very term that our entire project hinged on? In fact, arriving at a good working definition of retirement turned out to be a researcher's nightmare. The main issue is that many retirees continue to work, often for pay, but they still consider themselves retired. So, to conduct a truly comprehensive study of all retirees, we had to include both those who are working and not working. This brings us to another problem: how do you differentiate working retirees from nonretirees still in the workforce? We had to make sure we got this right; that we had retirees—working and nonworking—and nonretirees correctly classified, or our data would be useless. This was a very important issue for our research and a problem faced by other social scientists, so we had to come up with a sensible solution.

Social scientists believe that the definition of retirement has blurred, but it may be more accurate to say that the concept of retirement has evolved. Retirement is no longer seen as the complete end of work after a career of full-time jobs; instead, work is now seen as one potential element of the retiree lifestyle. However, there is a very important psychological distinction between employees still in the workforce and retirees who hold jobs. Working retirees tend to be less emotionally invested in their jobs and have more say as to the terms of their employment, such as the types of tasks performed or the number of hours worked. Also, retirees think of themselves as retirees. These distinctions—how they look at themselves and their jobs—are keys to coming up with a meaningful definition as to who is a retiree and who is a worker.

This may sound like a "fuzzy" or abstract concept—basing a definition on feelings—but its value may be illustrated clearly through a real-life example of two men who left their primary careers. Both did so in their mid-fifties: John as a police captain and Larry as a middle manager in a major corporation. After leaving the force, John took a position in his town as an assistant harbormaster, while Larry continued to work as an independent consultant for the company he left.

Despite their similar paths, Larry adamantly describes himself as retired, and John just as adamantly insists he is still working. In their new jobs, both work the same number of hours as in their original careers, but in fact Larry the retiree averages more working hours per week than John. When we discussed the differences between their perspectives with these two men, Larry explained that his decision to work was voluntary; he chooses the hours and days he works, and he could stop working at his own discretion. John, in contrast, believes he needs his job and as such has no choice in terms of task and time requirements, similar to other employees. Both appreciate the added income, but John feels he needs extra money to support his desired lifestyle; Larry doesn't feel that need since he is comfortable with his finances. In fact, both are at about the same levels financially and live very similar lifestyles; the difference between them is their perceptions of their financial status and not the actual amount of money they have, which have led to very different viewpoints as to which life stage each belongs to. So from the perspective of our research, Larry would be classified as a retiree, while we would classify John as a nonretired worker who only made a career change.

In large part, then, retirement is a state of mind—to be retired, one must believe he or she is retired, and that became part of our definition (along with having left their full-time career). Obviously, there are objective components to being retired: things like age and the termination of a long-term career clearly provide clues to someone's retirement status. But the subjective component, a personal sense or feeling that one is in fact retired, even if they are still working, has to be considered.

As the next in our long line of issues, we needed to find the most appropriate way to measure retirees' adjustment levels. Here we decided on a construct we will refer to repeatedly: *subjective well-being*. As background, social scientists have come to look at adjustment in a variety of ways, but there are really three key elements: physical health, financial stability, and subjective well-being. The first two may be considered the basic building blocks for a successful retirement. Among other benefits, good physical health gives you mobility and lets you focus efforts on building a retirement life; adequate finances provide a sense of stability and the resources to do what you like.

Subjective well-being is a more abstract idea. Very basically, it refers to happiness, how satisfied and content people feel in their lives. Subjective well-being is a pretty broad idea, and both physical and financial health can be seen as fitting under its umbrella and contributing to its achievement. For example, other things being equal, a person may be happy as a result of good health and sufficient funds, but being happy will not necessarily improve one's health or income.

Beyond health and wealth, subjective well-being is affected by many other factors. Productivity, self-esteem, feeling in control, having a sense of purpose, feeling connected to others, and the quality of other elements in one's life contribute to a person's overall subjective well-being. That being said, in order to make sure we covered all the elements that might play into subjective well-being, or happiness, we asked retirees how they felt about all the specific aspects of their day-to-day lives and how they felt about themselves.

As we set up our study, we took the perspective that retirement adjustment is a process, meaning that it may occur in stages over a period of time. Psychologists and sociologists have come to accept this, along with the thought that the process can vary from one person to the next: it may take anywhere from a few months to a number of years to establish a comfort level in retirement. Using this viewpoint, it would be helpful to talk to retirees with different lengths of time in retirement. We should be able to answer such questions as the following: "What emotional and psychological changes occur as retirees move deeper into the retirement lifestyle?" "Do retirees make adjustments to their lifestyle with more years in retirement?" "Do retirees with different lengths of time in retirement have different sets of problems?" The answers to these and other questions may be especially helpful to novice retirees, for example, since they might learn from more experienced retirees how to achieve a faster and smoother transition.

Amount of experience is certainly worth exploring, but researchers have also shown that one's adjustment to retirement can be affected by who that person is and where he or she comes from. Within this context, we made sure to include people representing the full range of work backgrounds and demographic characteristics. As an example, we thought it would be useful to look into whether those who retired at the conventional age had a different experience than those who retired younger (i.e., their early or mid-fifties). Older individuals retire with their peers, while those in their fifties often have to go it alone, and this could lead one or the other to have an easier time adjusting.

Our nationwide survey was conducted via the Internet among approximately 1,500 retirees and 400 people who are of the same age and other demographic characteristics as our retirees but still working. We realize that our decision to conduct online interviewing may raise a few eyebrows, primarily among other researchers, because of concerns regarding sample representativeness and scientific "control." These are two elements required in a research project for it to produce meaningful results.

Regarding representativeness of the sample, an Internet survey requires access to a computer and at least some experience with the Internet (though not a lot; modern online surveys are very easy to fill out). As such, there is the risk that respondents drawn in this manner could limit our ability to draw conclusions to only those individuals with computers and Internet access and not all retirees. As another possible concern, online interviews are completed in the privacy of one's home. Respondents are not monitored, so it is possible, for example, that someone in the household other than the chosen respondent actually filled out the questionnaire or that the survey was filled out with the input of others.

These are legitimate concerns for a researcher. However, Internet interviewing has in fact become the standard in market research, with billions of dollars worth of business decisions made annually from online surveys. The reason for the switch from in-person or telephone interviewing was based on practicality—online interviewing is much quicker and much less expensive. But that's not what really matters to a researcher. Most important, it's accurate. Internet interviewing was adopted only after researchers could prove its quality. Research companies and end users of market research have conducted tests to demonstrate that Internet surveys produce the same results as telephone and in-person surveys. As an example, Marketing Analysts, the research company responsible for this study, has consistently been able to make projections for new product sales with the same degree of accuracy using the Internet as with other interviewing methods.

But online interviewing also has a compelling point in its favor: some of our questions were unavoidably personal in nature, such as personal finances or sexual activities. Market researchers are well aware that people are reluctant to answer these sorts of questions at all in a personal interview. Or, if they do answer, they may not answer completely candidly. On the other hand, people answering online surveys, in the anonymity of their homes, show no such reluctance or lack of candor answering sensitive questions. In the final analysis, we feel extremely confident that our interviewing method produced the best possible results.

From the myriad data we collected from our nationwide sample, combined with all the work that has already been done by other social scientists, we set out to accomplish two objectives. The first of our objectives was to uncover the problems and issues retirees can face both before and after retiring. Through an in-depth look into each of the elements that make up the life of a retiree—activities, personal relationships, self-perceptions, and so on—we were able to see how some retired successfully and some less so or not at all. And that led to our second objective: to point out reasonable solutions to problems, the things retirees can do to handle issues as they arise, or maybe even to prevent some from ever arising. Through a better handling of their issues and problems, some retirees may be able to achieve a faster and smoother adjustment to retirement. And, along the way, they may end up feeling better about themselves and have a more fulfilling retirement.

• *2* •

Why We Can Retire

Half our life is spent trying to find something to do with the time
we have rushed through life trying to save.

—Will Rogers

$\mathscr{B}$efore we discuss our own findings, we'd like to lay a foundation based
on what is already known about retirement. Over the past 50 years, the body
of work done by social scientists on this subject has been extensive and far
reaching. Their efforts have led to a number of important discoveries and the
development of theoretical frameworks on retirement adjustment. Today, we
have a much clearer understanding of how the process of adjustment unfolds
and how it fits within the broader perspective of psychological development.
We are greatly indebted to these professionals for pointing the direction for
designing our own research and have attempted whenever possible to discuss
our own findings within the context of their discoveries.

To begin, retirement is a relatively new phenomenon. As recently as the
mid-twentieth century, workers typically just stopped working when they had
no choice in the matter as a result of factors such as declining health or loss
of job competency. This rather harsh state of affairs began to change around
the 1950s and has accelerated to the point that within the past few decades,
retirement has become the norm. Retirement rates for those 65 and older have
risen from about 50% at the middle of the twentieth century to about 80% by
the start of the twenty-first.

Not only has the number of retirees grown dramatically, but the very
nature of how retirement fits in our culture has shifted radically as well. In
comparison to the start of the twentieth century, retirement by the year 2000
had, in the words of Melissa Hardy, one of the many scholars on the topic,

"changed from a largely involuntary transition toward dependency to the increasingly voluntary adoption of leisure instead of work."[1]

The "how" of retirement is not the only recent development—the "when" is changing as well. Today the retirement pool has expanded to include relatively high percentages of people leaving the workforce before the traditional age of 65. In fact, many baby boomers now seek to·retire while they're still in their mid-fifties. In this regard, the United States appears to be following a trend that has been well under way for quite a few years overseas. International research has shown a dramatic decline in labor force participation among 55- to 64-year-olds in a number of industrialized nations during the past 15 to 20 years. For some European nations, retiring at 55 has become the norm.[2]

But just because we aim to retire doesn't mean we can: other factors, changes in support systems, for example, have to be in play to make retirement a realistic option. Two of the most important are improvements in medical care and greater prospects for financial security. Advancements in medicine have led to enhanced quality of life and extended life spans. Healthy adults can reasonably expect to live 20 or more years beyond the traditional retirement age of 65. And with the availability of pensions and social insurance (Social Security for one), postemployment income levels and health care coverage are adequate to provide most retirees with a reasonably secure quality of life. As a result, retirees have the opportunity to use their extended years to explore alternative life approaches, either fully in leisure or in pursuit of personal interests. Unfortunately, this relatively benign state of affairs may not remain in force indefinitely: longer life spans are likely to place ever-greater stress on social support systems in the future. But until then, at least in the short term and under normal economic conditions, current retirement patterns and trends are likely to continue.

There have also been some recent changes in the way our employers, particularly major corporations, think and act, and these may have added some momentum to the earlier retirement movement. As market research consultants, we have worked closely with many of the largest U.S. corporations over the years. Based on our experiences, there has been a noticeable change in the way companies conduct their operations. Corporations today—far more than even 30 years ago—are under relentless pressure to maintain profit growth, quarter after quarter, and to keep their operating costs as low as possible. At the same time, the business environment has become much more competitive—a glance at the number of brands on the shelf for every product category illustrates how difficult it is for companies to launch new successful products and be profitable.

Under such difficult conditions, many businesses have had little choice but to revisit their approach to staffing. Returning to our example of the market research field, concerns about the bottom line have led corporations to cut head counts in their research departments, so that more work is being done by many fewer people than was the case 30 years ago. Furthermore, there seems to be a tendency to believe that professional experience, determined by years on the job, is less important for corporate competitiveness. Younger employees, as an alternative, are seen as bringing fresh ways of thinking and higher energy levels to their jobs, and since they lack seniority, they generally get paid less. In contrast, by the time employees reach their fifties, their salaries are at the top of the pay scale, and their higher costs to a corporation make them more expendable. And, along with being more expensive, there may be the perception—rightly or wrongly—that as they move into their fifties, older workers are winding down their careers, becoming less productive as they do so.

To the extent that these points are true for many organizations, then strictly from the viewpoint of fiscal responsibility, it makes sense that companies favor younger employees over older ones for full-time work (moral, ethical, and legal issues are another matter entirely but are not part of our particular equation for this book). Obviously, "favoring" younger workers does not suggest that companies should—or do—drop their older employees outright. It is easy, though, to see the rationale that companies follow when they try to ease older individuals out of the organization by offering financial packages. And it is almost inevitable that when these packages float through a company, they are likely to make older employees feel highly insecure about their jobs. Consequently, especially when there is an option to work on a subcontractual basis, it can be in the best interests of some older employees to take a package and retire.

So with lower productivity and greater expense, older employees are more vulnerable to losing their jobs. And this job insecurity has led many to feel less satisfied with their careers in the later years. Tony, who recently retired as an executive in a major corporation after 35 years, was forced to take a retirement package at 59. He talked about the changes he has seen over those 35 years and how these have affected employee morale and, for older employees, have led to an inclination to just chuck it all and move on:

> As the pressure on corporate performance and profitability has intensified over the past couple of decades, so have expectations that financial objectives be met not just on an annual but a quarterly basis. The impact on how businesses seem to run now and how their employees are forced to operate in such an environment has been enormous.
>
> In my experience, these negative trends have had a tremendously demoralizing effect on the people working for these organizations who can remember when things were very different—anyone older than their late forties or so. On countless occasions, in speaking with work colleagues

around my age, I have heard comments like: "This just isn't fun anymore" or "There's got to be a better way" or "I don't know how much longer I can put up with this." I personally know several people in their early or mid-fifties who voluntarily left lucrative positions at their companies, citing these sentiments as the reason for their departure. Many others, who may not have the financial wherewithal, stay put, increasingly unhappy and frustrated, until they are able to (or are forced to) retire. There is no doubt in my mind that similar types of dynamics have been operating in other types of companies as well and that they are a major factor in older workers' decisions to retire from the workforce earlier than they had planned.

The older managers that I know at these organizations are mostly disillusioned. And as I write this, I realize that one of the reasons why I wasn't terribly upset at my forced departure was my own disappointment with how my company was conducting business. I don't think I've admitted that to myself before.

I'm going to try to be objective here and not sound like a bitter old man, but there is no doubt in my mind that, at least in the companies where I've worked, there is a clear preference for younger managers within corporate organizations. I certainly understand the financial reality of salary discrepancies—the fact that two or three 20-somethings can be hired for the same price as a 50-year-old senior manager. That's an issue that plays a key role in staffing decisions across corporate America.

But I'm speaking about something different and perhaps more insidious. I don't think what I've experienced has anything to do with the higher salaries or perceived lower productivity of older employees. The fact is that, at my own consumer products company, the insights and business perspective of younger managers were clearly favored over those of older, more experienced folks. Senior management was far more interested in the thoughts of a 30-year-old marketer who might have recently arrived from another consumer company than they were with the perspective of an individual with 20 years' tenure at our own organization. I think the in-going bias is that somehow the younger manager is savvier, is more attuned to the latest marketing innovations, and is more likely to offer up something that is new and different. No premium whatsoever was placed on the experience, familiarity with the business, and the exposure to myriad historical precedents that an older manager can bring to the table.

In my own case, I found myself avoiding invoking learnings from the past, never starting sentences with "In my experience" or "Back in the day." But the reality is that although my technical and people management skills were highly valued, I think, until the day I left, my perspective on marketing issues and key business decisions was less and less sought out the grayer my hair got. I think it's also telling that the proportion of 50-plus folks in the entire organization was extremely small (under 5%) and that within my department, the oldest manager other than myself was 46. But what's truly ironic is that, as a health care company, we were marketing products primarily for people 50 and older.

Nevertheless, many clouds have silver linings. Although from his experience Tony might not agree, the flip side of changes in corporate thinking may have led to a new kind of employment opportunity for older individuals. Corporations today are much more amenable to outsourced staffing, and companies have come to see the value of being able to bring in an experienced workforce for part-time or temporary work to meet specific needs. Ironically, these changes may have inadvertently contributed to the evolution of retirement—specifically, that it often includes work.

Such subcontracted, postretirement jobs are often advantageous for those able to get them. They serve as a safety net in the event that incomes from pensions, investments, and Social Security dip below desired levels. And companies benefit as well: they have an available workforce that does not require a full-time or long-term commitment. Furthermore, employees coming from the retired pool are likely to be willing to work for less because they tend to have supplemental income sources. So, between their lower financial demands and their years of experience, retirees make themselves very attractive to those looking to hire but not looking to commit.

Needless to say, there is often a downside to every rosy story. Some scholars argue that these changes in the corporate employment structure can marginalize workers, particularly older ones.[3] This perspective views the issue as a downward spiral: as employees lose their long-term commitment, they tend to be viewed as less valued by their companies. As their company sees them as less important, they may be more vulnerable to losing their jobs or, at the minimum, cannot be certain of holding these jobs for as long as they might like to. This of course may be true, but given that older workers tend to be more vulnerable to losing their jobs anyway, they are probably no more devalued as contracted workers than as full-time employees.

Apart from the marginalization debate, from many retirees' perspectives, the benefits of part-time or temporary work probably outweigh the shortcomings. For one thing, working retirees are often able to retain their retirement status—and at the same time maintain their income potential—in an economic downturn. Such "bridge jobs," as they have come to be known, also tend to offer favorable working conditions. Retirees can often have meaningful input into the terms of their jobs, such as the tasks performed, the number of hours worked, and when during the day work is conducted. Additionally, these jobs are often less stressful and don't demand the same degree of emotional commitment as one's full-time career.

Larry, a middle manager in a major corporation, retired in his mid-fifties and then worked contractually for his company, carrying out many of the tasks he did when he was salaried. His description is consistent with how many working retirees view their jobs in retirement—their responsibilities are the same in some respects, but there are differences, mostly in the attitude in how these jobs are perceived:

When I was working as a salaried employee, I was always concerned about my financial and job security. When I felt confident I didn't need the job anymore, I decided to retire. Once I committed to that decision, I stopped worrying about my job. Of course I knew there could be some financial bumps along the road, but pretty much I knew I could make it, and in leaving my job I eliminated a source of stress in my life.

When I went back to work for my company as an independent consultant, I didn't do it just for the money. The money of course was a nice bonus, good to have for discretionary spending. But I actually liked what I did for a living, so I didn't want to give it up completely. I wanted to work a little, but I was also interested in doing other things besides work. So when my company was open to hiring me back on a contractual basis, I went for it.

With the way my job is structured now, I don't have the same sense of commitment to it, and I don't feel the stress. I really believe it's because I already made the decision to be retired. If they told me tomorrow I was out of a job, I wouldn't feel too bad, certainly not how I might have felt if they fired me when I was a salaried employee. That doesn't mean I don't put in my best effort or that I have less enthusiasm for what I do. But now I do it because I want to and not because I have to. I certainly care about doing my job well, but I don't have to take any setbacks as seriously.

What's great about working like this is I am in control—that's the critical difference between being on salary and working in retirement. I have lots of flexibility as to what I do, how much I want to do, and when I do it. I might start work at 4 A.M., or I might start at 10 P.M. I work for about six hours per day on the days that I work, but the start and stop times are my call. Many of my assignments are ad hoc, in response to a particular issue or need on any given day. But I set the priorities for what I do, and even with a priority list I might choose to work first on something that has lower priority because it's a task that interests me.

Here's a good example of my working arrangement. Yesterday I was involved in some non–work-related chores around the house, which made me about an hour late for a conference call. I got on the call, and everyone was fine with it, and I certainly wasn't worried. But the truth is, what can they do about it? I work hard, and I'm respected, and I come at a good price to them. They can't fire me—I'm retired. So I pretty much run my own show.

But I want to mention that sometimes there are crazy days on my job: very tight deadlines, lots of pressure, just like the old days when they paid me a salary. When those days happen, I lose that sense of control, and all the good things about this job go away. If there's ever too many of those days, I'll have to reconsider things.

Larry's plan to "reconsider things" if conditions move beyond his control is an unveiled reference to quitting, at least this particular job. However, as long as conditions remain favorable, meaning that he feels less stressed and has some input into his job definition, Larry will, like many other retirees, continue working into the foreseeable future. Larry in fact liked the types of assignments associated with his job when he was working full-time, and it is this aspect that continues to attract him. This is not so surprising; research has shown that a number of retirees actually enjoyed their work and would not mind continuing in their career role if they could make some modifications. In fact, many would put off their retirement if they could redefine their jobs to have less stress, more choice in the tasks performed, and fewer working hours each week.

In summary, retirement has become a real option for many people, driven by the prospect of improved health and health care, greater financial security, and its evolution to include working under circumstances more favorable than a full-time job. But it's also a movement that may have been forced by changes in corporate employment policies and practices, unspoken as these may be. Nevertheless, one can also speculate that the drive to retire may be tied to a desire to get the most out of our lives. It can be argued that the prosperity of modern times, occasional economic downturns notwithstanding, has given us more freedom to think about living in terms of personal happiness and not just in terms of filling basic needs than might have been the case for people up to the middle of the last century.

But however one gets to retirement—whether forced by job circumstances or chosen because it's seen as offering a better lifestyle—a surprising number of issues can blindside a retiree, possibly leading to disenchantment down the road. The next few chapters will lay them out.

• 3 •

Why We Run into Problems

We've put more effort into helping folks reach retirement age
than into helping them enjoy it.

—Anonymous

$\mathcal{O}$nce a person has decided to retire, he or she will typically schedule an
actual retirement date, which can be anywhere from a few months to, in some
cases, as long as a few years later. While waiting for the big day to arrive, the
future retiree generally enters a wind-down period at his or her job, characterized by a weakening of career commitment and reduced emotional attachment
to the organization. Some retirees use this period to ponder the upcoming
lifestyle change and make plans for it. A few might even try to visualize what
retirement will be like by mentally placing themselves into the day-to-day
life of a retiree even as they are still working. That's one way they can help
themselves become emotionally prepared for the event.

When the day of their retirement actually arrives, most retirees tend to
start out on a positive note. They are likely to feel a sense of freedom and a
respite from day-to-day pressures, as though a burden has been lifted from
their shoulders. They may feel as though they've reclaimed ownership of their
life, that time is their own to use however they desire. It is a time to finally
catch one's breath and chill out for a while.

Unfortunately, within a relatively short time, many retirees begin to sense
some uneasiness. After the initial sense of relief, sooner or later they begin to
realize that there's more to retirement than the simplistic "stop work, go play."
Although retirement is a relatively pressure-free way of living, and many adults
truly look forward to it, studies have found that as many as 33% of retirees
have difficulty adjusting to the lifestyle.[1] Furthermore, as we mentioned very
early on, even those who claim to enjoy their retirement may not be content

21

100% of the time. They are instead likely to sense some discomfort from time to time, however short lived, as they adapt to a life without work. Rob's experiences illustrate how the euphoria in the wind-down phase at work and in the initial stages of retirement can dissipate quickly and lead to feelings of stress from an entirely different source—a lack of something meaningful to do:

> When I made the final decision and picked a date to retire, my view of my job changed completely. I no longer felt the pressure, the aggravation of having to deal with tons of issues every day. In fact, I pretty much left the job mentally and emotionally almost immediately. My retirement was still about six months away, but more and more I cut off communication with my staff and clients. In part this was to force them to rely more on the partners who would be running the company but also because I just had no interest in doing the work anymore. Plus, since I was leaving, this world would no longer be a part of my life. For the last three months, as soon as I came into the office, I closed my door and stayed in there alone virtually all day. I'd amuse myself on the Internet or maybe do a crossword puzzle, call some friends, and then at some point each day I'd go for a walk for an hour or so.
>
> Gradually I came to spend less and less time at the office each day. Actually, since I was really doing nothing constructive, what was the point of going in at all? Eventually I was getting really bored, but it never got to the point that I would do any work to make the days less boring. Finally, after more than 25 years, I didn't have to care anymore, and I wasn't going to change that.
>
> But thinking back on those last days, I now realize that I made a mistake. Despite the fact that I'm big on planning, I didn't use that time to lay out the specific steps that I would follow in retirement. I was so in love with the idea of having stress-free days and being able to do whatever I wanted to do that I didn't bother to think about what I actually would do when I was no longer working. I had some general ideas but nothing specific. So after I retired and the joy of no stress was gone, other problems set in—no structure, nothing meaningful in my life. I felt disconnected, no place to go, no direction, isolated. Then there was the boredom of nothing to do, a boredom that was at a whole different level from what I felt after the many years of doing my job. The emotional issues I dealt with during that time were pretty intense and wholly unexpected and, in retrospect, also very stressful.

Rob was just not aware of the myriad issues that lay before him. That's not to say the information isn't out there, just that it's not common knowledge or easily accessible. In fact, much work and many resources have been devoted to trying to help retirees adjust. The fact that so much effort has been expended suggests that smooth transitions from work to retirement are not very typical.

As early as the mid-1950s, psychologists and sociologists began research-ing the psychological aspects of the adjustment process.[2] In-depth exploration on the topic has increased dramatically in recent years, as evidenced by the 90 scientific references cited in this book. In addition to the scientific literature, there are many popularly written books and articles designed to bring discus-sions about retirement into the broader public domain. There is the inevitable *Retirement for Dummies* and, not to be outdone, *Making the Most of Retirement for Dummies*, along with 187 books, as of this writing, under the subject head-ing "Psychology of Retirement" on Amazon.com.[3] Many of these books use a self-help format in their attempt to help retirees, pointing out what they should do in an effort to make retirement a happy and fulfilling life stage.

In spite of the systematic attempt to uncover the factors that play into the adjustment process, it may not come as much of a surprise that there is some inconsistency across studies. There are bodies of evidence suggesting that retirement can have a positive effect on subjective well-being and some that suggest a negative one or a neutral one (i.e., not much effect at all). Some researchers have found that retirees exhibit poorer physical health, more de-pressive symptoms, lower activity levels, and less positive overall satisfaction and happiness.[4] Others have found retirement to have a positive impact on life satisfaction, physical health, and stress levels. Retirees in these studies have described themselves as calmer, less competitive, and less argumentative.[5] The absence of work-related stress, according to this body of work, apparently has led to less aggressive behavior, which in turn has led to more positive social interactions. Finally, other research studies suggest that retirement is a benign event with no or only a minimal apparent impact on one's health and well-being.

It may be tempting, in light of these inconsistent findings, to dismiss the work of these social scientists as misguided or wrongheaded, but that would be a serious mistake. The fact that some studies show positive and some show negative outcomes simply reflects reality: we don't live in a linear world, and there are no simple clear-cut solutions that apply to all retirees. Furthermore, the way a retiree feels will change depending on how long he or she is retired. If a researcher talks to retirees 10 years into this life stage, one is likely to draw very different conclusions about retirement than if one talks to those only six or nine months out of the workforce. So the fact that people are different and that the same people can feel differently at different points in time illustrates just how difficult it is for social scientists to come up with straightforward or one-dimensional findings.

Nevertheless, when one looks across the entire body of work, it's clear that researchers have isolated and identified many factors that interfere with adjustment. From there, paths to successful retirement are beginning to emerge. As a reasonable albeit broad conclusion, some researchers propose that retirement has two opposing directions. On the positive side, retirement can lead to the development of new goals and interests; on the negative side, it can lead to stress, anxiety, and depression.[6] Whether retirees achieve one or the other depends to an extent on the type of people they are and their individual backgrounds and characteristics but also on the amount of creativity, energy, and resources they are willing to invest in building a life without work.

There are other issues, however—it's not just a matter of effort and personal characteristics. For example, some benefits of working that may not be readily apparent while still in the workforce extend beyond a paycheck. When retirees give up their jobs, they are leaving an environment that offers opportunities for all kinds of psychological rewards, many of which are not easily or immediately replaced through the undefined retirement lifestyle.

In truth, even though a job at times may be a hassle, there is a lot of evidence to show that work is an essential component of American society. Researchers have confirmed what many Americans intuitively believe: that the United States is a work-driven culture, that one's job is a primary source of identity and a means of determining self-worth, and that the status associated with a job can contribute a great deal to one's subjective well-being.

Through their jobs, people also acquire a sense of purpose—even, for some, a reason for being. The feeling that life has purpose can be especially strong if one's job requires a variety of skills and the worker feels that his or her performance is valuable to other workers and to the organization. On leaving the work force, that sense of purpose and the feeling of making valuable contributions can be more limited, and retirees can start to think that they no longer play an important role in society. The loss of that role and the attendant feeling of being unproductive can adversely affect psychological health, weakening one's sense of self-worth and eliminating the basis of one's personal identity.[7]

With their well-defined routines, jobs also add structure to living by making us conform to daily schedules. Social scientists have demonstrated that the structured use of time can enhance subjective well-being by providing direction to a person's actions, along with a sense of working toward a goal. When people's time is not accounted for in a purposeful way, they can feel a lack of direction and loss of personal control over their lives, and this can lead to a decline in subjective well-being.[8]

Then there are the social benefits of employment. When people are employed, they have a variety of personal contacts and daily opportunities to interact with friends and coworkers. These relationships provide employees with emotional support as well as opportunities for social comparison and feedback about themselves. Along with being an important source of friendships, being in the workforce allows people to bond by sharing common goals. Working toward goals with others provides a sense of membership and acceptance in a group, and being accepted by others helps people maintain their self-esteem. When this opportunity for social contact and group membership is reduced or cut off, as can occur in retirement, people can feel isolated and socially disconnected.

Of course, not all jobs offer the same social and psychological benefits. Some retirees dislike their jobs for one reason or another, and for them, employment is not necessarily a better alternative than retirement. There is evidence that although the loss of a job that is stimulating or enjoyable can have negative consequences, leaving one that is demanding or unsatisfying can actually improve a retiree's health and overall happiness. When working conditions are truly disagreeable and a job is psychologically damaging, not working can be the better alternative.[9]

But not always, surprisingly enough: the benefits of giving up an unrewarding job may be short lived. Certainly, retirees are likely to go through an initial phase of relief when they first leave a miserable job: an unfavorable and possibly stress-inducing part of their lives has been removed. But as the bad memories of that job fade away, retirees may still face adjustment issues. Unless something of value is added to their lives—beyond just the subtraction of the bad job—they may not be happy, especially later on in their retirement. Rob experienced that exact issue when he retired. His decision to leave his job was based more on dissatisfaction and boredom with work than on seeing retirement as a destination with specific goals to pursue that were personally meaningful to him:

> As I mentioned already, I was not as prepared for retirement as I thought I was, and I didn't leave my job because I had something else to do that I was particularly interested in. I can look back on my decision to retire as being driven more by a need to just get rid of the stress of running a company. By the time I threw in the towel, I had had enough of dealing with employees and of worrying about keeping the business going. Furthermore, after more than 25 years in that role, I had come to look at the successes on my job as the minimum of what I expected and the failures and problems as more and more catastrophic—so I was getting very few rewards and lots of pain for my efforts. The final straw came when an employee attempted to sue me. This was an individual whom my partners and department heads wanted to fire for more than a year but whom I protected just because I never liked throwing anyone out of a job. Even though the suit was without merit

and eventually dropped, still it left me angry and bitter. In the midst of this nightmare, I called my partner and told him that I had enough of the whole thing; I wanted out.

I set my retirement date for about nine months after that phone call. During that time I made no specific plans about what I would do when I retired. Rather, I just used that time to distance myself from my job and to wind down. As I had mentioned before, I had a lot of interests, and I believed a general idea about how I would use my time was good enough to make my retirement fulfilling and enjoyable.

I couldn't have been more wrong. After the first two months or so, the elation of a pressure-free life subsided. At that point I had to scramble to find things to do, and that's when I started experimenting with a lot of new business opportunities. Because I had no clear direction and no structure to my days, I pretty much had to go back to what I knew—business. The reality was, even though I thought retirement was a great idea, the fact that I was running away from my job rather than running to something specific in a retirement life left me with very little when I was out of the job and into retirement. I have no regrets about the courses I pursued, but I probably could have saved myself a lot of trouble if I had really focused on putting together a structured way of living with some nonbusiness goals set up. Even though I'm big on planning, I just didn't realize what I needed to do to feel good about being retired.

Beyond losing the benefits of working, present-day adjustment problems may also be a function of time. In the past, workers retired much older, often from physically demanding jobs with longer working hours. And not only did they retire older, but their life spans were shorter than they are now. This compression from both ends meant that many retirees were likely to have only a few years outside the workforce before—to put it bluntly—they died. Worse still, while they remained alive, they didn't have the benefits of modern medical care, so their physical health was often much worse than that of modern retirees. This unhappy state of affairs meant that, for the short amount of time available to them in retirement, many retirees in the past may just have looked forward to some relaxation. But even if rest was not required, their retirement was simply not long enough for adjustment to be something they needed to worry about.

In contrast, the current generation of retirees can look forward to many healthy years outside the workforce—those retiring young may spend as much time retired as they did working. Because of the expanded time, psychologists and sociologists now consider retirement a new life stage, a normal and distinct phase of the life cycle and no longer just the start of old age. However, while those added years are a nice bonus, they are also the source of the problem— you have to fill them with something meaningful; some sort of structure has to be put back in place so you can feel comfortable in the many years to come.

But where will this structure come from? How is the new retiree to find it? There is little direction, no personal guide, and no designated path through the maze that leads to a place of personal meaningfulness, and this can leave retirees completely at a loss. Some, for example, may experience a condition of what psychologists call "learned helplessness." Because they are not sure how to proceed and lack a sense of personal control, they may be less motivated to move forward. As a result, they may develop a pessimistic attitude about retirement or, worse, depressive symptoms. Others may take a route of trial and error, experimenting with different ways of living and thinking, keeping those that are enjoyable and discarding those that are not. This approach is actually a good one to take, but it has its own set of problems—it includes the word "error" for a reason and is likely to entail considerable frustration along the way.

Trying to work your way through all the issues is the reason retirement is seen as an ongoing process. It plays itself out over an extended period of time and is not a single event with a clear beginning and end. The process can go on for months and possibly years before retirees can completely adjust to their new life stage, establishing clear direction and establishing a structure to their days. During that time, many retirees may feel as though they are on an emotional roller coaster, experiencing a series of emotional ups and downs. But we should keep in mind that this is to be expected since it is highly unlikely that one can leave a highly structured environment such as the workforce and enter an unstructured environment such as retirement without some period of emotional upheaval. That being said, acknowledging that there will be emotional turmoil and having to live through it are two entirely separate matters.

Although it's almost impossible to specify the time needed to feel adjusted, social scientists have been able to map out the stages of the process. Researcher Robert Atchley has proposed such a model, laying out the various phases that are likely to occur, each characterized by a particular set of emotions and thought patterns.[10] Although there are variations on this model, we have presented the four phases that deal directly and specifically with retirement adjustment:

1. *The honeymoon.* The very early stages of retirement, in which emotions are generally positive as retirees enjoy their new freedom from work and its schedules. This phase is often marked by vacations, exploring new interests, or simply rest and relaxation. Emotionally, retirees may experience the elimination of stress and some euphoria, feeling that they have reclaimed their lives for themselves and that their time is their own to use how they see fit.
2. *Disenchantment.* This phase can begin a few weeks to a number of months after retirement. It is a period during which retirees may experience an

emotional letdown and a decline in subjective well-being as they come face to face with the reality of day-to-day living devoid of direction. Situational elements, possibly unforeseen, may contribute to this letdown, such as a concern that financial resources are more limited than initially thought or that some activities are not as absorbing as they expected. Retirees may also feel the loss of the benefits provided by the workforce, as described above, such as a weakening of identity and self-worth, feelings of being disconnected and without a meaningful role in society, and a sense of living unproductively.

3. *Reorientation.* At some point, possibly as long as a few years after they first retire, retirees will begin a reevaluation of their circumstances. During this phase, attitudes about what it means to be retired start to change. Retirees come to a better understanding of retirement's social and economic components as well as a more realistic understanding of what it means to be retired. Many are likely to take a careful look at their lifestyles and begin to outline ways to improve the way they live.

4. *Stability.* Through the process of reorientation, retirees eventually come to terms and feel comfortable with the idea of being retired. At this point, the retiree has developed an alternative lifestyle that does not include work as a primary component. In addition, he or she will have abandoned the work role as a primary means of self-definition. New roles and patterns of living are likely to have developed, with routines and goals established to provide meaning and direction to their lives.

As a general model, this sequence of stages for retirement adjustment is certainly reasonable. It can actually be charted as an up–down–up mental and emotional path that moves from elation to disappointment to acceptance over time. But again, people are different, so this model does not precisely apply for everyone. For example, as we have already mentioned, some retirees experience virtually no emotional problems throughout the transition process. Additionally, researchers have not been able to pinpoint the exact times each stage begins and ends or even to show that every retiree actually goes through all adjustment stages. Some studies have found that the honeymoon can end as early as 6 months after retiring, while others have found emotional declines occurring 18 months or more after retirement. Furthermore, the degree of emotional upheaval at the different phases can vary dramatically, ranging from mild discomfort to depression.[11]

Anne, an education administrator, is a good example of a retiree who had gone through the honeymoon fairly quickly, about a month after retiring, and then moved into the disenchantment phase. She was caught unprepared by her emotional upheaval as her retirement progressed, which she linked to the lack of structure in her day-to-day living. Anne will certainly emerge from the disenchantment phase at some point, although it is difficult to say how long it will take her to become reoriented to her new life stage:

> I am surprised by my emotional experiences in retirement. I used to be the calm one, the one people sought out to solve problems. But now, I can't seem to get out of my own way, and everything becomes a big issue. The freedom of retirement is also the problem of retirement. Now everything "takes" more time. I seem to lack the sense of organization that I once had, and things are now overwhelming. I think that without the structure of my "work life," I tend to create a type of "daily work (retirement) life," and when anything intrudes upon that needed structure, I get thrown for a loss. I've lost my flexibility to handle the daily issues or problems that pop up. I am aware of this, so I am attempting to address the issue.
>
> I am on an adjustment roller coaster. At first, I loved retirement—so much free time; so many things I wanted to do; so many places to go and people to see. But then I started to experience negative feelings. I can't define these feelings as depression but rather as "I'm not as happy as I used to be." I used to sing (when I was alone), but when I am down, I was just disgusted with everything—including the weather. I can find fault with everything. The smallest issue could become a major tragedy—like a broken fingernail (seriously! especially if I had just had my nails done—holy cow, watch out world). The feelings do not happen every day but more frequently than when I was working. Once again, I had no time for the small issues when I was working; now, unstructured time allows you to waste time on insignificant issues. The ups are just me feeling like my old self—happy, confident, and yes, singing in the living room when I was alone. But no feeling, be it up or down, stays with me too long. If I were down for too long, I think I would seek help because it just doesn't feel good, and my family would not tolerate the "nasty Anne."

Anne's rapid movement into the disenchantment phase may have been driven by her strong devotion to her career and the personal rewards she received from it. In her mind, she gave up a lot in retirement. Others may experience shorter or longer times from one phase to the other—as we've said, it's difficult to know from one person to the next since people are different and so many other factors come into play.

But the issue of adjustment is deeper than what the model can describe: the stagewise approach only answers the question of *what* happens in retirement but not *why* the adjustment process unfolds as it does. To answer the "why," psychologists have looked to broader theoretical models of psychological development. Within this context, three approaches—continuity theory, life course perspective, and role theory—have been developed as theoretical frameworks guiding the research efforts of a number of social scientists.[12]

These theories look at the retirement adjustment process from different perspectives, but it's important to understand that they are not mutually contradictory and do not lead to different predicted outcomes for retirees. Rather, there is substantial support for each of these perspectives, and they tend to work together to explain why retirees experience emotional upheaval as they adapt to their retirement. They have also been very helpful in identifying mediating factors—the things that conspire against us in making the transition from work to retirement. We'll now take a brief look at each of these three approaches—they provide an interesting perspective on how we move from one life stage to another.

Continuity theory focuses on each person's ability to adapt to change and maintain a degree of consistency, or continuity, in his or her life.[13] Continuity refers to having situations or conditions that remain the same as a person moves from one life stage into another. Friendships outside the workforce, hobbies, and non–work-related activities are examples of elements that provide continuity—you take these with you when you leave a job. The key benefit of maintaining continuity is a reduced perception that one's life has gone through a drastic change. With many elements in their lives remaining in place, people who have maintained continuity can essentially carry on with many of their familiar patterns and routines.

Continuity may be a matter of degrees; that is, the more lifestyle elements are retained, the less one feels affected in transitioning to a new life stage. It may also be a matter of the strength of the elements retained. For example, if a retiree has especially strong family ties, the fact that these family ties are still available in the movement across life stages suggests that continuity would be maintained. A good example of maintaining continuity might be found among women who have children. Mothers tend to rely very strongly—and more so than men—on their nurturing roles. This role is still available to them when they leave the workforce and can supplant the worker role in retirement. Women in fact are likely to adjust better because their lives tend to be more multidimensional; that is, they are more broadly connected to things outside of work, so giving up their jobs need not be as big a loss for them as it is for men.

Although leaving the workforce is of course a major lifestyle change, retirees can nevertheless retain some degree of continuity as they enter retirement. For example, holding on to coworker friendships can be helpful in this regard, especially in the initial stages. Also from a social perspective, continuity can be preserved through nonwork relationships, including friends, a spouse or significant other, and other family members. Note that these are important elements in their own right—they allow us to feel connected to the world and are a source of emotional support.

Other ways of maintaining continuity can include leisure activities, hobbies, and other activities the retiree practiced in his or her spare time outside of work. Retirees might find that starting hobbies or some other activities before retiring and having them to go to after retiring may provide some sense of comfort because the degree of lifestyle change won't feel so intense. The idea that ongoing activities can help retirees feel adjusted actually suggests that continuity plays a role in putting structure into daily living. It's important for retirees to establish routines and keep to schedules just as they might have while working—and activities can help in this regard.

Some retirees may experience only a minor loss in continuity on leaving their jobs, most likely because they have many interests and strong personal relationships outside of work. However, it is likely that for retirees to feel truly adjusted, from a continuity perspective, a critical mass of lifestyle elements has to be retained after leaving the workforce. Unfortunately, this may be an unrealistic expectation, and to understand why a shortfall in continuity is likely, one need only consider all the ways a job contributes to subjective well-being. As we have already mentioned, work focuses one's time and attention, provides structure, allows opportunities to feel productive, provides a social environment, and for many is a primary means of self-definition. In retirement, it may be difficult or even impossible to find enough activities to provide the same types and amounts of benefits, especially in the initial stages. And for retirees whose social life is completely tied to work or whose interests outside of work are especially limited, there can be a dramatic loss in continuity, making the adjustment to retirement especially difficult.

Shortfalls in continuity may be contributing to the recent trend among retirees to take "bridge jobs," which we briefly discussed earlier. These jobs will be explored in detail in chapter 8, but in the present context they can be seen to smooth the transition into retirement, especially for those who had been highly committed to their careers. They offer a way of maintaining a sense of purpose and productivity as well as social contact through friendships developed at work.[14] The fact that more and more retirees are turning to these bridge jobs suggests that they have not been able to put enough elements into place to achieve adequate levels of continuity after leaving the workforce.

The second perspective, role theory, focuses specifically, as the name suggests, on the importance of roles—ways of defining ourselves—to subjective well-being. Each of us has multiple roles we use to define who we are as people and to connect us to the outside world, such as parent, club member, friend, and, of course, worker. Once a particular role is taken on, identification with that specific role becomes central to how a person lives. Roles tend to drive our attitudes, self-image, behaviors, and decisions.

The worker role tends to be very strong and firmly embedded in each person's psyche; indeed, it is a role we hold on to for the majority of our adult lives. Its strength is driven in part by the highly structured nature of the role itself. The worker role has its variety of rules and behavior patterns and is further reinforced by the tendency for others in a worker's peer group to hold that role as well. In this regard, the worker role makes us feel connected to other workers.[15] There are other factors that cement the worker role and that, as with issues of continuity, are tied to the psychological benefits of working and to the fact that the role leads to a paycheck.

Role theory looks at the transition from employment to retirement as a loss of role identity.[16] Some retirees, especially those who use their career role as their singular identity, can have a particularly hard time after leaving the workforce. These retirees can have a sense of "rolelessness" when they retire—a lack of a meaningful way of defining themselves. Roleless retirees can feel disconnected, unproductive, anxious, or even, in severe cases, depressed. Retirees can remain in a roleless state for some time or at least until a new role is adopted, such as community or club member, or until other preexisting roles become more prominent, such as parent or family member.[17]

Not all retirees react the same way to losing the worker role. Role theory actually points to two distinct patterns, depending on the degree of career commitment and feelings about one's job. Those who were highly involved in their careers, identified strongly with their role as a worker, or believe they lost a personally important role are much more prone to experience role loss. Conversely, those for whom their job was burdensome, unpleasant, or stressful or who are looking forward to involvement in alternative roles are likely to be happy to depart the workforce and drop their worker roles. These retirees are less likely to feel roleless and to suffer the attendant emotional negatives as they enter retirement. Instead, the opposite can happen: retirement allows them to escape from an unpleasant or unrewarding role and provides the freedom to pursue other interests and activities—and strengthen other roles—that are more personally meaningful.[18]

Retired men may be more prone to suffer the pitfalls predicted by role theory, the sense of occupying a "roleless" role. Men tend to be more emotionally tied to their jobs than women, possibly because they have more continuous time in the workforce and are more likely to have the traditional role as breadwinners in their households. For women, in contrast, researchers hypothesize that because they are more likely to move in and out of work based on changes in family responsibilities (e.g., childbirth and maternity leave), their lack of continuity makes them less prone to develop a worker identity and hence suffer less of a loss in retirement. But they may also be less affected by losing their worker role because women tend to be more socially integrated. In other words, they tend to occupy multiple roles at the same time and are less locked into one role in defining themselves. With greater reliance on their nonworker identities, role theory would predict an easier transition into retirement.

However, this does not hold for all women: there are many who are just as career driven and have just as many uninterrupted years in the workforce as men. Women with these employment histories are likely to suffer the same sense of role loss as men when they enter retirement. Anne is a case in point. When she gave up her position, the resulting loss of that role weakened her self-esteem. But importantly, without that role for guidance, Anne felt a loss of direction in her life:

> I definitely feel a loss of identity since I retired. I was one of those "supermoms"—a wife, a mother, a professional, a student—and I never missed a holiday at my house, which meant dinner for from 6 to 23! I worked hard to raise the status of women, and before I retired I thought that I had made a positive contribution. I worked even harder to get my doctorate, and I was thrilled to have the title "Dr." in front of my name.
>
> While working, I had a very positive self-esteem and an "I can get the job done" attitude. Not so in retirement. I don't get as much done, and I tend to be crabby if there are too many tasks to get accomplished. My career structured my life. It provides built in goals with time limitations; you can't put things off til tomorrow, and there are so many tasks that you can't sit and "awfulize" about every little thing that goes wrong. In retirement, any little thing can become a tragedy. Retirement is like moving to a new neighborhood—you have to relearn a lot that you didn't expect you would have to.
>
> I've also lost my colleagues, and those relationships helped to define who I was. I also feel that my status in retirement is less than it was while I was working. For example, no matter how often I introduce myself as "doctor" everyone calls me "Mrs." Perhaps this is not a big issue in itself, but no one refers to my husband (who also has a doctorate) as "Mister." While working, I controlled curriculum for 16,000 students and oversaw teachers and administrators in 27 buildings. I had an important job and a certain status in my profession, which gave me lots of reasons to feel good about myself. But now that is gone.

The loss of direction that can accompany an important role loss, such as Anne experienced, is not surprising if one keeps in mind that roles do more than just provide an identity. They put structure into our daily living because roles have a corresponding set of behaviors and responsibilities. Accompanying your worker role are the various tasks you are required to perform on your job; as a parent, you have the job of raising your children.

Role theory would argue that retirees may have a smoother adjustment if they reduce their reliance on, if not drop completely, their worker role. In its place, they pay more attention to their alternative roles, particularly that of retiree. Over time, as these alternative roles strengthen, retirees are more likely to pick up the patterns and responsibilities associated with these roles, thereby allowing them to feel more connected to the retirement world and less to the worker world.

The third theory, life course perspective, is a very broad approach that takes into account all the elements in one's life. This theory proposes that adjustment to retirement is affected by the full gamut of past experiences, the individual's social and cultural environment, personal characteristics, and relationships with others. A critical feature of the life course perspective is that a person's past *matters*, and the adjustment to a life stage such as retirement must be considered within the context of all of their experiences.[19]

The life course perspective also considers the transition to retirement within the framework of what social scientists call ongoing trajectories. Trajectories are the paths that one's life has taken or is expected to take in the future. People's lives generally have a number of trajectories going on simultaneously, such as being a parent and maintaining a career. Each trajectory has its own specific set of associated responsibilities, rules, and patterns that guide our behavior. And as individual paths, they provide structure, direction, and purpose to our lives, very much as we found for continuity and roles.

The life course perspective, also like the other two, has meaningful implications for the retirement decision. It presumes that individuals will take into consideration all the various aspects of their lives as they decide whether to stop working. They might consider whether their children are living at home, whether a working spouse is planning to retire at the same time, whether they have specific other plans, and so on in deciding if and when to retire.[20]

According to this approach, how well and quickly a person adjusts to retirement depends on all the factors of that person's life. These can include retirees' ability to cope with change, feelings about their job and career, involvement with other nonwork roles and trajectories, the quality of their health and finances, future plans, and the quality and importance of relationships with other people, such as friends and family members.

The life course perspective sheds light on the retirement adjustment process by suggesting that individuals will develop a comfort level and achieve subjective well-being in retirement over time and will come to enjoy this phase of their lives. There may be some dissatisfaction in the initial transition stage, possibly because of unrealistic expectations or worries about having sufficient resources (economic or otherwise). But as these retirees redefine and refocus their lives—that is, pursue other trajectories—and come to grips with their resource strengths and limitations, their emotional state is expected to improve.

As a particular point related to this perspective, retirement can be viewed as a disruption of an ongoing trajectory—your career. In the event that such a disruption is expected and planned for, retirees have the opportunity to immerse themselves in other ongoing trajectories or develop new trajectories or paths to follow. In such situations, leaving the workforce is more of a voluntary termination than a disruption of a trajectory. However, through this perspective it is easy to see, for example, why those forced into retirement or retiring too early can face difficulties. The career trajectory, which guided their day-to-day patterns, has been abruptly and involuntarily removed. While they have other trajectories they can pursue, these may not have the same rewards that work provided and hence may not serve as adequate replacements. If these other trajectories were equally valuable, these retirees might well have already retired, provided that their finances suggested that possibility. Or, at the minimum, they would have an easier time making the transition even if forced to retire.

As with continuity and role theories, the life course theory suggests the same up-then-down-then-up-again emotional roller coaster we talked about earlier. All three approaches assume an initial satisfaction with retirement due to achieving a sense of freedom and loss of stress. Within the framework of the life course perspective, there may then be some decline in psychological well-being because the retiree has been removed from a structured environment. But ultimately there is recovery as the retiree moves further and further from his career state of mind and establishes a new life and new pathways (e.g., goals, interests, and activities). In comparison, for role theory, the role loss resulting from leaving the workforce may lead retirees to feel anxious or depressed initially but will recover over time as new roles are adopted. Continuity theory proposes that initial loss in continuity may undermine the retiree's sense of identity and lifestyle but that subjective well-being will improve as new identities and patterns emerge and the perceived loss of continuity diminishes.

All three frameworks share another aspect as well, and this is a point we have mentioned repeatedly: the length of the retirement adjustment process, the steps involved, and the degree of comfort one feels while moving through the transition all depend on the myriad things that make up your life. And further confounding the situation are expectations regarding what retirement is like and how one's life will play out in the absence of something as all-absorbing as work. In the upcoming chapters we will look at all of the variables in detail and how they work to enhance or inhibit adjustment, first at the decision stage and then after retirement.

But before delving into each of these issues, we need to take a step back and examine, in very broad terms, how people fare in general as they progress through this life stage: how many are happy and well adjusted in retirement and whether and to what extent various emotional or psychological issues emerge as a result of being retired.

Consistent with what other social scientists have found, our survey confirmed that adjusting to retirement is not without its problems. Of the 1,477 retirees we interviewed, only 44% described themselves as completely adjusted to their new lifestyle, and only 53% felt their adjustment was easy to accomplish. At the opposite end of the spectrum, we found a rather large group who are having major issues—about one in four retirees say they are having a very difficult time or feel they are only a little or not at all adjusted to being retired. The remaining 32% of retirees are in a sort of retirement limbo—they're not having major adjustment problems, but they're not completely comfortable with their new lifestyle either.

New retirees seem to have a particularly rough time of it—only 18% of those retired six months or less feel they are completely adjusted. These percentages rise to 35% with two years in retirement, to 41% with three to four years, and to 55% with five or more years. But that's about as far as it seems to go: ratings of being completely adjusted get to only 59% when retirees reach 11 or more years, and almost one in five of the most experienced retirees still feel only somewhat adjusted or worse. So while adjustment problems tend to get solved over time, for many retirees they never seem to go away entirely.

This is not to say that all or even most retirees are miserable. In fact, three-quarters claim they are happy with their decision to retire, and a further 17%, while not happy, at least claim to have no regrets about leaving the workforce. Even spanking-new retirees share these same feelings despite their evident difficulties adjusting. Additionally, three-quarters of all retirees say they feel less stressed in retirement, and 55% rate their overall quality of life as excellent or very good. Notably, this is about the same proportion we found among those who are working.

And there is evidence that retirees do eventually achieve levels of happiness similar to those they felt when they were working. Earlier we presented the idea of an up-down-up pattern of subjective well-being (i.e., happiness) that social scientists theorize should occur over time in retirement. To review, all three theories discussed earlier predict that retirees will initially experience a honeymoon phase, followed by disenchantment, which is in turn followed by adjustment and improved subjective well-being as retirees get used to the lifestyle.

When we first looked at retirees in total, we could not find that up-down-up pattern. This was not completely surprising since not all research studies have clearly shown this pattern, and some researchers have suggested that it may not apply to all retirees. That being said, we decided to dig a little further into the numbers, at which point we did indeed find the pattern. To get there, we had to focus only on retirees who were in good health. We realized that as retirees spend more time in retirement, they are also getting older. That obvious fact has some major implications. With increased age, health problems become more prevalent, and the quality of health has a profound effect on a person's happiness. But by focusing our analysis on only healthy retirees, we could eliminate the confounding effect that declining health might be having our results. In other words, when we looked at healthy and unhealthy retirees together, ratings on overall happiness stayed the same. This turned out to be because healthy retirees' ratings were going up and unhealthy retirees' ratings were going down, so they averaged no change over time. But when we looked at only healthy retirees, taking out health issues as a confounding variable, we were able to see what happens to retirees specifically as a result of how long they have been retired.

Focusing on ratings of their perceived quality of life, a measure of overall happiness, we found that in year 1 of retirement, healthy retirees rate their overall quality of life slightly higher than those who are still working. This is the period of euphoria, the honeymoon, as the pressures of working are eliminated and the retiree has complete freedom of movement.

But very quickly, somewhere between years 1 and 2, retirees hit a low point. Their overall quality-of-life ratings fall sharply, down to almost half that of those retired one year or less and those still working. Beginning in year 3, their quality-of-life perceptions start to recover—but only slowly—and it's not until they are eight or more years into retirement that we finally see their ratings improve to their starting levels, that is, when they were still working.

So we have a good news/bad news story. As the good news, there is hope—eventually retirees come to terms with their retirement, accepting it for what it is. The bad news is it can take quite a while to get there. In fact, among those who are completely adjusted, 54% have been retired for more than five years—among those who are poorly adjusted, the same percentage have been retired for less than three years. Said another way, well-adjusted retirees have been retired for about six years on average; the poorly adjusted averaged only three years.

And, unfortunately, there is some more bad news: many retirees show some key losses regardless of how long they are retired. For one, 45% say they miss their jobs, and except for the newly retired who are probably still in the euphoria of their newfound freedom (among whom only 36% say they miss their jobs), this number does not decline even 11 or more years into retirement. Such an attitude would suggest that many retirees have not found enough things to occupy their time that are as fulfilling or engaging as their job once was.

When we looked at how retirees feel about themselves, we found that some can experience psychological difficulties. As an overview, there is a sense that some retirees have almost shut down and closed themselves off, that retirement is not only about stopping work but to some extent also about stopping *living*. Some of their attitudes almost mirror a mild form of depression: as is the case among those truly suffering depression, they're aware of their listlessness but lack the energy or the will to help themselves out of their funk. (We hasten to add that we are *not* suggesting that all retirees who have adjustment problems are literally clinically depressed—although some are likely to be: retirees are twice as likely as those still working to be on antidepressant medications, and one-third of these retirees started taking them after retiring. Our point, instead, is to emphasize just how much difficulty some retirees can have in their adjustment by noting that, *in some respects*, their problems echo those of people whose issues call for psychological counseling.) Some of their attitudes suggest a weakened self-esteem, a loss of direction and purpose, and much-reduced levels of motivation and open-mindedness. The latter two of these are particularly troublesome since, if nothing else, retirees need to have a good deal of drive and a willingness to experiment if they are going to build a fulfilling life after leaving work. Here are the more important differences we found between retirees and those who are still working:

- Relative to those in the workforce, retirees as a group are much less likely to believe their lives have been a success, to feel they are useful or productive, or to be optimistic about their futures.
- They are more likely to have bouts of loneliness and have lower energy levels and greater difficulty getting motivated. They are less prone to have goals and more likely to report having too much free time, yet they are less likely to see retirement as a time to get energized to pursue new goals. Relatedly, while they have a harder time finding interesting things to do, they are much less open to trying new things and claim they have difficulty coping with change.
- Interestingly, the newly retired (i.e., retired six months or less) tend to be more optimistic about their futures and to feel more motivated, but their motivation and optimism start to decline by the time they are three years or more into retirement.

For some of these findings, we cannot assume causality—it may be the case, for example, that those who retire are different in their psychological makeup from those who choose not to and that retirement per se does not cause these changes. However, it is interesting to note that motivation weakens as people spend more time in retirement—this would suggest that the retirement lifestyle, with its limited demands, does in fact cause retirees to have less interest in doing at least some things. Nevertheless, regardless of whether attitudinal differences are caused by retirement or are inherent in people who want to retire, the ways of thinking held by some retirees can make adjustment a difficult proposition.

But again, it's not a problem for all retirees. The 44% who claim to be completely adjusted seem to have found their way to a satisfying life. These folks don't have the psychological weaknesses we found for all retirees relative to those still working. In fact, in some ways, they have a healthier profile than those still toiling at their jobs—they tend to be more self-confident and optimistic about their futures, for example. They also tend to do a number of things well in their day-to-day living, and the paths they choose help to illustrate what it takes to achieve a successful retirement. So it is for this reason that in the upcoming chapters, we will use these well-adjusted retirees as a comparison group as we discuss the most effective means of dealing with the many issues that can impede adjustment and detract from subjective well-being for the less well adjusted.

II

PRERETIREMENT: WHAT TO KNOW BEFORE YOU GO

How We Decide

Before deciding to take early retirement from your job, stay home a week and watch daytime television.

—Anonymous

$\mathscr{T}$he decision to retire and when to do so is one of the most important choices most people will make in their later adult years. And it often isn't an easy one, partly because of how big a step retirement is but also because of the sheer number of considerations that need to be weighed. As part of the process, retirees are likely to undertake a mental assessment, laying out what they see as the advantages and shortcomings of retiring versus staying in the labor market. They'll typically examine aspects of their career as well as personal characteristics and background. In the end, the way that retirees arrive at their decision can influence whether and to what extent they are in the right frame of mind for the retirement lifestyle. Some elements leading to the decision can help retirees be well prepared for the event, increasing the odds that their adjustment will be smooth. And there are some that operate against a smooth transition.

How would-be retirees get to their retirement is important, for it determines the in-going mind-set: how the event is perceived. In that regard, social scientists and economists have come to look at the decision process in terms of "push" and "pull" factors.[1] Pull factors are the ones that lead a person to decide to retire voluntarily, while push factors force people into retirement through no choice of their own. In general, pull factors are enticements: retirees enter retirement with a positive state of mind, and this is an advantage in terms of adjustment. Push factors, on the other hand, tend to be negatives, often leaving the retiree less well prepared mentally. This push/pull perspective can be applied to almost all of the elements would-be retirees need to consider in their decision process.

Of all potential factors, finances and health are the paramount considerations in the decision process. Retirees must believe they have the resources to survive without a regular paycheck; their savings, pension, and Social Security must be adequate to see them through their remaining years. Feeling financially secure unquestionably works as a pull factor. With adequate income, retirees can essentially enjoy freedom from want. They can then decide to retire on the grounds that the benefits of the retirement lifestyle, with its reduced responsibility and lack of constraints, outweigh the benefits of unneeded added income. Once the retiree has achieved economic critical mass, he or she is not obligated to continue working, so the anticipated lifestyle benefits of retirement serve to pull him or her out of the workforce. In contrast, those without adequate financial support, because of either limited savings or pensions or the presence of financial obligations (e.g., children still living at home), are not at all in a position to retire.

Health, on the other hand, functions mostly as a push factor. To be sure, it is possible that some people might consider retiring because their good health allows them the mobility to live well in retirement. Under these circumstances, health works as a pull factor. But the reverse is more often the case; that is, poor health will tend to push people to consider retirement. At worst, in cases of failing health, such as serious illness or functional impairment, workers who are no longer capable of doing their jobs may be forced to view retirement as the only feasible alternative.

But the above is clearly a worst-case situation—a potential retiree doesn't have to suffer a totally debilitating illness in order to feel that his or her health is not good enough to keep working. For example, as they get older, workers may sense that they have lost a degree of effectiveness at their job, perhaps because of a physical manifestation such as reduced stamina, especially when compared to younger workers. Their perceived loss of competency could detract from their confidence, possibly making them feel vulnerable to losing their jobs. They may then come to view their occupations as undesirable and unfulfilling and at worst may feel pressure from younger workers to retire "voluntarily."

For some, this realization may serve as a welcomed relief—a good excuse to take the plunge into retirement. In this context, there is both a pull and a push since these retirees may have only wanted a little justification for retiring but didn't want to make that decision on their own. In reality, it is likely that retirement already had some allure for these people. For others, though, their perceptions of reduced or failing competency may lead to feelings of being forced out of their jobs, even if not overtly in the sense of being fired but certainly as an end result.[2]

Beyond money and health, a person's occupation and working conditions play a role in the decision to retire. These typically operate more as "a push out of work" than "a pull into retirement." We have to presume that positive working conditions and an enjoyable occupation provide more motivation to continue working than to move into retirement. On the other hand, research has shown—and common sense would suggest—that jobs that are seen as unpleasant are likely to push workers to consider retirement. That's what makes a bad job more of a push—retirees are more interested in escaping an undesirable situation than in going to one that they see as rewarding.

However, working conditions are only one side of the equation. Regardless of how they feel about their jobs, would-be retirees still need to determine whether their lives would be better outside of work. So, assuming that their financial situations are secured, retirees make their decision by assessing the pluses and minuses of the two options. The extent to which an occupation is viewed positively or negatively on its specific features, weighed against the perceived benefits and shortcomings of retiring, will determine whether a worker feels he or she is better off continuing to work or entering into retirement.[3]

Obviously, weighing the options is a complex process, but there's still more to be taken into account. Even if the benefits of a given job outweigh its shortcomings, that *still* may not mean staying in the workforce is the best option. There must be a perceived sense of security that a job can be held into the foreseeable future. If, for example, you work in a declining industry, such as certain manufacturing sectors in the United States, or if your company is looking to cut staffing, then you might really have little choice but to consider leaving the workforce. This is especially the case if your financial resources are sufficient or a financial package is offered by your company or if trying to get a job in another company is not a realistic option.

Having an uncertain future career path usually pushes people out of the workforce but not always—there can also be some pulling into retirement. For example, preretirees not immediately forced out of their jobs have the option to decide to stay at work for as long as possible. If they decide to leave without being forced to, then there must be something about being retired that seems attractive. Of course, if a person tries to stay on the job until the bitter end in a declining industry, then he or she may eventually be pushed out once the job is eliminated.

Along with finances, health, and the job itself, there are personal factors to be considered in the retirement decision. These can relate, for example, to a person's values, aspirations, and the potential he or she sees for a life outside of work.[4] More often than not, personal reasons act as pulls since they suggest that retirement is seen as offering a better lifestyle. As one example, someone who retires for personal reasons may be interested in pursuing new goals. This in turn implies a positive perception of retirement as well as the presence of specific plans and activities already in mind, all of which make for a smoother and faster adjustment.

Personal reasons may be particularly relevant to those who retire while still in their fifties. Young retirees are likely to leave the workforce because they want their lives to take a different direction. In other words, they are pulled into retirement because they sense something positive in that lifestyle rather than seeing it as something they have to do because they're getting old. Of course, they may be bored with their careers or maybe want less stress in their lives, but generally they have something in mind that may be more personally fulfilling, and retirement allows them to go after these goals. And with their relative youth, they are likely to have enough energy and drive left in them to bring their new plans to fruition.

But not all personal or emotional considerations work exclusively as pulls into retirement—some can have both pull and push qualities, and some can actually work more as a push out of work. Leaving a job to eliminate stress or because it is disliked are examples of this push–pull duality. In this case, the motivation to quit work can be seen as a pull into retirement because the individual wants to move into a better living situation. Research has shown that those retiring from jobs that are psychologically demanding, stressful, unrewarding, or unpleasant are happier in retirement because of the relief it provides—at least initially.

However, this scenario is not fully a pull into retirement. There's a piece missing: how retirement is perceived. As a singular thought, "get me out of my awful job" is just another type of push out of work; to make it a pull, it has to be accompanied by a perspective that retirement would be a great destination. In other words, leaving a bad environment just to "get out" is a very different proposition from moving to a new environment because of its expected benefits. Retirees who in effect simply flee their unpleasant jobs might enjoy being retired initially since they've eliminated a source of unhappiness, but their lack of attention to developing a new life could leave them ill prepared to enjoy their retirement in the long term. If you decide to quit work because you hate your job, search for the meaningful positives about retirement before making the leap.

The timing of retirement is also important. Researchers point out that retirement needs to occur by choice and at a predesignated time. People whose retirement is expected and planned for will have had an opportunity to examine their retirement within the overall context of their lives prior to it actually taking place. When a person is forced to retire in an "off-time" way, that is, earlier or later than expected, that can be a stressful or disruptive experience.[5] Worse still, if other important elements are unfavorable, for example, family life and marriage, or if no new life paths have been adequately developed to replace the career path, as mentioned in our discussion on the life course perspective, then it is even more likely that the retiree will run into adjustment problems.[6]

As we mentioned, looking at the retirement decision in terms of the various pushes and pulls makes a lot of sense. And while it should be obvious by now, we nevertheless want to state it explicitly: as a general rule, pulls are good, and pushes are bad—for retirement and for subjective well-being. Being pulled into retirement means you have a choice; being pushed out of work means the decision is forced on you. When retirees are pulled into retirement, they are more likely to find the whole idea of retirement attractive—they see it as a destination, full of promise and opportunities.[7] To them, retirement is the logical next step into a life stage they look forward to.

Beyond just feeling good about retirement, voluntary retirees have a few advantages over those forced to retire. They tend to be more open to new experiences and are likely to have done their homework and to have made specific plans for their retirement. By doing so, voluntary retirees help to ensure that they keep a sense of direction and purpose in their lives once they leave their jobs. They have an easier time making plans because they feel personally in control of their futures, and that sense of control over their destinies allows them to adapt more quickly to their life outside of work.

Voluntary retirees also have the benefit of knowing in advance when they will retire. They don't have the stress of an off-time exit, so they have a better opportunity to plan their futures as well as adopt the right mind-set about retirement. Both adopting a positive attitude and making preparations for retirement help to make the transition a little smoother. At the same time, voluntary retirees can begin distancing themselves from their careers while still in the workforce. They are likely to use the last few months at work to loosen their commitment and break down emotional connections to their jobs while building up their connections to the retirement role.

In contrast, retirees who have been pushed out of their jobs and forced into retirement are more likely to run into adjustment problems right from the start. Regardless of whether the retiree is forced to retire for personal reasons, such as poor health or family problems, or because of organizational changes, the end result is generally the same—they are mentally and emotionally unprepared for retirement. Their sense of having little or no ability to affect their own circumstances can lead to feelings of anxiety and despondency. They may feel angry, resentful, unappreciated, and abandoned. These feelings may emerge while still working, but even if they don't, they are likely to emerge in the early stages of retirement.

Furthermore, forced retirees tend to have little advance warning, sometimes only a few weeks, from the time they discover they are being retired and the event itself. In comparison, voluntary retirees may have a transition period of a year or more between their decision to leave their jobs and their actual retirement. With less advance notice, forced retirees have far less time to adjust their mind-set—to become retirees in their heads. Consequently, when they retire, they are more likely to hold on to their worker role, not having the time or maybe even the inclination to emotionally break from their careers. And without strengthening their reliance on other identities, they have a greater tendency to find themselves falling into the "roleless" role predicted by role theory. Their lack of time also hurts their chances of planning a retirement lifestyle. With no plans, forced retirees can feel disconnected, especially early on in retirement. Without a clear-cut path to follow, they may suffer a loss of direction or meaning to their lives.[8]

What we have just described for forced retirees is a worst-case scenario—a worker who has absolutely no idea that his or her job is nearing an end and for whom retirement is the last thing on his or her mind. To be sure, this happens every day, but there are also many forced retirees for whom the situation is not so dire. They like what they are doing, don't intend to retire soon, but have an inkling that retirement may be thrust on them. When it happens, they are not completely caught off guard and may have already kicked the idea of retirement around in their heads if for no other reason than having read the writing on the wall. Some may even have come to terms with the inevitable even before it becomes a reality and started preparing themselves for the lifestyle change. They are likely to have a very different retirement experience, at least at the onset, than those retirees in the worst-case scenario.

We have encountered two retirees who represent the opposing ends of the spectrum. Both were forced out of their jobs, but they had very different outcomes because of differences in their degree of preparedness and perspective on retirement. The relative experiences demonstrate that while not all pushes into retirement are entirely negative, some can be psychologically devastating.

Tony, a corporate executive, truly looked forward to the day he would retire, although he had no immediate plans to do so. As a result, even though his retirement was forced, he entered this life stage in a positive frame of mind. Consequently, he did not look back disappointedly to the job he lost but instead was ready to move in the direction of building a new life:

> Word came on a Monday morning when my boss called my office and asked me to join her in a conference room. I instantly realized what was about to happen. Sure enough, when I arrived at the conference room, my somber-faced boss and an HR person were waiting. Within seconds, the dreaded but expected words were spoken: "your position has been eliminated." I have to say that the whole event was handled professionally and

with a good deal of sensitivity. My boss, whom I had known for 20 years, was actually more upset than I was. And as we left the conference room, I found myself comforting her rather than vice versa.

I actually chose to stay in the office for the remainder of the day and was gratified by the steady stream of coworkers who came to visit as word spread through the organization. Not that I needed the blow to be softened, but their kind words made me feel good about the job I had done for my company.

I fully understand what happened to me that Monday morning, as it happens hundreds of times a day in corporate America— workers in their fifties are asked to leave in spite of their continued dedication, strong work ethic, and ongoing significant contributions to their organization. It is, of course, inherently unfair. Would I have liked to continue working for at least a couple more years? Absolutely. Nevertheless, I felt at the time—and still do—that for so many reasons, *I was one of the lucky ones.* My severance and retirement package—pension, health care coverage, etcetera—were generous. College tuitions were behind us, and our finances were in good shape. My wife was working. Most importantly, it happened when I was 59. My heart goes out to folks whose careers are ended in their early or mid-fifties. For me, had I been even two or three years younger, things would have been dramatically different. I don't think I would have been emotionally ready for retirement at, say, 56 or 57. Nor would I have been as prepared financially. And I would be faced with the daunting prospect of job hunting, knowing the chances of being hired at that age were minuscule in spite of decent credentials and a pretty good reputation in the field. But finding another job at my age was the last thing I wanted to do—I love being retired.

On the other end, Charles, a police chief in a small town, provides some insight into how disruptive forced retirement can be. In his case, Charles was prevented from enjoying his retirement for a number of years because of difficulties in coming to terms with the events that led to his retirement:

I did not plan my retirement. In my mind, retirement was for everyone else. Although after 20 years of service I did find myself checking and double-checking the amount of money I would receive down the road, I loved my job and had no plans to leave. But years of long hours, working side jobs most of my career, poor nutrition, and family problems were catching up with me. I was good at what I was doing, but when you are running a business that never closes and overseeing 36 employees, it takes its toll. Then at the 20-year mark, I went through a divorce and took full custody of my three children. Somewhere around that point, I suffered a heart attack that I was too busy to know I had. I still never thought seriously about retirement.

But then the situation at work changed. A job as police chief has its political side, and there are times you will find that you are expected to sacrifice your principles and ethics. My entire life I played by the rules and was not about to change or to bend those rules. Things became so bad because I refused to play ball that I even hired an attorney for my protection. I knew I was defeated, but I hung in for a few more years even though I knew I didn't belong there anymore. But after an extended time recovering from a heart operation, I made a decision to retire. After 28 years in a job I loved, I was thrown into retirement.

I left that job angry. I found that people I worked with for years, the same people that once came to me for a job, didn't even stop by my office to say good-bye. Nobody cared. I was sad that so much had changed, but I looked forward to leaving so that I could heal my many wounds. I remember locking my office door for the last time and quietly leaving.

But it wasn't over for me. I was consumed with the way my career ended. I was running the work lives of a number of people and now nothing. No more calls sorting out issues, making decisions. Instead, all I had were the thoughts of how things ended up. These thoughts ran my head all over the place. I had no peace. I was an unemployed chief of police—it was not just a job to me; it was my life and identity. It was too much for me to accept because I didn't come to that out of my own choice. My sleeping patterns were a problem . . . sleeping way too much. I started a routine of going out to pick up coffee and hanging out with my dog. She is a little dog that came to work with me every day and sat on my desk. I would walk that dog and think about what had happened, how I had been betrayed by some of my closest friends. I walked that dog so many times that one night I looked up my house address on some satellite imaging website, and there we were . . . me and the dog in front of the house. It took years for me to finally give all this up and start living again.

The experiences of Tony and Charles illustrate how different forced retirement scenarios can have an impact on adjustment and subjective well-being. But here we should point out that gender plays a role in the retirement decision as well. Satisfaction in retirement tends to be lower for women who feel pushed out of the workplace. While they tend to have other nonwork roles and more disruptions in their work histories, these do not seem to help them make an easy transition from the workforce under the specific situation of forced retirement.[9]

At this point, we need to shift our focus away from the issues faced by preretirees themselves because typically they are not the only ones involved in or affected by the decision to retire. The fact is most adults have a spouse or significant other in their lives, and the decision to retire is typically explored jointly, not solely by the retiree. Couples talk to each other before moving forward, and their decisions generally take into account each other's needs, desires, and expectations. They are also likely to discuss the obvious issues of affordability, the impact on other family obligations, what they will do in retirement, and the specifics of when the event should take place.[10]

Within both single- and dual-worker households, couples will also consider the quality of their relationship in the decision process. Where the relationship is positive, there may be greater motivation to retire because doing so promises more time together and a sharing of joint activities. For couples in this happy situation, retirement is a positive event that has the potential to enhance the subjective well-being of both partners.[11]

For potential retirees who find themselves in unhappy marriages or relationships, on the other hand, leaving the workforce becomes more problematic. Remaining at work provides an avenue of escape for both the worker and his or her partner, whereas retirement requires these couples to spend more time together in an unpleasant situation. If both partners in this sort of relationship are happy in their careers, the decision is a relatively simple one—stay on the job and maybe find a second one. But under conditions where a job is seen as stressful or unsatisfying, the worker is left with the dilemma of having to choose between the lesser of two evils. Neither choice is likely to lead to a satisfying retirement unless the couple can find diversions that allow them time apart from each other.

But for all couples, whether happy or unhappy, the decision to retire is likely to bring out some concerns as to how marriage and home life will be affected. In other words, retirement might be a scary proposition for a retiree but no less so for the one you are retiring with. These concerns focus on retirement's impact on the dynamics of the relationship, the distribution of household chores, how each will live with the other with so much free time on their hands, and so on. Angela clearly expressed many of these fears when asked how she views her husband's retirement. Angela, 51, has been out of the workforce for about 10 years, while Larry, 63, an entrepreneur, is still working full-time but is likely to retire within the next few years. Despite a happy marriage, Larry's retirement is a source of anxiety for Angela. Her concerns are for her husband's happiness but are also very much—if not more so—about how his retirement will change her life:

> I think there are some positives about Larry retiring. I look forward to spending more time together. We'll have more time to travel, we can sleep later, and we'll just have more time to do what we want. But I don't think this will be a bed of roses. First, I have concerns about Larry. He needs to keep busy at all times, but he doesn't have a lot of outside interests other than work. He has no hobbies; he plays a little golf, but he can take it or leave it. So I think retirement for Larry is going to be difficult. He has worked forever, and he loves it. I just don't know if he'll be happy.

As for me, I have lots of activities to fill my time. I love to cook, have dinner parties, read, go shopping, have lunch with friends, and get my spa treatments. I take care of the house inside and out, and I plan all of our traveling and social activities.

So when I think of Larry retiring, I really worry about how it will affect me and my life. I want him to find things to do without me so I can continue doing what I want. I don't want him to feel he needs to be with me 24/7. The truth is, I really love my personal time and doing things at my own pace.

One of my biggest fears is money. We are financially ready for retirement, and with what we have, we can continue to live the same lifestyle for the rest of our lives. But I've seen men change when they stop bringing home a paycheck, and that scares me more than anything. I really believe that's going to be the biggest challenge for both of us. My personality is to spend, and his is to save. It's a good mix because we usually end up somewhere in the middle. But I think when the paychecks stop, it's going to be more difficult to get the things I want. For example, if I want to change something in the house like drapes, bedding, rugs, or something in the yard, he'll give me a hard time. When Larry retires, it's going to be harder to get him to spend. Maybe I'll have to find him a part-time job.

While Angela was worried about her own future when Larry retires, still she was able to see some positives, such as added time together. For some wives, however, there are aspects of their relationship that are problematic before retirement and are likely to become more so when their husbands spend more time at home. Lynne left the workforce years ago to raise children and run her household, and her husband retired a few years ago. Most of her friends have also been out of the workforce for quite some time, but their husbands are still working. Lynne asked these women over dinner how they would feel about their husbands retiring, and they were of one voice in rejecting the idea. As with Angela, these women's fears revolved around how they would be able to use their own time, but they also expressed strong concerns about their husbands' lack of support in maintaining the household—concerns that they fear would only get worse when their husbands actually *do* retire:

> Many of my friends' husbands are a few years away from retirement, but when I asked if they were looking forward to celebrating this stage of their lives, it was apparent from the looks on their faces that this was not something the six of them were happily anticipating.
>
> Joan just stared at me for a moment, then followed that disgusted look with the fact that her husband thinks he has retired already. He does not do anything around the house anymore. He, although home before she is, will not start dinner, do laundry, or even clean up or load the dishwasher with the dishes that weren't there when she left in the morning. When she

can't see her Yorkie in the backyard, it's time for her to call the teenager next door to mow. Her husband goes to work, comes home, and "retires" for the remainder of the night/weekend.

Donna's husband is a TV buff. It doesn't really matter what's on; he just enjoys sitting in front of it. If she has household chores—like vacuuming—he is very understanding and tells her to go ahead and vacuum—it won't bother him. She so looks forward to his errand day. He prefaces every one of those excursions with "I have some things I have to take care of. See you later." She is always hopeful that he will be out for a couple of hours so that she could just be alone in the house for a little while, but sometimes he's back within 20 minutes—or so it seems. It's not even enough time for her to take a bath, read the paper, or vacuum without guilt.

Arlene, Nancy, and Maria are not working now. They are all financially comfortable, so they do not have to worry about their entertainment expenses—shopping, tennis, lunch with friends, manicures, pedicures, movies, etcetera. They even enjoy being able to tackle household chores at their own pace. If they want to get up and have coffee and just stare at the kitchen table, they can do so without being asked why they are doing that. On occasion, when their husbands are home, Nancy and Arlene said that, if they are going out, they have to answer questions first, like "Where are you going?," "What time will you be back?," and "What do you want to do for dinner?"

Maria, on the other hand, has created a very interesting pastime—blogging. She includes photos of certain foods she cooks, flowers she's grown, as well as books she's read and places she has traveled. When not creating or experiencing subject matter for her blogs, she is actually writing and editing her work. Needless to say, when she and her husband are not traveling, she spends her days in front of her laptop. If her husband is home, he always asks what she's got planned for the day. If she answers in any way related to blogging, he always makes a comment about wasting time or that she acts like this is a job. Now, when she knows he is going to be home, she uses those days to do errands or lunch with friends.

These women are not in the workforce, and while they may not be happy about their husbands' pending retirements, they are likely to have some input as to when they will do so. The same is typically true for dual-worker households—retirement is handled as a joint effort, and both partners have at least some say as to when to retire. However, in practice, the decision often focuses more on the husband's aspirations. Researchers have found that if the husband is interested in retiring, he may pressure his wife to do the same, although the reverse is not typically the case. Rather, her decision to retire is more likely to be driven first by her husband's decision.[12]

But this is not the ideal situation for women. The greater the extent to which a working wife bases her own decision on her husband's plans, the more likely she will find herself at a disadvantage. Research has shown that wives are less happy in retirement if they feel their husbands drove their decision to retire. Without equal input, she may feel more pushed out of the workplace than pulled into retirement and thus may not be fully prepared mentally or emotionally for leaving her job. As a result, she may have a harder time adjusting and may experience declines in subjective well-being that might have been less likely to occur if she felt the decision was her own.

Men and women are notably different here: women are not just concerned about having input into their own retirement; they also want a say when it comes to the decision for their husbands. For retired husbands, whether their wives influenced their retirement decision has little impact on how they feel in retirement. But wives, if they feel they were part of their husband's decision, tend to be happier about their husband's retirement as a result. Wives' need for input on both ends makes a good deal of sense—working women operate fully in two worlds, work and home, while nonworking women typically manage their homes on their own. For both, their lives tend to be affected by their husbands' retirement at the household level. But for whatever the reason, these findings suggest that a happier retirement—for both men and women—will result if the wives feel they have input regardless of who is retiring.[13]

That pretty much sums up what social scientists have to say about how we make our decision to retire. In our own survey, we looked into all of these issues in detail to see if there were perspectives or elements we might add—specifically, how retirees arrive at their retirement decision and how the factors weighing on their decision affect their adjustment and subjective well-being.

We found that push and pull factors were indeed likely to lead to different retirement outcomes. But we also found that many retirees do not fall neatly into one camp or the other. Rather, for a relatively large proportion of retirees, there is often a combination of both forces at work—from our survey, 34% completely retired by their own choice (i.e., were pulled), 36% describe themselves as completely pushed out of the workforce, but 30% gave answers to our questions about the "why" behind their retirement that clearly suggested they felt they were both pushed and pulled into retirement.

The fact that both push and pull factors play a role for such a large percentage of retirees is understandable. As we alluded to previously, whether a retiree is pushed or pulled is not always that clear-cut—Tony, our forced-out retiree who didn't mind retiring, is a good example of a person who is both pushed and pulled. Some factors, such as wanting a stress-free life, can be seen in terms of being both a push and a pull into retirement—the push is the job being too stressful, and the pull is the expectation (or at least the hope) that retirement will not be very stressful. Furthermore, some retirees, even though they may feel retirement has become their inevitable fate, may also look on that life stage as an opportunity to build an enjoyable life without the pressures of work.

When we asked those who said they retired by choice why they retired, roughly 4 in 10 mentioned they just wanted to stop working and were looking for more free time. But quite a few mentioned reasons indicative of being forced into retirement: 4 in 10 also wanted less stress, and 2 in 10 mentioned that health problems caused them to retire. As such, although they classify themselves as being pulled, the reasons they give suggest that some pushes were present as well. Similarly, among those who were forced to retire, about half mentioned health, and one-quarter stated their job was eliminated, but 15% also mentioned a pull factor, such as wanting more free time. In total, our survey found that both pushes *and* pulls were present in the decision for almost a third of retirees.

But remember: the 30% who mentioned *both* push and pull factors in their retirement decision actually classified themselves as falling into only one group: some say they were forced to retire and some as having retired by their own choice. What seems to determine how they classify themselves is whether they feel retirement offers them new opportunities. In other words, those feeling they retired by choice look on retirement favorably, while those feeling forced to retire see fewer positives to leaving the workforce. Whatever their perspective, it is reasonable to assume that, among those mentioning both push and pull factors, some were more pushed than pulled into retirement and some were more pulled—relatively few were equally affected by both forces.

That being said, whether retirees were completely pushed, completely pulled, or a little of both, our results showed a more positive outcome for those who were pulled into retirement. First of all, when we took a look at those who are well adjusted to retirement, 68% felt they retired by their own choice, but only 31% of the less well adjusted made that claim. Less well adjusted retirees also found their forced retirement to be particularly upsetting and felt that it interfered in their ability to enjoy retirement.

We looked a little more closely at those who labeled themselves as retired by choice to get an idea of the ways they do better in retirement. For one, how they felt about their jobs gave us a sense that those retiring by choice (i.e., pulled into retirement) were mentally ready to leave the workforce. Although both liked their jobs equally while they had them, 59% of those forced into retirement claimed to miss their jobs as compared to only 32% who retired by choice. Furthermore, 29% of those forced out claimed that, if they had the option, they would prefer to be back at work, but only 3% of those retiring by choice held that perspective.

Not surprisingly, before they retired, those who chose to retire had a better view of what retirement would be like—95% expected retirement to be positive as compared to 73% who were forced into retirement. But more important, 70% of choice retirees felt their positive expectations had been met as compared to only 35% of those forced into retirement—in other words, those who were forced into retirement not only expected less but also got even less than they expected. And once into retirement, those there by choice fared better:

- Among those who retired by choice, 69% are satisfied with their retirement lifestyle as compared to only 36% of those forced into retirement. About 55% describe themselves as completely adjusted, but only 31% of those pushed into retirement feel that way. Those retiring by choice also report much lower stress and a better quality of life and are happier with how they spend their time in comparison to forced retirees.
- Retirees who chose to retire are more likely to be self-confident and optimistic about the future, feel connected to the world, and feel productive. They are also much less likely to be taking antidepressant medications than are those who felt they were forced to retire.

Those retiring by choice have other advantages. For example, they had about 11 months from the time they decided to retire until they actually did so, much more so than the roughly five months available to forced retirees. So choice retirees had about twice as much time to get their mind-sets right and make preparations for their retirement. And they seemed to use their added time as well as could be expected—47% made plans for their retirement prior to leaving work, but only 28% of forced retirees did so, and choice retirees were much more likely to achieve the goals they set for themselves.

The phrase "as well as could be expected" that you may have noticed in the previous paragraph was meant to signal a potential problem. The planning efforts for all retirees, even many of the successful ones, tend to focus mostly on finances, and this is also true for those retiring by choice. As will be discussed in a later chapter, many retirees, seemingly through a lack of awareness, miss critical areas in their planning, and what they miss can have an effect on how well and how quickly they actually adjust to retirement.

Choice retirees have more going for them than just time to prepare. They are much more motivated to pursue the various aspects that make life fulfilling. For example, they tend to be more active, participating in a variety of social and personal activities, and are more passionate about their activities. They are also much more likely to find their activities rewarding—even more so than their jobs were. Those forced to retire, in contrast, are much less enthusiastic about how they spend their time—they are more likely to feel they cannot find interesting things to do and just don't know what to do with their time. Socially, although those retiring by choice have the same-size social circles as those forced, the way they interact with their circle is much more rewarding: they spend more time with friends and are more emotionally connected to their friends in and out of the workforce. As a result, they are much more likely to feel satisfied with their social lives, which they believe have gotten better since retiring.

So it would seem that retiring by choice—being pulled into retirement—is a much better situation. However, before we accept that blanket statement, we need to point out that there are two other important areas where choice and forced retirees differ—money and health. Forced retirees are less healthy and have a harder time covering their expenses. As we mentioned, roughly half of those forced to retire cite health issues as the reason, and forced retirees also have much lower annual incomes—$48,000 versus about $64,000 for those retiring by choice.

As will be discussed in a later chapter, health and financial status can have a major impact on quality of life and subjective well-being regardless of whether a person is pushed or pulled into retirement. With that said, we wanted to be completely sure that those forced out of the workforce are less happy in retirement solely because they had no choice but to retire and their unhappiness did not actually stem from their health or finance problems.

To answer this question, we looked at only those who retired for reasons other than health, and we compared forced and choice retirees with the same income levels. We found exactly the same results—even when health and income were taken out of the equation, those who retired by choice were happier and better adjusted in retirement and seemed to have developed a lifestyle that was much more satisfying and fulfilling as compared to those forced into retirement.

Regardless of whether leaving work by force or by choice, what seems to differentiate successful retirees from less successful ones is their positive attitude and higher motivation. There are some well-adjusted retirees who are forced into retirement and some retirees who claimed they retired by choice who also had push elements working in their decision, a few of whom even reported health problems. But choice retirees embrace the idea of retirement, do not seem to dwell on the negatives of being displaced from the workforce, and take a more proactive stance in their handling of their retirement.

Forced retirees, in contrast, are particularly vulnerable to a letdown in subjective well-being. Because retirement is not their choice, they tend not to approach it in a positive state of mind. This negative attitude, in turn, may deter them from seeing the benefits of retirement and may limit their motivation to create a personally meaningful lifestyle. Worse still, because the interval between learning about their retirement and the actual event may be relatively short, they have less time to focus their thoughts on building a retirement lifestyle. The brief interim may also inhibit their ability to make the emotional break from their roles as workers, potentially stranding them without a role that would serve them better in retirement. Our earlier account regarding Police Chief Charles clearly illustrated how, in being pushed out of one's job, the opportunity to make the mental adjustment to retirement can be impaired, especially if one continually dwells on their unfortunate situation.

In contrast, those retiring by their own choice have a better chance of entering retirement on solid footing. They maintain a positive frame of mind and view retirement as a favorable life change. This is indeed a good start, but it doesn't mean they're invulnerable—even these retirees are likely to run into adjustment problems over time. They can, for example, experience disenchantment as a result of unmet expectations. To improve their odds of achieving a successful retirement, these retirees must use the time after they decide to retire but while still in the workforce to accomplish two objectives—manage their expectations as to what retirement is all about and plan, very specifically, how they will live outside the workforce.

For those forced out of their jobs, having realistic expectations and making plans are likely to be even more critical for success. But these retirees must take a few additional steps to get their retirement started off on the right foot. Forced retirees can best serve themselves by coming to terms with their circumstances as soon as possible. They should attempt to embrace the fact that retirement is their only option and stop fighting the inevitable. This includes coming to a realization that they must begin the process of breaking their emotional connection to their jobs—stop missing them, for example. Additionally, an assessment of their financial situation is called for, and it is hoped that this will achieve two important goals: first, to ensure that retirement is a realistic option, and, second, to let them feel confident with the idea that they can afford it.

Once they have fully accepted their fate, forced retirees need to adopt the appropriate frame of mind. At this point, their efforts should focus on the positives of the retirement lifestyle. Obviously, analyzing the trade-offs of the advantages versus disadvantages of retiring no longer serves any purpose—their retirement's a done deal, and they have to get on with it. Instead, they need to turn their attention to how they will live in retirement, first by imagining the freedom from stress and schedules and then looking for future opportunities.

Beyond their personal mental preparation, retirees can also help themselves by preparing their significant other. Assuming that the retiree is retiring by choice, both partners should have input into the decision so that each feels some control and responsibility for the event, not that retirement was forced on them. The next not-so-obvious step should include open and frank conversations about life together without the diversion of work. Since healthy relationships require time together and time apart, there is the issue of managing expectations. A retiring husband must acknowledge that his non-working partner has established her own patterns and ways to spend personal time and that his retirement does not put an end to that. From the husband's perspective, he should develop and pursue his own interests so that he is not completely dependent on his wife for his entertainment. Then each partner also needs to understand what is expected of the other with regard to shared time—and with shared responsibilities around the home. Husbands who retire should consider that their wives are likely—and rightly so—to expect greater sharing of the household burdens. By discussing who will be responsible for what, couples can avoid becoming disappointed with each other.

In short, preretirees need to weigh many mental and emotional factors in trying to decide whether to leave the workforce. The extent to which one's options are fully understood and the positives and negatives are thought through carefully will have a lot to do with whether the decision to retire is ultimately the right one. But, of course, that's not enough—there are lots of other issues to be aware of. In the following chapters, we discuss the importance of having not only a positive state of mind but also an accurate perspective on what retirement is all about and then how one should prepare for all that free time.

Preconceptions and Misconceptions

The only way to avoid being miserable [in retirement] is not to
have enough leisure to wonder whether you are happy or not.

—George Bernard Shaw

$\mathcal{A}$fter the decision to retire is made, the last few months in the workforce
are the time to prepare for retirement. Regardless of whether soon-to-be retirees are pushed or pulled into retirement, they are likely to begin to establish
expectations about what retirement will be like while they're still working.
For those looking forward to the event, one might think this would be a time
to indulge in pleasant dreams about freedom from responsibilities and stress,
about finally having time to relax and pursue things they've always wanted to.
One might also think, on the other hand, that those forced into retirement or
who dread the prospect of leaving their jobs may be having nightmares. Their
thoughts might be expected to focus more on worries or fears about no longer
being involved in meaningful tasks, losing a source of self-esteem, and becoming disconnected from coworker friends. They may also wonder how they'll
ever be able to fill all the free time without meetings, assignments, and so on.

While both scenarios are intuitively reasonable, the fact is that even
people looking forward to retirement may approach the event with a degree of
trepidation. Researchers have found that a large percentage of pending retirees
have negative expectations about retirement, possibly because their futures are
uncertain. They are likely to focus less on the good things, such as reduced
stress and personal freedom, and instead tend to overestimate potential problems, such as the prospect of poor health, a potentially unsatisfactory social life,
or inadequate finances. These thoughts can lead to considerable anxiety and
even to second-guessing their own decision to retire.

Negative expectations can also be driven by preconceptions about how retirement would make you see yourself. And these preconceptions can create such poor expectations about retirement that they prevent people from ever considering it. In this regard, we came across an issue that has not as yet been covered much by social scientists. There seems to be a fear that retirement would make you feel old, that it puts you one step closer— maybe too close—to the grave. Rather than being seen as an opportunity to take life in a new and exciting direction, retirement appears to lead some to sense their own mortality, consciously or otherwise. This notion may have a historical basis; we probably can't help but think of retirement as a phase that only old people go through and that they don't stay in that phase very long.

But even if would-be retirees won't openly admit to a feeling that retirement means the reaper is knocking at the door, some harbor concerns it might sap their vitality for life. Such concerns are clearly expressed by Linda, 62, who is currently employed as a teacher. She links retirement with feeling old and in turn with feeling marginalized and unproductive. Linda also has the added concern of identity loss if she no longer works:

> The idea of retirement is somewhat alien to me. I tend to think of retirement as a point in my life when I can no longer do what I love doing and not as a time of freedom from the daily grind. I suppose at retirement I fear I may lose the feeling of vitality that comes with daily involvement/connections with young people and the sense of purpose that comes with my profession. I also fear that free time would feel meaningless and mundane if all time is "free." It's working all week that makes me appreciate weekends; it's teaching all year that makes summer so special. If every day is "free," does free time lose its luster?
>
> I would hope that retirement would provide an opportunity to widen horizons in terms of pursuing other/new areas of knowledge, activities, purpose, etcetera, perhaps leading to a less one-dimensional focus. It would be an opportunity to take on some of the challenges and develop some interests that have been put on the back burner too long. But I am concerned that without my professional identity to fall back on, I may view myself differently. For myself, I tend to equate retirement with being elderly. I suppose I fear being viewed in retirement as a "dinosaur" with nothing worth contributing. The elderly are often not respected in our culture as they are in many others. Our culture, it seems to me, is notorious for putting the elderly on a shelf or at least taking them less seriously regardless of their mental capacity and abilities. The elderly often become not only diminished but invisible. I suppose I fear becoming expendable and dispensable, although I know realistically we all are.

Linda went on to mention that in retirement she fears she might become lethargic and demotivated in the sense that laziness can breed more laziness. Linda is likely to continue in her job for as long as she can because her preconceptions act as deterrent for her as they might for others. In fact, similar concerns were expressed by one of the authors, Dr. Lou Primavera, as reasons why he prefers not to retire. To Lou, retirement is perceived as the start of a downward spiral, instigated by a weakened self-image and a preoccupation with illness and death:

> I always saw retirement as the end of life, the time you give up being who you are and move into an ambiguous position while you wait to get sick and die. My role model for life was my father, who was a tailor. Dad worked until the age of 88 and was forced to retire because my mother pushed him into it. Retirement did not go well for him. He seemed to be lost and unsure of where he was going. He had always been a very stable, wise, and involved person who loved his family and his work. Retirement seemed to have left him without an identity. His last years were not good; he just seemed lost much of the time.
>
> I feel much the way my dad did. I love my family and love my profession. When I think of retirement, I wonder what I would do with the time. There is not one activity I would engage in that could fulfill me. I have a number of health problems, and I think that if I were retired, I would spend a lot of time focusing on my health issues and spending a lot of time focused on dying. Now, I have no time to do that.
>
> Retirement and "old" have always been the same for me. I think of elderly as a state of mind combined with a degenerating body. Elderly means that you are stagnant and unproductive. It is not strictly correlated with age but more related to your thoughts and ideas. But if I didn't work, my thoughts and ideas would turn negative, to sickness and dying. My dad went downhill slowly when he retired. He didn't have the same verve for life in the end. I would rather go down fighting.

Since Linda and Lou are still working, their perspective is based on presumptions rather than personal experience. But Tony, our retired midlevel executive, also talked about feeling older when he retired. But instead of feeling demotivated or demoralized, Tony believes that the presence of a "ticking clock" actually helps to spur him to action:

> Retirement has changed my perspective on life in a critical way: it has underscored the fact that I'm getting older. I certainly don't feel old. Nor do I think of myself as old. A typical boomer, I still think of myself as somewhere in my mid-forties, even though in reality I'm 15 years older. But

retirement has made me keenly aware that my remaining time on the planet is limited. I'm certainly fortunate in that my health is good, and there's no reason to think that I won't live to a ripe old age, but even 20 or 30 years doesn't seem like a terribly long time when I think about all the things I would still like to do. So I'm feeling a sense of urgency to get those things done while I still have the quality of life to do them.

Both Lou and Linda love their jobs, and that, coupled with their negative views of retirement, suggests they will stay at their jobs for as long as they can. While Tony also enjoyed his career, he saw retirement as an opportunity for new experiences. Although retirement has made him feel older, an unexpected negative, these feelings do not deter him from moving forward—actually, they motivate him. The fact is that if retirees persevere in their quest to retire in spite of their worries, research suggests that they may actually be happier in retirement than they might believe. On the positive side, note that these retirees' lower expectations mean that they are not as likely to experience a sense of disappointment.

But some will delay finding out whether they will like being retired for as long as possible because more often than not, a negative perspective on retirement works as a deterrent. We surveyed people still in the workforce who have no plans to retire and compared their attitudes and opinions to working people who plan to retire within the next one to two years. Many of the differences between these two groups were predictable. To begin with, their financial situations are much different—reported annual income is about $88,000 for those wanting to retire as compared to $68,000 for those preferring to stay at work. With lower incomes, those planning to continue working have a harder time covering expenses and are more worried about their financial futures. They are also more likely to have children still living at home, adding to their financial burdens. So their resolve to keep working is driven in part by money—many of these retirees don't have the financial wherewithal to leave their jobs.

But money is not the only issue blocking their retirement—they *want* to keep working. When asked about their interest in retiring if they could afford to, these workers are still much more likely to state they would continue working right now as compared to those planning to retire. In fact, they claim they would retire only as a result of being forced out of their jobs, either through ill health or company cutbacks. And even if they lost their jobs, they say that they are likely to find another job immediately in retirement.

So, they love their jobs, right? Well, actually, no; it's not that those planning to stay at work have a greater affinity for their jobs. Of the two, those planning to retire have higher status occupations—they tend to have white-collar jobs that they regard as prestigious, and as a typical link to such occupations, they are more likely to rely on their career role as a way of defining themselves. And while those wanting to retire are more likely to describe their jobs as stressful, they also claim their jobs require problem-solving and decision-making skills, characteristics that tend to make them more challenging and stimulating. But be that as it may, both those who want to retire and those who want to stay at work say they like their jobs equally.

Seems a bit confusing, doesn't it? Here we have a group with seemingly more appealing jobs but wanting to retire, and over there we have a group wanting to stay at work but not finding their jobs any more appealing than those who want to retire. Very early on, we mentioned that the quality of a job and its personal appeal *can* play a role in deciding to retire. Obviously, we've demonstrated that that is not always true, and from our results we have to conclude that some other factors must play a role in differentiating these two groups of employees.

What does distinguish these two groups from each other is *how they regard retirement.* Those who plan to continue working feel retirement offers little by way of an improved quality of life. When asked if they would be happy in retirement, 29% of those planning to stay at work say "yes" as compared with 58% of those wanting to retire. Furthermore, only 35% of those who will keep working say their quality of life will get better in retirement versus 65% of those planning to retire. Those who prefer to keep working tend to associate retirement with a few negative outcomes, seeing it as demotivating, boring, socially isolating, and largely without enough interesting things to do. Those who want to retire, on the other hand, tend to see retirement as a destination, an alternative lifestyle from work that allows them to pursue new paths and goals. These would-be retirees claim that retirement is a time for rejuvenation, a time to be productive for one's own purposes, without the stress and constraints of a job.

What makes retirement so unappealing to those who want to stay in the workforce might have something to do with their current lifestyle—they have less going on outside of work. Relative to those who plan to retire, those who prefer to work are much less active and have fewer nonwork interests. In contrast, those planning to retire are much more committed to their personal interests—they have a number of activities they are passionate about and are constantly searching for more and open to trying new things and having new experiences. From a social perspective, employees who want to keep working are less connected with friends in and out of the workforce, take part in fewer events and activities outside the home, and are less likely to describe their social lives as satisfying. Finally, they also tend to have less satisfying marriages, rate their overall quality of life worse, and are not very optimistic about their futures. With such a profile, it's no wonder they don't want to retire.

On the other side, those who want to retire have a lot going for them, so retirement makes a lot of sense. They will enter that world with a positive disposition and seemingly with some direction and a lifestyle that promises a variety of diversions. But there is a concern—maybe they're a little *too* positive. In truth, expecting too much from retirement may be more of a problem than not expecting enough. Even if they dislike their jobs and believe that a life without work is better than one with work, overly optimistic retirees may be disappointed by the day-to-day realities of retirement. This can happen very early on for those who approach retirement overoptimistically; they can fall into disenchantment and emotional distress right from the start.[1] It's not that positive expectations are in themselves a problem; it's more that retirees often tie such expectations to a sense that things will just come their way with little or no effort exerted on their part.

Two studies demonstrate how unrealistically positive expectations can complicate the transition into retirement. A study conducted by Oishi and colleagues in 2009 found that retirees who in effect tried to move to Paradise, that is, who relocated to an area with warmer climate and more recreational facilities, were less happy after they made the move than they expected to be. In contrast, retirees who placed more importance on practical elements in deciding where to live, such as easy access to medical services or daily convenience, felt happier and more at peace.[2] An earlier study, conducted by Perry in 1980, focused on travel in retirement and showed that retirees did not enjoy traveling as much as they had expected to after they retired.[3]

In both of these studies, retirees seem to have overestimated the personal value of seemingly wonderful choices after leaving work. While working, of course, the prospect of travel or of spending hour after leisurely hour in a warm climate surrounded by golf courses and beaches represents the ultimate escape or break from the workplace. This dynamic changes after retirement, though: when their job and its stresses are no longer part of daily life, retirees may feel less of a need for a break from their routine. Hence, one of the main originally anticipated benefits of retirement—escape or a break from routine—may no longer be applicable, and the rejuvenation benefits of travel and warmer climates may no longer seem quite so wonderful after all.

Realistically, expectations cannot be avoided, even if they come with the potential for disillusionment. But in spending time thinking about their future retirement, retirees must try to arrive at expectations that are realistic. Researchers have found that accurate expectations about what retirement entails and a grounded understanding of the ramifications of that lifestyle from the perspective of day-to-day living are important for retirees to feel comfortable in the beginning stages.[4]

Unfortunately, a realistic set of expectations is hard to come by. Most retirees admit they cannot, before the fact, get an accurate picture of day-to-day retirement living since there are so many unknowns about how it feels not to work. Therefore, given what we've seen are the pitfalls of overoptimism, the goal should be to avoid becoming disappointed, which can lead to feelings of disenchantment with retirement. For some retirees, this can be demotivating and lead to second-guessing about their retirement decision. This in turn can interfere with establishing goals and plans for their future because the idea of enjoying retirement becomes harder to visualize. Social scientists claim that if retirees have realistic expectations or don't expect too much, they are more likely to feel satisfied when first entering into retirement.

To get a handle on whether expectations about retirement are accurate, we again looked into the opinions of those who are still in the workforce and plan to retire. This time we compared their views on retirement to those of actual retirees, and we started from the assumption that the best predictor of future behavior is past behavior. In other words, regardless of what those who plan to retire *think* they will do or feel when retired, they will in all likelihood, on actually retiring, behave just like people who are already retired. Such an assumption on our part is reasonable since the opinions about retirement among those still in the workforce are just that: only opinions and not based on actual experiences. It is not until they enter retirement that they can truly understand and react to the forces around them, and at that time the evidence suggests their actions will be different from what they expected while still working.

So, does our analysis show that preretiree expectations are realistic? Unfortunately, no, it doesn't. On the contrary, expectations about retirement among those who are working appear to be a little over the top. Without the work-related pressures and time constraints, retirement seems to look like greener pastures to many of these workers. In fact, some preretirees' expectations seem to be so unrealistic that we feel we are previewing a train wreck, with lots of potential for disappointment. For example, 75% of preretirees believe they will find their lives satisfying in retirement, but only 54% of retirees had that experience. Almost 7 of 10 preretirees say retirement will be positive. But when retirees were asked to think back to their expectations while still working, only 47% claimed to remember expecting retirement to be positive—our guess is that their memories have been distorted by their experiences. Two-thirds of preretirees expect their quality of life to improve in retirement, but only 56% of retirees actually feel that it did.

We do not mean to imply that preretirees are living in a fantasy world. In fact, it is entirely possible that the positive expectations of some would-be retirees are accurate, and they will achieve a good deal of satisfaction in retirement. But for the rest, it is likely that their overly positive perceptions may be clouded by how they are living now while still in the workforce. For example, preretirees have a good deal of self-confidence and a generally positive disposition and sense a bright future ahead. However, a glance at retirees' self-image suggests that the lifestyle changes that occur on retirement may result in a weakening of that image—some of the bloom might come off the rose. And, unfortunately, many of these changes might not be foreseeable when looking in from the outside.

For one, there is the issue of money. A high income can provide a sense of security, heightened self-esteem, and a feeling of optimism about the future because money provides lots of options to those with enough of it. While working, those planning to retire have much higher incomes in comparison to retirees—$89,000 versus $57,000, respectively. And with more money, they feel more comfortable financially, having a relatively easy time covering both their basic and their discretionary spending needs without touching their savings. But then comes actual retirement; once that regular paycheck stops, some would-be retirees probably won't feel quite as financially secure, and this in turn could lower their self-esteem and their perceived prospects for the future. Such a downturn in perspective could result in a less satisfying view of retirement, as we found among actual retirees.

If the financial going gets tough, would-be retirees are more likely to believe they would take a job if they needed extra money—more so than retirees would in the face of financial difficulties. But what preretirees may not be aware of is that motivation to work diminishes on retirement and continues to decline as one spends more and more years in this life stage. For example, 82% of preretirees claim they will work in retirement as compared to only 27% of all retirees who actually do so. Willingness to work is 47% among those retired six months or less, but this percentage drops to 36% when retirees hit the one-year mark and to 26% by the time they are retired three years. This is not to say that all retirees don't work—actually about one-quarter hold a job. But that's still far lower than the 82% of preretirees claiming they will work in retirement.

In this vein, it appears that would-be retirees presume the energy and drive they possess while working will remain at the same levels in retirement. But the reality appears to be quite different—motivation to do a lot of things seems to decline when one retires. Whether it's from lack of direction due to inadequate planning or lack of a perceived need to accomplish anything right away (or ever), less is likely to get done, not more.

When they're looking in from the outside, it's difficult for preretirees to know that they are likely to experience a reduction in drive—the feeling of wanting to accomplish things—when they retire. Nevertheless, it's there, and it gets worse with more years in retirement. For example, would-be retirees are more likely to describe retirement as a time when they will feel productive, motivated, and rejuvenated, and 57% say they view retirement as an opportunity to plan new goals—but only 38% of retirees actually plan new goals for themselves. Moreover, 88% of preretirees claim they will put in the effort to find activities they will thoroughly enjoy in retirement, but only 48% of retirees say they actually made that attempt. Finally, 48% of those still working say they will retire specifically to pursue their passions, but only 13% of retirees remember actually retiring for that reason.

Beyond motivational issues, would-be retirees are more optimistic about how much they will enjoy their leisure activities. Those still in the workforce are almost twice as likely to believe that they will find activities to be passionate about once they retire as compared to what retirees actually experienced. And this may be due in part to how they view their leisure activities now— those planning to retire but still holding jobs find their leisure activities more enjoyable than do retirees. However, what's missing is perspective—for retirees, leisure activities are their *life*; for those in the workforce, such activities are more like a diversion from work. When the diversion is no longer needed and these leisure activities become more routine, they may not be quite as appealing—as Rob discovered about his interest in painting.

And there are likely to be disappointments from a social perspective as well. While still working, would-be retirees are pretty satisfied with their social lives. In comparison to retirees, they have much larger social circles and spend more time interacting with friends. But in retirement, the size of that circle will shrink, in part because of the loss of coworker friendships. Retirees claim to have about 13 friends in their circle as compared to 20 for those planning to retire but still working. And the time they spend interacting with friends is likely to decline, too—from 30 hours to about 17 hours per month. While they are likely to spend more time with their friends outside the workforce once they retire, this added time will not be enough to make up the difference caused by the loss of workplace friendships. Instead, they will make up the time through increased interaction with family members and their spouses at the expense of valuable peer interaction time. Furthermore, in all likelihood the time spent interacting in person will also decline, and they can expect to feel less emotionally connected to their friends in and out of the workplace, probably because of reduced time and quality of their interactions.

In marriage, those still in the workforce spend more time in joint activities with their spouses than retirees and are more likely to feel their marriage will improve further in retirement. But we have to keep in mind that these people are still working, so their time with their spouses is likely to be more limited than for retirees. Once they leave the workforce and they are with their spouses for more hours per day, they may experience some changes in their relationship. Again using retirees as a reference point, their preference for joint activities is likely to diminish, as might other elements, such as sexual intimacy (we will discuss the impact on marriage in more detail in a later chapter).

There is at least one positive feature about the attitudes of would-be retirees, at least among those who want to retire. They will certainly enter that stage in a favorable state of mind. This is an important step in the transition from work to retirement, although it should be noted that the "right mind-set" is more complex than just rosy expectations. Rather, we would suggest that people should go into retirement open to its possibilities, a mind-set best achieved through a positive attitude grounded in realistic expectations. If retirees can attain that perspective, they at least have the potential to be less disappointed and better able to stay motivated to pursue a course of action that can lead to longer-term retired happiness.

But questions remain. If retirees develop their perceptions of retirement while living in the stress- and energy-filled world of work, can they come up with realistic expectations? And if their expectations are not entirely accurate, does that doom them to disappointment in retirement? As a reasonable guess, the answer to both questions is no. As we pointed out, it may be too much to expect a person to know what a life stage would be like before living it— there are a lot of subtleties to day-to-day living that are likely to go unnoticed or whose true impact would be hard to envision without direct experience.

From here we have to conclude that most people will go into retirement with inaccurate expectations. Some will be overly positive and some overly negative, and maybe just a few will hit it dead on. For those preretirees who can't get it right, there may be some mental exercises they can perform before retiring to arrive at some semblance of reality. First, they can begin with an acknowledgment that retirement is not likely to be as exciting or fulfilling as a career that offers constant social contact, challenging tasks, and an established routine. Second, they can try to imagine what a lifestyle without work is like: living day to day with very little structure, direction, or challenge. If they can take this mental image far out enough into the future, they might get a sense of the gaps they are likely to have in their days, and these will have to be filled with something meaningful.

If that approach doesn't get you there, then we suggest it is best to err in the direction of expecting too little rather than too much. It is often more difficult to overcome disenchantment due to overoptimism than to live with the pleasant surprise that it's not as bad as you thought it would be. However, we must return to the point that, whether your expectations lean to the negative or the positive, it is important to keep an optimistic attitude, a feeling that you can make your retirement a great experience. Going in with low expectations *and a negative attitude* will more often than not lead you to exactly the type of retirement you are expecting. A positive mind-set, on the other hand, will keep you motivated, an important mental state for rebuilding a life.

To reiterate, motivation is the key—it's what gives you the potential to set goals for yourself and accomplish things that are meaningful to you. As will be seen in the following chapter, goal setting is at the core of a satisfactory retirement. And at the core of goal setting is a detailed plan of action. If retirees put in the effort to plan how they will actually live day to day in retirement, they can improve their chances of having a satisfactory retirement. Of course, there is still the problem of knowing what to plan for. With the inability to foresee all the subtle issues that can arise, making plans that are all-encompassing can be quite difficult. So in the next chapter, we look into some of the specifics that have been found to be lacking in the plans of retirees, even for the very few who attempted to be completely thorough in their preparations.

· 6 ·

The Devil's in the Details

Don't simply retire from something; have something to retire to.

—Harry Emerson Fosdick

$\int$o far, we've seen that a positive state of mind and realistic expectations are important starting points on the path to retirement. But the path has many stages, and the benefits of positive thinking and accurate expectations play a part mostly in its initial stages. They have little impact over the long term—positivity and realism alone do not necessarily translate into taking the appropriate steps to building a retirement lifestyle. Rather, retirees need to think very seriously about what they will do with their lives if they are going to ensure a happy and fulfilling retirement. In short, they have to plan ahead and set goals for themselves. And they really ought to start planning and setting goals early, even while they're still in the workforce. Researchers[1] have found that the benefits of planning ahead, of setting goals for retirement before you do so, are multidimensional:

- Setting goals provides retirees with the framework they need to create a fulfilling lifestyle, one that includes activities that have some personal value.
- Goals or more specifically the activities undertaken to meet them, put structure in retirees' day-to-day lives and yield a sense of control over their lives, both of which might otherwise be lost on leaving the workforce.
- The mere fact of going through the steps of planning before actually retiring offers an opportunity to live vicariously in retirement prior to the reality; in essence, it allows people to mentally rehearse how they plan to live and starts the process of adopting the retirement role.

• Finally, by achieving their goals, retirees give themselves opportunities to create a positive self-image and to feel more connected and committed to the retirement lifestyle.

Retirees who fail to prepare and make plans for retirement risk leaving the workforce with no path to follow. Once they do retire, they will have no structure to their days and may come to feel a loss of personal control over their lives. From here, some retirees may eventually move into a state of "learned helplessness" whereby they don't want to move in any direction because regardless of what they do, they just can't be sure of the outcome. And things spiral downward from there: reluctance to act can lead to negative feelings about retirement, which in turn can lead to depression and weakened subjective well-being, to say nothing of poor adjustment to the life stage.

Setting goals has another useful benefit: it helps to focus one's attention on something that is personally meaningful. When retirees focus on meaningful goals, they become personally invested through the process of working toward their goals. In doing so, they accomplish a few objectives—they put direction in their lives, and they put in place the means to redefine themselves as retirees by connecting with that role. Without meaningful goals and a sense of moving in a purposeful direction, retirees are less likely to have the opportunity to develop those important alternative roles to replace their worker role—in essence, retirement goals help make you feel like a retiree.

Planning itself has a number of dimensions. First, there are the specific things you should plan for. Social scientists point out that retirees give financial issues most of their attention in retirement planning because they lose their weekly income. There is no doubt that financial planning is highly important, but it is far from the only issue that needs to be considered. Planning for your retirement needs to include all the various elements of daily living. That is, some of your goals should be short term, designed to establish a routine that puts structure into your life. As we have seen, routines and a structured use of time are often lost after leaving a job, and they need to be reestablished in retirement.

Within this context, one set of goals should revolve around establishing daily activity patterns. This can include setting up a schedule for doing household chores or handling basic responsibilities but also taking part in personal leisure activities, such as hobbies, and something social, such as visiting a local café or other location where you can be around other people, do some reading, or just sit and relax. The point here is to establish a regular routine: come up with a plan that makes for meaningful use of your time each day.

Note that the social activities, such as visiting cafés and the like, play into another goal: retirees can strengthen non–work-related roles that will help them adapt to their new lifestyle. Focusing on relationships outside the workforce, such as friends or family members, or joining clubs or volunteer groups provides a good way to redefine oneself in retirement. These relationships help to keep you feeling connected to the outside world and serve as a basis of emotional support, which we have seen to be important for subjective well-being.

Daily goals such as these help establish a comfort level early in retirement. Retirees may also want to consider establishing broader, longer-term goals, though. These keep retirees invested in their futures, give them something to look forward to down the road, and can enhance subjective well-being. Rob has used long-term planning as one means of maintaining a positive outlook on his future:

> I have learned that, whenever I felt a particularly strong lack of purpose or direction at different points in my retirement, making plans for the future helped me quite a bit. Often times these long-term goals would focus on travel, one of my passions. I would plan a trip to take place one year or so later, usually involving a group of friends. Having so much free time at my disposal, I would typically do all the legwork for everyone who wanted to come along. Once a destination was selected, I would become highly focused, almost obsessed with the details, which could consume weeks of my time. I even took to writing my own travelogues, which I then bound and gave to all the attendees. Along with describing what we would see and do, my travelogues included funny anecdotes and comments about my fellow travelers, which made for more enjoyable reading and writing. These trips and their travelogues not only added some excitement about what was ahead for me; they gave me something to be committed to and to care about. They also made me get closer to my friends by having all of us work together toward something that would be fun, traveling together.

For planning and goal setting to be of any real value, a few things have to be kept in mind. For one, research has shown retirees' plans have to include the details, not just general ideas: the steps needed to reach their goals must be laid out. If done right, the creation of this retirement map will result in concrete plans and a clearer overall path. Better still, because the plans are specific rather than vague, there is a better chance they will actually be implemented. Ultimately, retirees whose plans are focused and specific will have a better understanding of where their proposed course of action will take them. Not only will they know whether their plans meet their needs in terms of personal fulfillment, but they'll also be able to get a sense of the effort that will be required to achieve their plans—are the specific goals in mind worth the effort it will take to reach them? Such a question cannot be answered accurately unless you know precisely the steps you will have to take to get there.

This leads to the crucial second element—goals must be realistic. As retirees lay out their plans step-by-step, they have the opportunity to go through a reality check as to whether their goals can be attained. If goals are realistic, retirees can have confidence that what they plan to do can actually be accomplished and can then realize the resulting benefits. Unrealistic or grandiose goals, on the other hand, are likely to lead to one of two outcomes: plans that are never implemented, maybe never even tried because the tasks involved are too daunting, or failure of even bothering to initiate the plans because you probably know in your heart they are unachievable. Both can undermine a retiree's confidence, along with his or her motivation to move in any direction, because whatever path you take, you can't be sure you will be successful.

Rob went through a process of unrealistic goal setting early on in his retirement. Afterward, he realized that he actually cared less about what he wanted to accomplish and was more concerned with just using up time, something he had too much of. Rob also felt he lacked a source for maintaining his self-esteem when he left his job, so doing anything that smacked of productivity was acceptable at the time:

> About six months after I retired, I realized I still had a need to do something that was productive, and with my particular view of things, that was in terms of making money. I was only 51, and the prospect of getting paid for something still interested me, especially since I thought I could do it on a part-time basis. But after 30 years in my career as a researcher, I just didn't want to do the same thing. So I decided to try my hand in other businesses, ones that I knew absolutely nothing about. While I knew I had a lot to learn, that would never have stopped me.
>
> I got involved with a few people from Italy importing organic foods, with others in developing pet products, and still others in creating a fashion jewelry line. Along with that, I got involved in breeding and racing thoroughbred horses and helping my wife set up a women's boutique. The pet thing is particularly amusing since no one would ever accuse me of being a pet lover. Before long, I had six separate companies going, and for each of these I jumped in with complete enthusiasm. I could spend a day tasting new foods, making cold calls on retail outlets for the jewelry line, then delivering fliers door to door for the boutique. Sometimes I would laugh to myself, particularly when making cold calls for jewelry, because I would think back to when I was a kid and the Fuller brush man would come by our house, and I realized that was now me.
>
> As it turns out, my enthusiasm for these businesses had more to do with just wanting to have something to do rather than starting up a new full-time career. This is not to say I didn't take things seriously—I really believed I wanted to make these new opportunities successful. But I also knew I just didn't want to work that hard. If I had sat down and thought

about it for more than a few moments, I would have realized I would never have put the in effort that was required. From my own experiences of having developed a company, each of these new businesses would have taken years to develop, and only if I was willing to put 60 to 80 hours of work per week, and that's per business. So what I thought I wanted to do was not at all what I wanted, and it could not have been accomplished anyway—my goals were not only unrealistic; they were outright ridiculous.

That little lesson cost me quite a few bucks. But still I am glad I went through the process—if I hadn't, I would have wondered if I could have been successful in any of these businesses or would have enjoyed them. Really this was all about experimenting, as silly as it all was and as silly as I felt in the midst of it. In the end, I most enjoyed shutting them all down and knowing that I was completely through with the idea of doing anything like that again.

In the above, Rob's goals were unrealistic, mostly because he was never motivated enough to carry them through to completion. This brings us to a third requirement for realizing the benefits of setting goals. Researchers have found that retirees cannot take a halfhearted approach either to developing their plans or to implementing them. In fact, the depth of retirees' commitment to carrying out their plans may actually be more important than the specific content of the plans. If one is strongly committed, there is a much greater chance that plans will actually be implemented, and from there, there is a greater likelihood that they can be brought to fruition.[2] On the other hand, without follow-through, plans are essentially just a nice way to daydream.

It should be fairly obvious that the absence of any one of these dimensions—laying out the details, being realistic, and being motivated—reduces goal setting to nothing more than an intellectual exercise. Over time, the positive effects of planning alone tend to dissipate and will be very short lived if retirees are unrealistic in their goals or inaccurate in their expectations or fail to follow through. Successful retirement hinges on making sure that one's plans are grounded in reality, based on a true understanding of what the retiree hopes and wants to accomplish, and following through with the appropriate steps to reach one's goals.[3]

Given its importance for putting structure into an unstructured world, we wanted to find out just how much planning and goal setting actually goes on before retirees leave the workforce. Our results suggest that the answer is not much, as it turns out. We discovered that fewer than 4 in 10 put even a moderate amount of effort into making plans for their retirement, and a very small percentage—fewer than 1 in 10—claim to have given a great deal of consideration to how they will live outside of work. We then probed further, specifically among these "heavy" planners, to find out how much detail went into their plans—and once again the answer came back: not much. In fact, only 13% actually laid out the individual steps they would follow to achieve their goals.

And what about carrying out their plans to completion? Unfortunately, and possibly because there was not enough attention paid to the details, only 47% had actually achieved the goals they planned on. While one might expect that goal achievement would be a matter of time (i.e., the more years in retirement, the more retirees would feel they met their goals), we found that in fact time has only a moderate impact. Achievement of planned goals climbs from about 42% among those retired two years or less to 53% among those six or more years into their retirement—which of course means that even after six years, almost half have met very few of their goals.

We also asked retirees how they felt about the amount of effort they put into planning for their retirement while still in the workforce. Between retirees' admittedly limited focus on the details and the fact that only half achieved their goals, our findings should come as no surprise: fully half of all retirees admitted in retrospect that their retirement planning was inadequate. Retirees seem to realize at some point in their retirement that they should have done more to get themselves ready for it, but this admission in itself suggests many are not feeling comfortable with how they are living. If things were great, they would not feel the need to have planned better.

These results are not very encouraging—a relatively small percentage of retirees make plans, and those who do haven't put enough focus on the details to allow them a good chance for success in reaching their goals. Although we cannot be sure whether this is a fault of goals being unrealistic or whether retirees lose their motivation to follow through, it is likely that both play some role. But the acknowledgment that their planning was inadequate also suggests that there may be other factors involved, and our research uncovered some elements that may be missed by many retirees during the planning stage.

For one, retirees don't seem to make plans in all the right aspects of their lives. We found that retirees who claimed to plan for their retirement focused heavily on finances, almost to the exclusion of anything else. Among all retirees who made plans, 68% say they planned financial aspects, but fewer than 3 in 10 mentioned setting up plans for their personal activities, social life, travel, recreation time, or even something as basic as where to live. Importantly, only 16% mentioned planning their retirement social life, an aspect of daily living that is dramatically affected when leaving the workforce. Of course, money is of paramount concern, but in the end, those whose plans are only about finances have actually made very few plans for living—they simply looked at whether and how they can afford to retire. Although necessary, it is far from sufficient in creating a purposeful lifestyle.

Now, does this mean that retirees didn't even try to do a better job in their planning? Not necessarily. Rather, we believe it is probably more the case that goal setting is easier thought about than done and that it is difficult to grasp fully the subtleties of day-to-day unstructured living before they are experienced. In fact, it is very likely that retirees intended to work out some of the various aspects of their daily living before they left their jobs. Our evidence for this comes from those still in the workforce. Preretirees are more likely to claim they will plan their retirement down to some very fine details—61% of those who are still working say they will put time and effort into planning their retirement as compared to 38% of those who are actually retired who say that they did so. Furthermore, while they also focus strongly on finances, they are much more likely to claim they will address issues of travel, social life, and personal interests than retirees report having actually done.

But that's not as encouraging as it might sound. We have to point out that even though preretirees *intend* to be better than retirees in getting their retirement house set up, they're probably not going to be much better. The percentages claiming they will pay more attention to daily living elements are still low—only 39% will focus on their personal interests and 30% on maintaining their social lives.

Furthermore, good intentions notwithstanding, unfortunately it remains true that the best predictor of future behavior is past behavior. Therefore, we would expect that those still working are likely to behave just like other retirees when they stop working. In other words, based on what actually occurs in retirement, the odds are against preretirees coming up with detailed plans for retirement much beyond the money or, at the minimum, carrying through on many of their plans once they finally retire.

Still, regardless of the fact that retirees don't plan enough (or well, for that matter), we wanted to see whether and in what ways planning actually makes a difference in adjusting. Here we looked into the planning efforts of well-adjusted retirees and compared those to the less well adjusted. What we discovered was not exactly earthshaking but is certainly consistent with what we've already seen—in short, *getting* something done has much more value than *thinking about* getting something done.

These two groups actually approached planning in similar ways—well-adjusted retirees were only a little more likely to have made plans overall and to have laid out the specific steps for their plans. They also tended to focus on the same issues as the less well adjusted—mostly finances. But where we found very dramatic differences—among the most dramatic in our entire survey—was in their ability to see their plans through to completion. Among well-adjusted retirees, 68% claimed that they actually achieved the goals they set out to meet as compared to only 12% of the less well adjusted. And when asked if they felt they adequately planned out their retirement, 80% of less well adjusted retirees admitted they did not, while only 29% of well adjusted had that opinion.

If well-adjusted retirees are only as likely as less well adjusted retirees to make plans, why are they so different in terms of carrying out their plans? A little digging into personality characteristics reveals that well-adjusted retirees are armed with a variety of mental coping skills, along with a great deal of energy, and with these they can operate effectively on the fly. In truth, these retirees may not even need specific plans—their confidence, open-mindedness, goal directedness, positive attitude, and ability to be flexible allow well-adjusted retirees to find a way to establish and then pursue their goals as they go. We get the sense that goal creation and pursuit is actually an ongoing process for these retirees, with each new goal continuously following on the heels of an achieved goal. However, for those with less drive and fewer coping skills or who tend toward procrastination, there is probably a more pressing need to lay out the specific steps up front in planning.

All in all, we are unhappily forced to conclude that many retirees' planning efforts are woefully inadequate and somewhat misguided. Realism, carry-through, and details are important, but so is the choice of which elements receive consideration in one's plans. The emphasis on money is understandable and certainly critical, but money only provides permission to retire. Retirees need to pay just as much attention to the elements that really make up day-to-day living, such as one's activities or social life. Before entering retirement, it's possible retirees are just not aware that a well-developed social life and a repertoire of meaningful activities are vital to their subjective well-being. Or they might mistakenly take these elements for granted, assuming they will simply fall into place on retiring. Social interaction and structured activities are the essence of the workplace. But in the unstructured world of retirement, these are not likely to be readily available without some directed focus by retirees, plans that ensure they are part of their daily routines.

As one suggestion to build planning and goal setting into your regular routine, consider keeping a calendar or a "to-do" list. In this way, you will treat your retirement lifestyle very much like a job, keeping track of the personally meaningful things you want to pursue, your social engagements, and the more mundane chores and responsibilities. Probably the better option is a calendar since it more clearly illustrates what you have planned for each day and points out the gaps—the periods of time when nothing is planned and that you might want to fill. Each morning should routinely start off with a review of your calendar or list so that you know what the day ahead holds for you, and if nothing's there, then you start filling in the blanks. One of the more obvious traps a retiree can fall into is a loss in motivation to do something—and that's exactly what could happen if structure and direction are not self-imposed. When structure is missing in your life, it may be difficult to summon the energy to make plans without a plan of action to follow. But if you maintain a written schedule, you're less likely to fall into the "What do you want to do?" "I don't know, what do you want to do?" pattern, which can end in either doing nothing or settling on something of low interest just for the sake of having anything to do.

Of course, even if retirees diligently keep a record of their plans, they still need to have a better idea what to plan for. In the following chapters, that is exactly what we will try to provide: a better idea of what retirement actually involves. We will delve into the details of the retirement world, concentrating on the various pitfalls that can arise. We will address how a poorly developed social life, insufficient activities, and obstacles in other aspects of daily living might conspire against a successful adjustment. And whenever possible, we will offer some strategies to help overcome the problems that can surface in the hope that our advice may help more retirees have a better quality of life.

III

POSTRETIREMENT: PITFALLS AND AMBUSHES

• 7 •

Health and Wealth

Retirement is like a long vacation in Las Vegas. The goal is to
enjoy it to the fullest, but not so fully that you run out of money.

—Jonathan Clements

*W*ithout question, good health and sufficient finances are the most important foundations of a successful retirement. Over and over, research shows that
retirees who enjoy good health and perceive their income to be adequate tend
to be happier in their retirement.

Good health provides everyone, not just retirees, with the basic physical
tools needed for an active life; it's much easier to have a positive disposition
when you're not worrying about your body breaking down. Healthy retirees
can be as active and involved as they want to be. They are not constrained in
their movements, nor do they have to limit themselves to either completely
sedentary activities or, at best, to those that make minimal physical demands.
Healthy retirees' mobility puts them in a better position to develop a satisfying lifestyle and reap the accompanying benefits to their subjective well-being.
Good physical health has direct emotional benefits: it is associated with higher
life satisfaction because it allows people to pursue valued goals and to take part
in activities they enjoy.

Poor health, on the other hand, can make life and retirement miserable:
with its associated physical discomfort and high costs, it can severely restrict a
retiree's options. It is well documented that poor physical health is closely linked
to poor mental health, often leading to depression. For retirees, the situation is
worse because of the way poor health can undermine all the necessary adjustments to the retirement process. Health problems lead not only to lower activity
levels but also to reduced social contact, undeveloped non–work-related roles,
and an inability to participate in events and situations that are of personal value.[1]

85

Happily, though, we found from our own survey that 78% of retirees claim to be in good health. Although not quite as good as the 89% we found among those still in the workforce, this still suggests a sizable percentage of retirees consider themselves to be healthy. Furthermore, only 17% of both retirees and workers claim that health issues inhibit their ability to participate in physical or social activities.

We also found that 7 in 10 of both retirees and workers have health insurance, and most believe it is adequate to cover their expenses—only 16% claim they have to use money they planned to spend other ways to cover their health costs. And, as an unexpected twist, retirees are not overly worried about covering their future health care costs. In the absence of steady income, one would think that such an unpredictable expense would produce some consternation among retirees. To be sure, health insurance is more of an issue to those new in the game, retired less than six months: for those with less retirement experience, financial issues may be a little more problematic because of their uncertainty. But once retirees enter their fourth year, these concerns start to dwindle.

So, who *is* worried about this issue? People who are still working: future health care costs are a greater issue to the currently employed, especially those who are not planning to retire. In fact, worries about health care coverage and future expense are a big factor that inhibits plans to retire—64% of those planning to stay in the workforce claim the uncertainty of future health care coverage makes them worry about retiring, far higher than the 39% seen among those planning to retire.

While health is not a primary reason for most retirees to leave their jobs, it does appear that it has "pushed" some into retirement, and it does play a role in adjustment. For example, those claiming to have health problems tend to be less well adjusted in retirement—among those completely adjusted to retirement, only 28% claim health forced them to retire as compared to 48% making this claim among the less well adjusted. There is also a tendency for the less well adjusted to view their health as having deteriorated since retiring—38% of these retirees mention declining health since retirement compared to only 19% among those who say they are completely adjusted. We also found the reverse for those completely adjusted: 36% felt their health actually improved since retiring as compared to only 18% of the less adjusted making this claim. On the surface, then, it seems that health can interfere with how well a person feels about retirement.

But it's possible that things are not that straightforward. For one thing, the cause-and-effect question remains unanswerable here: we can't know whether retirees are not adjusted to retirement because of worsening health or whether health deteriorates because retirees are unhappy in retirement. While the former seems to be the most reasonable answer, there is a good deal of evidence that stress or unhappiness can actually cause one's health to deteriorate. If that is true, then being unadjusted or unhappy in retirement can lead to declining health.

There's also the possibility that just being in retirement causes one to think or worry more about their health. One of our respondents, Lou, mentioned earlier that he preferred not to retire because he felt he might dwell too much on his health issues. So the quality of one's health can also be a perceptual thing, meaning it's not really better or worse in retirement but just seems to be because you think about it more. It's probably safest to conclude that the truth lies somewhere in between—some are unadjusted because of poor health, and some have declining health because they're unhappy in retirement.

However, in the end it may not matter either way. Whether one's health problems are real or imagined, the result is the same—poor health may get in the way of being happy. But just to be sure about this conclusion, we compared people suffering from poor health to people describing themselves as healthy. Our survey completely validated the findings of other social scientists: whether people are retired or working, poor health is debilitating. Our data show that those in poorer health have resigned themselves to an unhappy future and lack the energy, social support groups, and resources to get back on track. Compared to those in good health, we found that retirees in poor health face a number of difficulties in many aspects of their lives, including the following:

- They have more fragile financial positions and tend to have blue-collar jobs. Because of their weaker financial status, they are much more concerned about their financial futures and more likely to need to dip into their savings to cover basic expenses. And because they can expect continually escalating expenses, they are especially concerned about covering their health care costs in the future.
- They are less likely to be married. But if they *are* married or intimately involved with someone, they are more likely to describe their relationship as unhappy and to have worsened since retiring. Tied in with health and a deteriorating relationship, they are much less sexually active and rate the quality of their sex lives much less positively—and this, too, has gotten worse since they retired.
- They are more likely to be taking antidepressant medications and medications to help sleep and are more likely to have started using these medications after they retired.
- They are much more likely to have lost their jobs because of poor health, would prefer to be back at work rather than retired, and feel

that being forced out of their jobs has affected their ability to adjust to retirement. They are also more likely to feel that their health issues have made it difficult to enjoy life in general. As a result, they are unhappy in retirement, feel their quality of life has declined, and have found their adjustment to be difficult.

- They are much less active and spend more hours at home alone, whiling away the hours in sedentary activities such as watching television or just sitting around the house. Although they claim that they would like to find things to do that interest them and have even tried to find such activities, they have not been successful at it. However, they may not have tried very hard: they are much less open to new experiences and trying new things and more likely to see retirement as a time to do nothing.
- Socially, they have fewer friends in and outside of the workforce and spend less time interacting with the friends they have, and this has become more pronounced since retiring. And they tend to be dissatisfied with their social lives in general and to feel they have gotten worse since retiring. But here, too, there are signs of some internal contradiction: while they claim their circumstances do not afford them the opportunity to meet new people, they nevertheless are not motivated to do so in any event.
- All things considered, it seems almost inevitable that retirees in poor health will suffer psychologically. They are especially likely to feel their lives are a failure, have low self-esteem, and be pessimistic about the future. Furthermore, they tend to be lonely, don't feel useful or productive, and lack the energy and motivation to pursue goals. At the same time, and probably contributing to their unhappy state of affairs, those in poor health have a very difficult time coping with change—such as that which occurs when moving from work to retirement.

Unfortunately, apart from wishful suggestions to get better, there is little guidance to be offered on how to improve the unhappy future faced by retirees suffering from completely debilitating health problems. But it is not likely that all of these retirees reporting poor health suffer illnesses to that degree. Rather, many are likely to be mobile and functioning at relatively high levels. For all but the bedridden, there are things they can do that might help to improve their life quality, working to address weaknesses outlined in their profiles.

For starters, they need to acknowledge that a satisfying social life can have positive effects on how they feel about themselves and life in general—many people are just not aware of how important this is to their subjective well-being. They can make improvements here simply by increasing the amount of time they spend interacting with friends, and in this regard they should look to personal meetings, not phone or email conversations. Additionally, they should consider placing themselves in social situations, areas where people tend to congregate—just the act of being in the company of others, even strangers, can be stimulating and help improve one's connectivity to the outside world. In this way, they give themselves an opportunity to meet new people without having to feel the pressures of joining clubs or organizations.

An improved social life has the benefit of enhancing one's self-esteem, which in turn helps to increase one's drive to do other things—motivation to improve one's life is also a key to subjective well-being. So a good next step might simply be to find something to do. Given that those in poor health tend not to have found nonwork interests that are worthwhile, they probably won't do so at this point either. As a recommendation, if their health permits, they might consider some type of work, either a paid job or a volunteer position that is within their physical capabilities and is limited in time and pressures. The benefits, as we have discussed already, include an enhanced sense of productivity and usefulness, social contacts, and structured use of time, not to mention some additional cash, all of which further enhance self-esteem and subjective well-being.

There is one more health-related suggestion *all* retirees should consider — the importance of exercise. Because the lifestyle can be more sedentary, health may deteriorate in retirement—and it doesn't help matters that retirees are not getting any younger. From our survey, only about one-third of all retirees claim to exercise regularly, but it is important to note that this percentage is 41% among well-adjusted retirees and only 22% among those who are less adjusted. The physical and psychological benefits of exercise are well known, and this activity should be part of the daily routine of every retiree. Join a gym—in addition to feeling better physically and psychologically, there are social benefits to be realized from being in a public place with other people having the same objective, namely, to get in shape and stay healthy.

Turning from health to money, financial status dictates the answer to the very first question about voluntary retirement: "Can I do it now, or not?" If the answer is "No, I need more money," then keep working if you can. But even if the answer is a happy "Yes, I have enough money set aside to retire," that doesn't mean that financial concerns go away from then on—far from it. As in all aspects and stages of living, money plays a vital role in the quality of the retirement experience.

A number of studies have documented the beneficial role of money on quality of life, retired or not. The list of benefits is a long one: adequate finances have been linked to better physical and mental health, greater longevity, lower rates of infant mortality, lower frequency of having children drop out of school or become pregnant as teenagers, less frequent victims of violent crime, and fewer stressful life events. Financial problems have been tied to depression and poor adjustment in retirement, while across a variety of countries and cultures, wealthier people are more likely to be satisfied with their lives.[2]

Truly, it is hard to overstate the benefits of having adequate money in retirement. Virtually all professionals working in an advisory capacity first suggest that retirees carefully assess their financial status prior to considering a move into retirement; many retirees use these professional services for money management counseling. Books on the topic abound. There are at least 600 available through Amazon.com covering the financial aspects of retirement planning. Advice on the Web is also seemingly endless. If you Google "retirement financial planning," you'll get more than 21,000,000 hits—and that's just one search.

Retirees who are financially stable have the resources to take part in an abundance of social and leisure opportunities. Income and financial status determine the degree to which retirees can pursue various courses of action as they choose. Being able to live as one chooses has been found to contribute to subjective well-being and satisfaction in retirement. Financially comfortable retirees are also likely to enjoy emotional benefits. They may feel a degree of security about their future because two potential sources of stress, money and work, are eliminated from their lives. In comparison, retirees who have inadequate income or face financial uncertainties are likely to feel stressed and as a result are more likely to be unhappy in retirement.[3]

Our survey clearly documented all the previously mentioned emotional and psychological benefits of money besides the obvious ones of being able to afford more things and worry less about expenses. In comparison to those with lower income, our upper-income respondents were indeed healthier, happier overall and in retirement, more self-confident and optimistic about the future, and more likely to be married (and happily so) and had better sex lives. With respect to the latter, lower-income people were more likely to report their sex lives had actually gotten worse in retirement. One can speculate that increased time together, combined with the fact that their lower income limits their entertainment options, may put some added pressures on the relationships of these retirees. It also suggests they are not using all the extra time at home with their spouse in a very productive manner.

We also found that upper-income retirees have different personality characteristics and ways of living than lower-income people, not all of which are a result of simply having more money. We do not know whether these traits contribute to their ability to earn higher incomes or are a by-product of being more successful (success here is defined not only in terms of income but also by having held more prestigious jobs). Nevertheless, however they come to be the people they are, their ways of thinking and living allow them to get the most out of life. Relative to lower-income people, we can characterize those with higher incomes as follows:

- They are much more active and personally invested in their various activities, allowing them to find these activities more rewarding. They tend to have a wider circle of friends and feel socially connected and to be more satisfied with their social life. In contrast, lower-income people, with less social involvement, tend to feel their social lives have gotten worse since retiring and are more likely to feel isolated and suffer bouts of loneliness.
- They are more prone to describe their careers as having been personally rewarding, despite being stressful, and more likely to have defined themselves by their work. But they are less likely to miss their jobs— they have moved on to other things and have adopted the retirement lifestyle. Lower-income people, on the other hand, are more likely to wish they were back at work.
- They are much more open to new experiences and to be searching for new things to do because they are energetic and consider retirement as a time to pursue new interests and not merely as a time to relax. Relatedly, they are constantly setting new goals for themselves and are more likely to achieve these goals. Lower-income people are less likely to have made specific plans for how to live in retirement and, perhaps worse, are painfully aware that their preparation was completely inadequate.
- They are more likely to have retired out of choice, looking to reduce their stress levels and wanting more free time to pursue other interests. Lower-income people are more likely to have been forced out of their jobs, a fact that they feel affected their ability to enjoy their retirement.

With such a profile, it's no wonder upper-income people are happier in retirement and have had an easier time adjusting than lower-income people. A particularly important differentiator seems to be their higher energy levels—this provides the juice to make ongoing improvements and adjustments in their lifestyles. Upper-income people are just plain motivated to succeed. But even these retirees struggle with the magnitude of the change represented by retirement—only 51% of our affluent retirees report to be completely adjusted. Clearly, having money is a good start, but it is hardly the sole determinant of a retiree's happiness.

So, just how much money *is* enough to retire on? That's a fair question, but, unfortunately, it's not as easy to answer as it sounds (and no, "there's no such thing as enough" isn't a good answer). Bad enough that it's impossible to predict the course of the economy: will there be inflation? Recession? Will the stock market tank? But even beyond that, there's a very tricky subjective element at play here as well. With money, as it turns out, security is in the eye of the perceiver. Research has shown that *it's not the amount of money one has that matters as much as a belief that whatever one has is adequate for one's needs.* This includes having confidence that one can afford the essentials and still have enough discretionary income to pursue one's interests.[4]

Many retirees tend to worry about their finances because this may be the first time they will not have a regular paycheck coming in. And without a regular paycheck, one's money supply after leaving the workforce is likely to be less predictable—and it's almost certainly likely to *feel that way.* The downturn in the economy starting in 2008 is a case in point; it easily justified fears that the cost of living and earnings on investments might be less than expected as compared to the time even a short while earlier when the decision to retire was made.

But even if retirees ultimately come to realize their finances are sound, many will not see things that way in the very early stages of their retirement. For one, new retirees will lack personal experience handling their money under no-paycheck conditions, so there is some uncertainty about how much they can spend without putting themselves at risk. Some may question whether they have adequate funds to do what they would like in addition to covering normal living expenses. As a result, they may initially limit their discretionary spending for fear of running short of money. And if they feel constrained by money, they are likely to be dissatisfied with their new living arrangements. And for those with less money—and even for some with lots— retirement can entail dipping into savings or earnings on investments; this can be scary because it means money is going out without a supply coming in.

In our survey, we found that retirees do in fact worry about money—6 in 10 are at least somewhat concerned, and only about 10% claim that they are not at all concerned about their finances. These worries are more prevalent among women, blue-collar workers, and those with lower income, but even those with higher income are not immune to these fears—roughly 4 in 10 affluent retirees in our survey are at least somewhat concerned about their financial futures.

Financial worries are not found only in the early stages of retirement, as we had anticipated. We discovered that the deeper into retirement, the more retirees seem to be worried about their finances, regardless of their income. Mentions of being extremely or very concerned are made by 18% of those retired one year or less but steadily climb to about 30% for those six or more years into retirement—this is in spite of the fact that income does not vary much with the number of years retired.

So what's at the root of all this? We had expected to see financial concerns decline as retirees gain experience in retirement living, but the opposite appears to be the case. One possible explanation has to do with how retirees would handle financial problems should they arise. As a follow-up question to financial worries, we asked retirees whether they would consider going back to work if they had a financial shortfall. We found that about 30% of those retired one year or less claim they would do so, but this figure drops to just 19% for those retired six years or more.

Their growing desire to avoid work implies that, as the years pass, retirees come to accept and like the undemanding retirement lifestyle. But longer-term retirees may also feel that their opportunity to work diminishes over time. Retirees are likely to lose their business contacts as they are farther away from their time in the workforce and may believe that finding a job would be difficult. Newer retirees, on the other hand, are likely to be more connected to the worker lifestyle and their job network, so work may be more accessible to them. Additionally, the greater willingness of new retirees to take a job offers another advantage—they have a built-in safety net in the face of money problems. This may be one reason why they are less concerned about their financial futures.

It is interesting that those who are still working are as worried about money as retirees, presumably resulting in part from the economic woes prevailing when we conducted our survey. But it's also fascinating to find that those who are still working are more likely to claim that, when retired, they would go back to work if they had money problems—57% say they would do so compared to only 21% of all retirees. The differences in these attitudes underscore the point that those still in the workforce really don't understand the mind-set that accompanies retirement—that returning to the workforce out of necessity seems to be a pretty distasteful thought, especially as retirees get further and further into the lifestyle. Consequently, their intentions notwithstanding, when they actually leave the workforce, they are very likely to adopt the same attitudes about working as other retirees—a lot less interest in it than they thought they'd have.

As we mentioned earlier, money has a perceptual component, and not all retirees' financial concerns are well founded. One of the retirees we interviewed, Patrick, explained what he went through with money as he wrestled with the "perception versus reality" problem. We should point out that Patrick's concerns about finances did not go away over time but rather were still running strong seven years into his retirement. Patrick was a successful businessman with a net worth of about $7 million when he retired. During the 2008 recession, his nest egg shrank to about $5 million. On top of that, his former company, which was providing him with money through a buyout for another few years, was itself struggling to survive the recession. Still, $5 million is a lot of money, and his finances were perfectly adequate for retirement by anyone's reckoning—except his own:

> When I first retired, I didn't worry much about money. I had made the calculations dozens of times and felt comfortable. I believed I had enough to do whatever I wanted. I expected that I could spend all the interest I made on my investments each year and never touch the principal, no matter how long I lived. However, when the economy went down I started taking a closer look at my spending patterns. At that point, I began to worry. Actually, panic is a better description. I started to find ways to cut down. I quit my country club, traded down our two luxury cars to something more moderately priced, put our oversized house on the market and moved into a modest condo, and cut down our visits to restaurants.
>
> Then I started wondering: if things get worse, how could I make money without having to go back into the workforce full-time? Maybe my former company would give me a part-time job. I was always pretty handy around the house, so maybe I could become a handyman, doing odd jobs. These ridiculous thoughts occupied my mind every day and kept me up at night. I knew deep down that I was being irrational, but that didn't matter. I resorted to talking to friends about my financial situation to get their opinions, and I always ended these conversations with, "You don't think I'm going to end up homeless, do you?" I discussed this often with my accountant, and when I finally asked him if I had enough money, he replied, "You will never have enough money." At that point I realized I had better calm down, I'm being irrational. But of course that did not make me feel any different. And I also knew I was not alone. I once discussed this issue with an uncle. He knew my financial status and was also retired. When I mentioned my concerns, he told me he never really got comfortable with the idea he could afford to be retired.

Now, it is difficult to feel sympathy for Patrick given his financial picture—and he made it clear to us that he wasn't looking for it. He obviously was far better off financially than most people, even in a down economy, and at some level he realized that. But the point here is that regardless of the amount of money retirees have, they must *believe* they have enough before they can feel truly secure. Only then will they have the freedom to pursue their goals without feeling financially constrained. And Patrick's worries, exaggerated though they may have been given his actual finances, are shared by many retirees in all financial brackets—and the constraints these often groundless worries can cause are widely shared as well.

Of course, unlike Patrick, some retirees' worries are *not* groundless—some really don't have enough money to live the lives they want to or even to cover all their basic needs. The loss in spending power is fairly dramatic after leaving the workforce. On average, retirees in this study reported an annual income (i.e., money from earnings or pensions that does not include the principal of their savings) of about $56,000 versus $78,000 among those still in the workforce. Blue-collar retirees have especially low annual incomes: about $44,000 versus $67,000 for those who held white-collar jobs. (In case you're wondering why the incomes of our respondents are higher than that found in the national population—which is roughly $50,000—we interviewed only people at retirement age or approaching it, that is, 45 years of age or older. They tend to be at the upper end of the pay scale for their jobs, whereas the national population includes younger people just starting their careers and therefore earning less.)

Furthermore, almost half of all retirees say they are only partially able to cover their basic living expenses, and two-thirds have a hard time meeting all of their discretionary spending needs from their incomes alone. As a result, about 4 in 10 have to dip into their savings in order to live comfortably. The extent to which retirees can meet either their basic or their discretionary financial needs very clearly affects their overall quality of life and how well they feel adjusted in retirement. For example, among those who feel they are completely adjusted, 69% report having enough income to meet their basic needs compared to only 28% of their less adjusted counterparts.

Some retirees' financial worries are imaginary, but for others they are quite real and can be a major roadblock in the way of their pursuit of a satisfactory lifestyle. Nevertheless, there are ways one can come to terms with his or her finances and maybe establish a better comfort level. First, those who feel uncertain about their finances must first find out which camp they fall into—are they needlessly worried about money, or are their fears justified? To assess if there's a basis in reality for their worries, retirees should seek advice from independent financial consulting services. For some, like Patrick, whose irrational fears prevent them from making an objective evaluation on their own, such professional assistance is vital.

Among other things, professional recommendations may include having retirees keep a ledger of monthly expenses and income, just as would be done if one were operating a business. Putting the numbers down on paper can help to clarify retirees' thinking as to whether they are truly operating in the black or the red. Our survey found this practice to be encouragingly common: about 6 in 10 retirees already have a ledger system in place to help manage their finances.

However, we also found that 34% do nothing concrete to monitor their spending, preferring instead to keep track of the numbers in their head. Not surprisingly, those who are less well adjusted and have lower incomes—those with the greatest financial fears—tend to operate in this manner. For those who are uncertain about their finances, this is probably not a good way to proceed, especially given how difficult it is to remember *anything* when one reaches retirement age, at least based on the experiences of the authors. Taking the paper-and-pencil route instead appears to have a few important advantages—even though their incomes are the same as those using the "I keep the numbers in my head" approach, our survey showed that those keeping a ledger were better at covering their basic expenses and discretionary spending without using their savings and were more likely to report they are retired comfortably, at least where money is concerned.

This is not to say that keeping a ledger, by itself, is a cure for money fears. We found that those who keep a paper ledger are just as worried as those who are doing nothing concrete to monitor their expenses. But the difference is those who systematically keep a written record of their income and expenses may have their concerns more grounded in reality and can plan their spending accordingly.

While we are not financial experts, it is reasonable to assume that, to make an accurate assessment, income and expenses should be recorded for an extended length of time—six months or so seems sensible. This will ensure that the numbers include the variations that can occur from month to month. Major one-time or occasional expenses, such as travel or holiday gift buying, need to be recorded; they can throw off an evaluation if they are not included. After keeping a ledger for several months, tally it all up. If you find yourself in the black, that is, your income is equal to or surpasses your expenses, then you can relax; you've proven to yourself that you can afford to retire. But keep the ledger going anyway. Although it's a bit of a chore, it's a good way to ensure that you have not varied your spending patterns and that you are still living within your means. And if at times you again start to worry about money, you can always refer back to your financial records to again achieve a comfort level—or, perhaps, discover that your situation has changed and you need to adjust your spending patterns.

Along those lines, if their financial assessment points to a shortfall, where expenses surpass income, retirees who cannot adequately cut back on their spending may have no choice but to reenter the workforce to supplement their income. While again this may be distasteful for many, some may just have to embrace the horror. And the fact is many retirees work in some capacity and actually find it enjoyable. The evidence suggests that such "bridge jobs" can provide quite a few benefits with respect to psychological well-being. Of course, it has to be the right job, one that has the characteristics that make working in retirement a positive experience and still leaves the retiree feeling retired. It is to these bridge jobs that we turn our attention next.

· 8 ·

Retired and Working

Everyone who does not work has a scheme that does.

—Munder's Law

*E*arlier we pointed out that the definition of retirement is no longer restricted to just stopping work altogether. The fact is, lots of retirees go back to work in some capacity after they retire. Research shows a very interesting pairing of recent trends. On the one hand, people are tending to retire earlier in their lives; on the other, over half of retirees, especially younger ones, hold jobs at some point after leaving their full-time careers. This development, which shows no signs of slowing, may simply be the natural evolution of how we think of retirement. As a relatively new social phenomenon, it is not surprising that retirement may take on new looks as retirees find ways to maximize their comfort and fulfillment—and it seems as though work is becoming one of them.

And as was also mentioned earlier, social scientists refer to working in retirement as "bridge employment." More formally, it is defined as a job held after leaving a full-time career, with the intention of gradually withdrawing over time from full labor force participation.[1] The term derives from the way that these jobs smooth, or "bridge," the transition from the workforce into retirement. This is something of a psychological sleight of hand—retirees continue to see themselves as retired while at the same time reaping the rewards and benefits of working that we've covered in previous chapters.

A bridge job can take many forms. It can be part-time, self-employment or working for someone else, or a "temp job," as long as it starts after full-time employment ends and before permanent retirement begins.[2] Bridge jobs generally entail shorter working hours, less emotional commitment to the job, the decision to work more out of choice than necessity (although sometimes

97

financial considerations force people into bridge jobs), and some degree of control over the kinds of tasks involved. These characteristics distinguish bridge jobs from conventional jobs held before retirement, and they make this type of work more enjoyable and less stressful without completely eliminating the benefits associated with retirement. On the whole, bridge jobs can be healthy for some retirees and can contribute to their subjective well-being.

A number of practical and psychological factors enter into the decision to take a job in retirement. On the practical side, assuming health problems are not a deterrent, there may be financial considerations. Retirees may elect to take a bridge job out of a desire to achieve a specific standard of living or increase their discretionary income. Whether a spouse or significant other has continued to work may also play a role in the decision. Retirees with working spouses may be limited in the types of nonwork activities they can participate in since many of these activities are typically done as a couple.

It's not all that unusual to find retirees who may be inclined to work simply because they actually enjoyed their careers. Bridge jobs allow them to continue using their skills without the stressful negatives of a full-time commitment. Some are likely to feel that a bridge job complements their retirement, with work time fitting in between nonwork pursuits.[3] These retirees can therefore stay busy with something they enjoy and at the same time maintain regular social contact with their coworker friends.

Bridge jobs fit nicely within the framework of role and continuity theories that we reviewed earlier, helping retirees adjust by letting them continue in their roles as workers. There is a certain "have one's cake and eat it too" aspect to this. Retirees can retain the worker role as a means of defining themselves while simultaneously feeling at least somewhat distanced from the workforce. Furthermore, by allowing retirees to live simultaneously in the two worlds of retirement and employment, bridge jobs help them to feel more socially integrated.[4] Research has demonstrated that people are better off psychologically when they are involved in a number of roles. If we keep in mind that each role you have gives you a reason for being, then multiple roles will give an added to boost to your feeling that your life has some purpose and at the same time make you feel even more connected to the outside world. When retirees add paid work to their list of retirement-related activities, they are much better off than those who retire without roles and relationships to compensate for what was lost after leaving the workforce (though of course paid work is not the only way to attain these benefits).[5]

Anne, a retired educator, discovered how taking on some work helped her feel more comfortable being retired. She initially found retirement to be a welcome break. But over time, she felt it to be unfulfilling, and she needed to find a way to feel productive. But it was not just about being productive because she soon realized that the social component of work was also very important to her:

> At first, being retired felt like every night was Friday night. No pressures to get up early. No particular place to go. Freedom to do as I pleased . . . a long vacation—at home! I quickly discovered that the five-minute breakfast that I used to eat before I went to work now became the two-hour coffee break. I was up at 7:00, but by the time I looked at the clock, it was 10:30. How could that be? Time flies when you're not doing anything, and soon it started to grate on my nerves. I needed something to do to keep me active. Lunch with my friends was nice, but you can't fill your days doing that . . . the thrill wears off. Time for myself was nice, but after a while I needed to feel productive. So I sought work.
>
> I first took an at-home job creating curricula for the state education system. It gave me something to do, but working alone on my computer was still not fulfilling. It was nice to be productive and to make money, but there was something missing. I needed the people, the students, the problems, the everyday aggravation that I had come to know as my job. I applied out as an interim administrator and found a two-year position in one school district, followed by a second two-year position at another. These interim positions helped to carry me over the rough spots and bring me to where I am today. I am retired but still available to consult to school districts. I work at my leisure but still feel productive.
>
> I think that was my biggest negative—when I was not working, I did not feel useful. Consulting for even a few days a month makes me feel like a professional. I need that because of who I am and because of my professional training. I can never see myself sitting on a rocker on the front porch. The biggest positive about retirement is the freedom to manage your own time. It enables you to do what you want, but it also reminds you of how little is left, so don't waste it. But all that time may be its biggest drawback. Actually, I believe that when people say that they want to retire, all they really want is a long vacation. At least, when I left public education, that was what I wanted, until I became bored and restless.

For retirees who have a particularly hard time making the adjustment to retirement, a bridge job is an especially good idea. Often, these retirees cannot make the emotional break from their field or organization, are uncertain about their retirement plans, or have not developed enough nonwork interests. Because they do not have an acceptable replacement for work, a bridge job can minimize the stress that can result from feeling unconnected to the retirement lifestyle.

But bridge employment is not for everyone. For one thing, it seems to suit men more than women, especially in the case of part-time positions.

Recent research has shown that women, unlike men, are often less happy in retirement if they take on a bridge job. (Of course, this is hardly a universal truth, as can be seen from Anne's positive experience.) Additionally, regardless of the retiree's gender, bridge jobs have less value for retirees who enjoy the freedom of the retirement lifestyle, have a well-developed social sphere or interests outside of work, or have found their careers or work in general to be too stressful.[6] For these retirees, having to return to work would likely be fairly painful.

Additionally, neither all types of bridge jobs nor all reasons for continuing to work are created equal. The classic case here is the retiree who is forced to work because he or she needs the money. These unfortunate retirees don't work out of choice and because of that are not likely to be in any position to exert control over their role as employee. Consequently, they can find themselves back where they started: feeling the stresses and pressures of their job just as they did before retiring. In fact, things may be even worse under these circumstances because now, every day they go to work, they're forced to confront the fact that they've tried to retire and weren't able to. Clearly, bridge employment under these circumstances is not likely to help anyone feel good about retirement (apart from the benefit to one's finances) or improve their subjective well-being.

Research suggests that when looking for a bridge job, one shouldn't stray too far from the familiar. If a retiree takes a job in a field or industry that is different from his or her primary career, research has shown the beneficial effects of bridge employment may not be readily available. Retirees-turned-employees have to learn new tasks and responsibilities if they enter a field they're not familiar with and may have to make a variety of adjustments in how they approach work mentally and physically. In such a case, the bridge job can become a source of pressure and stress, and that certainly doesn't help anyone feel adjusted to retirement.

Then again, sometimes a new field can be a good idea, such as when it lines up well with a retiree's lifelong passion (e.g., a wine lover working in the wine industry). On the surface, the advice would be to go for it. This sort of change can provide an opportunity to enhance the retirement experience and the retiree's subjective well-being.[7] But you still have to keep in mind that it is still a job, with responsibilities and required learning, and there will be expectations about performance. In other words, it will have its associated demands and stresses and may not be as much fun as it appears. Still, such jobs might be worth trying as long as one is prepared to jump ship if the going gets rough and the expected rewards do not outweigh the negatives.

Rob's experiences illustrate the potential pitfalls of a decision to take a job in a new field. From the first day of his retirement, he immersed himself in new fields that he thought he would enjoy. However, each of these turned out to be a lot more than he wanted to handle. In the end, though, he was able to find his way back to his true work-related passion:

> When I first retired, I immediately began to look for business opportunities in other industries. I felt bored with what I had done for a living for the past 30 years, but still I loved being in the business world, and I thought it would be fun to try a new field. Over the following months, through associates I became involved in fields I had absolutely no experience in. And I did not consider limiting my pursuits. Before I knew it, I was involved in five companies in fields as diverse as fashion jewelry, organic foods from Italy, skin care treatments, home fragrances, and pet products. And nobody would ever describe me as a pet lover.
>
> While I thought my experiences as a market researcher prepared me for launching new products, I was completely naive as to what was entailed in developing formulations, and I had no experience at all with import regulations, international shipping, and the like. Furthermore, even though I had already gone through the process of building a company, I had forgotten about the amount of effort such endeavors require.
>
> While I went through the motions of building these businesses, somewhere in the middle of it all I began to admit to myself that I was not really up to the challenge—I just didn't want to work that hard. So after some sleepless nights, I began to question why I was bothering with all this. How could I expect to develop one company, let alone five, on a part-time basis? And honestly, did I really want to count cans of freakin' tomatoes for the rest of my life? I started thinking of myself as a Ralph Kramden, hatching one new get-rich-quick scheme after another. So at that point I knew what I had to do: shut these companies down and go back to what I know—research. Interestingly, through this process, I fell in love all over again with my original field: research in the social sciences. And the best part of this new pursuit was I no longer had to deal with employees.

The above description illustrates still another aspect of bridge employment, and it is one that pervades all aspects of successful retirement—the need to experiment. Even though Rob considered some of his endeavors to be harebrained schemes, he still could grasp the value in going down each road, mostly as a means of eliminating them as options. Charlie, our ex–police chief, also tried a few different options until he came to one that satisfied his need to put something meaningful into his life, something that he could become passionately involved in. As with Rob, it took Charlie some time to get there, with a number of false starts and wrong steps. But he continued in his pursuit, and in the end he came up with a fantastic opportunity:

> About a year into my retirement, things were not going well at all. I remember my father retiring from NYPD, and he was a basket case for

years. This man, once a homicide detective, started making wooden boxes with dried beans in them as some kind of decoration. My entire family reluctantly took these things, but after a year or two they bred bugs. The thought of ending up that way scared the hell out of me.

Then I gravitated to other retired cops and police chiefs. We would meet up and discuss retirement. We were all dealing with it differently, and while some seemed happy and content, most were uneasy with their new life. This was not helpful at all, but misery loves company. I needed to get away from that, so I tried to think back to who I used to be before becoming a cop and police chief. But I was so locked up in what I did that I didn't know how to be something else. That didn't work. I was checking the obits daily to see who was dead and just sitting around. That was not the old me.

I knew I had to move on, so I started looking into my options. I would become a private investigator. That lasted about 12 months, and I packed it in because the only business I was getting was to follow cheating spouses around. After a short while, I found myself telling potential clients, "If you know they are cheating, why do you need me? Get a lawyer. At the very least, you don't trust them, so why do you want to stay married?" That attitude was not very good for business.

My next move was to send my résumé everywhere I could in the hopes of finding a job that fit with my background. As it turned out, it seems that some people felt I was worth an interview. But when they called, I would not follow up with them. What was this all about? I thought I wanted to work, but it seemed that the damage caused by my previous job was still there. I could have done most of the jobs being offered to me when I was younger and done them well, but now I felt I simply no longer had the heart or the stamina.

So then I started looking around for other jobs. There were many that surfaced that had nothing to do with my training and education. Looking back, I am embarrassed to even say what they were. I will only say they involved a minimum wage–type situation. I thought at the time that maybe doing something different and menial would solve my head issues. I never pursued these seriously, but still I knew I was open to considering anything.

For a couple of years, I kept looking, searching through the classifieds over and over again. I was sending my résumé everywhere on earth. But the way I pursued this was pretty strange—I would go to the interview, but sometimes I would leave the building before the interview took place. Other times I got the job but would say no thanks or just not show up at all. I once went on an interview at our community arts center as the parking manager. I was interviewed, and this kid that interviewed me gave me the job. But I was never to be seen again. My wife didn't like that my new job title had the word "parking" in it.

Now that I knew I could get a pretty good job, I took it up a notch. I was applying for large corporation international security jobs. These jobs are usually swallowed up by retired FBI guys, so this was now a real challenge to get into the big time. I never made it to an interview, but I did try very hard. I especially liked the ones that provided me with a corporate jet.

Then I decided to look into running the town I live in. Being the town manager had a certain poetic justice to it given how I was thrown out of my police job. I took some municipal courses at the local university for certification. When the town manager was ready to leave the job, he called and said, "It's yours if you want it." My reply was, "No, I am too busy."

What did all this mean? Was I that confused? Finding a job and getting the nod was keeping me going. It became my job to try to get a job but not to actually take one. I feel very foolish as I look back on this behavior.

But then I found my answer in volunteer work. I joined a program that had 170 retired cops from all over the country. Our mission is to locate and solve missing-children cases, cold cases if you will. I make my own hours and schedule, and I am once again working alongside retired guys who think and act like I do. After years of hunting, I finally found something that works.

From our own survey, we confirmed the results of other social scientists—but not in all respects, as we did uncover a few twists and turns. To begin, we found that about a quarter of retirees currently hold a job, a relatively high percentage for a group that attempted to stop working. Job holders are mostly new to retirement—41% of those who are retired six months or less are working, and this proportion drops to about one in four when retirees hit the two-year mark and to only a bit over 1 in 10 by the time retirees are 10 or more years into retirement. While part of the decline is probably age related, it is also likely that over time, retirees become more comfortable with their retirement lifestyle and have less and less need for the diversion of work.

Early in retirement, though, it appears that work does help some make a smoother transition, bridging the gap between the two extremes of all work and no work. Many working retirees seem to enter retirement feeling energetic. In comparison to nonworking retirees, they are more active and prefer a faster-paced lifestyle. And they tend to be more motivated—working retirees are interested in finding things to do that would interest them and view retirement as a time to pursue new goals. However, they also tend to feel that retirement was not what they expected, possibly because of its slower pace. They haven't fully embraced the relaxed lifestyle, and as a result they are not as happy or as adjusted to retirement as nonworking retirees. In fact, when we looked at which retirees are working, 19% of well-adjusted retirees hold jobs compared to 36% of the less well adjusted. As such, they may view work as one way of making them feel comfortable—if not with retirement, then at least with themselves.

There are a few other factors that make working an appealing prospect to these retirees beyond just dissatisfaction with the retirement lifestyle. First, working retirees are more likely to have a working spouse. Although their marriages are sound—or at least as good as the marriages of those who are not working—that means they spend more time alone and have fewer opportunities to socialize or engage in certain kinds of activities, such as travel. So working is a good way to use up time and probably avoid confrontations with their spouses. Second, when working retirees were in the workforce full-time, they held more prestigious positions, were much more career oriented, and got a lot of enjoyment from their work. Although they don't miss their full-time jobs any more than their nonworking counterparts, still their careers provided a number of benefits for them in the past. The warm place that working holds in their heart, coupled with feeling unfulfilled in retirement, makes working a better way to go for these individuals.

But it's not all about self-fulfillment—for many working retirees, it's also about money. Financial considerations definitely play a role in the decision to work—6 in 10 working retirees mention financial benefits as a reason for taking a job. Financial insecurity is part of this: working retirees are less likely to think they have enough money to be comfortably retired than nonworking retirees. In truth, working retirees' income is higher than that of nonworkers, but apparently this is not enough to make them feel as financially secure as their counterparts. They may in fact have greater financial needs, but, as we discussed in a previous chapter, money is very much a perceptual issue; working retirees may be more likely to succumb to the feeling that they need more money than they have, no matter how much they actually do have.

But, as we've seen, money is not the only motivation to take a bridge job. About two-thirds of working retirees look for emotional and psychological benefits from their jobs, such as feeling productive, feeling good about themselves, and having an opportunity for social contact. And these benefits seem to be realized—working retirees are more likely to believe they live a productive life and are in a better place from a social perspective. Because coworkers are readily available to them, they can hold on to these friendships. The result is a larger circle of friends with whom they maintain strong emotional bonds and fairly frequent interaction.

With such benefits, it's not at all surprising that working retirees truly enjoy their work—85% rate their jobs positively, and only about 5% regard them as stressful. The latter is an extremely low percentage, especially when compared to the 42% who felt stressed in their full-time careers. Working retirees are evenly split between those holding a job in a new field versus their old familiar industry. Necessity rather than a desire for new challenges seems to drive the move to a new field; retirees who changed fields were more likely to have come from a shrinking industry and to have been forced out of their jobs. While they had to do a lot more hunting to find the right job, they ultimately found one that was just as likable and stress-free as one from their original field.

So taking on bridge jobs can be rewarding—they help to maintain social connectivity, are a constructive use of time, and pay emotional dividends, such as feeling one is productive and a contributing member of society. However, simply taking a job, even one that is liked and stress free, does not guarantee that all these benefits will be reaped. Rather, it appears that one has to take a job for the right reasons.

We came to this perspective after looking at the factors that led retirees to get a job. Specifically, we broke out three segments of retired workers based on their reasons for going back to work—those who sought psychological and social benefits (such as contact with coworkers, to feel productive, and so on), those who primarily needed the money, and those who went to work out of boredom, not knowing what else to do with their time. Only the first of these actually achieved the benefits that bridge jobs are expected to provide. The two other groups—those who work out of financial necessity and those who work out of boredom—have not achieved a more comfortable feeling in retirement.

It is interesting here to note the parallels with the "push" and "pull" factors that lead to the decision to retire—these also operate in the decision to take a bridge job. The need for money and the desire to avoid boredom work as "pushes" since one is trying to *escape from* unsatisfactory circumstances; the desire to find psychological and social benefits are "pull" factors based on a desire to *move to* more positive circumstances. And, just as we saw in the decision to retire, "push" reasons often lead to unsatisfactory outcomes, whereas "pull" motivations tend to yield more positive results.

Let's look first at the most successful working segment: those seeking psychological and social benefits from their jobs. These are highly motivated people who look for work to enrich their lives and possibly fill gaps in the retirement lifestyle. While not quite as adjusted to retirement as those who do not work at all, they are much better adjusted than those who are motivated to work because of money or boredom. They are much more likely to feel emotionally connected to other people, possess a good deal of self-confidence, feel useful and productive, be optimistic about the future, and feel good about how their lives have turned out. Working has provided them with a very good way of coping with retirement.

On the other side of the spectrum are those who have taken a job for financial reasons. Their situations are unfortunate since they tended to be forced out of their jobs and had not actually planned for retirement. Worse still, they did not enjoy their jobs while in the workforce, and if they had a choice, they would not work. In fact, they tend to regard retirement as a time for rest and relaxation and would prefer to live a more passive, sedentary lifestyle. But their lower incomes—$51,000 versus about $63,000 for those who do not work or do not work specifically for money—make it tough for them to cover both basic living and discretionary expenses. Possibly because they work out of necessity, they tend to like their jobs less and find them more stressful than those working for other reasons.

The problem with working only for money is commitment. Retirees who take a job primarily out of financial need are motivated by external rather than internal reasons. When employees are only externally motivated, they don't feel emotionally connected to their work, the organization, or their coworkers, so they take themselves out of a position to reap psychological benefits. Consequently, these retirees feel less socially connected, valued, or productive. And, tied in with this, they rate their overall quality of life as poor, feel that their quality of life has gotten worse in retirement, are not happy with how their lives have turned out—and are less adjusted to retirement.

On the other hand, people who work for internal reasons—for example, because it makes them feel good about themselves, feel productive, and so on—tend to take ownership of their jobs. They are usually more motivated, take more pride in what they are doing, and feel emotionally connected to the job and their coworkers. As a result, they tend to get a lot more enjoyment out of their work—and get the psychological rewards.

What we found for the third group, those who work primarily to avoid boredom, is perhaps somewhat counterintuitive. One might think it reasonable to assume that if someone is bored in retirement, working should be the cure. Just by being back in the workforce, the psychological and social benefits of working should be readily available. But, as with working only for money, this isn't the case for bored retirees, and the by-now-familiar "push versus pull" dynamic might hold the key. These working retirees' dissatisfaction may have something to do with having approached work with the wrong mindset. Many of these retirees may have taken on a job not as a means of achieving a more fulfilling or productive life but more as a way to escape the undirected, unstructured world of retirement. Again, it's important to keep in mind that it's a vastly different thing to look to escape an unpleasant situation (e.g., the boredom of retirement) than it is to take on something (e.g., work) because you seek its rewards. In other words, they were pushed to escape something negative rather than pulled into something they saw as positive, and pushed is not a good thing.

But maybe these bored retirees also needed the money and *that* contributed to their dissatisfaction with their bridge jobs. Not so; we found that bored retirees don't seem to need the money. Their incomes are actually similar to those who do not work or who work for psychological benefits, about $63,000 per year on average. Also, like those who consciously sought the psychological benefits of a job, bored retirees are also more likely to have working spouses. And although their marriages are not quite as satisfying as for other retirees, the fact that their spouses are out of the home may contribute to their feelings of boredom.

In some respects, retirement was not their fault—bored retirees tended to be forced into retirement. With that, they were more likely to feel that those uncontrollable circumstances interfered with their chances of enjoying retirement. Certainly this is unfortunate, but still they seem to do little to improve their situation. For example, while they have as large a circle of friends as other retirees who are working, they tend to be less emotionally bonded to them. Possibly as a result, they feel less socially involved and less satisfied with their social lives and tend toward bouts of loneliness and feelings of being isolated. Furthermore, because of how they approach their jobs, they are less likely to feel valued, useful, and productive, the readily available by-products of working. With all this going against them, they tend to have weaker self-confidence, are not satisfied with how they are living, and are pessimistic about their prospects for the future.

Certainly this is not a happy situation. But we do get the sense that with either a greater realization of what jobs can offer or a greater personal commitment, these retirees might fare better. As was pointed out, if it's done for the right reasons and with the right frame of mind, bridge employment can offer quite a few benefits. So it should be noted that care must be taken when going down this path. To make sure the work-related benefits are realized, retirees must actively seek out the easily attainable rewards of working—a sense of being useful and productive as well as an opportunity for being socially connected and a member of a team. At the same time, however, the job has to be the right one to avoid the potential problems of feeling stressed, overworked, or even unretired.

We've discussed some of the types of retirees who might make particularly good candidates for a bridge job—those who enjoy working, have working spouses, who have not developed satisfying retirement lifestyles, or who want more challenges yet who understand that reaping the benefits of working requires some personal commitment. But there's another group for which such jobs might be especially important as a haven, one that we haven't focused on yet: those who retire at a relatively young age. These retirees are likely to face issues that are unique to their age-group, and we'll explore them in the next chapter.

· 9 ·

Taking Early Retirement

When is the right age to retire? When you dread going to work.

—Mary Bright

$\mathcal{A}$s noted in previous chapters, the number of people retiring while still in their fifties has been growing over the years throughout the United States and Europe.[1] Researchers point to a number of factors contributing to this trend, many of which can most easily be understood in terms of the "push" and "pull" qualities discussed earlier.

To review, environmental factors push some people into retirement. Here we are referring to corporate downsizing or restructuring, which means employees won't be able to count on staying in their jobs for the long term. Under these circumstances, it makes sense for them to retire early, as long as their personal finances are adequate. Early retirement may be even more tempting for those lucky enough to get a financial package or to find bridge employment on a subcontracting basis with the same company or within the same industry.

Pull factors presume retirees see retirement as a destination, a place to go to because it offers some allurements. We began our investigations with the assumption that many early retirees are pulled into retirement (as we'll see, though, that's far from always being the case). After all, if there weren't some compelling positive reasons to retire (and of course assuming no major "push" factors are present), they probably would not have left the workforce in the first place. Pull factors can result from positive expectations about the retirement lifestyle. For example, early retirees may sense that in retirement they could satisfy their personal needs and aspirations to a greater extent than they can in work. They may be interested in pursuing new paths or looking at the greener pastures of a life of leisure.

However, sometimes it's not so clear whether pushes or pulls are operating. For example, there is the possibility that some early retirees just do not like their jobs. When their feelings are considered in the context of personal finances and future employment opportunities, retirement may turn out to be a better option. They are not necessarily pushed out of work; instead, they may leave their jobs because their personal finances allow them to do so.[2] But if their decision is based just on their negative feelings about work and retirement does not lure them in with its opportunities, then the effect is to be pushed out of their jobs, and that can have negative consequences. Retirement has to be a destination in itself for retirees to be pulled.

If early retirees are pulled into retirement, they would seem likely to be well primed for the event. Retirement—and its timing—is their personal choice, so they probably look forward to being retired. With a positive state of mind, these retirees can improve their odds of success. Additionally, based solely on their having retired early by choice, it can be presumed that younger retirees were not too strongly tied emotionally to their careers. Instead, they may have already developed strong and stable nonwork roles or may simply be flexible enough to adopt new retirement-related roles quickly, both of which are advantages. They may in effect regard retirement as the next logical step in their lives and may have set up specific plans for goals they want to achieve.

Some early retirees are also likely to have a few personal characteristics and mental coping strategies that help them make it through life stage transitions—some of these may have even helped to make early retirement a possibility. For example, if early retirees held jobs that entailed considerable problem solving or task flexibility—the sort of responsibilities often found in white-collar occupations—then they would be used to dealing with change or undefined situations. Their entry into the undefined world of retirement might be a little easier since their experiences in the workforce have given them practice jumping through hoops. And, given that they are likely to have set aside enough money to retire—voluntary early retirement without enough savings is unusual, for obvious reasons—they have the freedom and flexibility to pursue various interests and activities.

However, whether or not early retirees actually manage to *have* an easy adjustment in retirement is another issue entirely and has not been fully assessed by social scientists. Most of the research on young retirees has focused on the factors leading to their retirement decision rather than how well they actually make the adjustment. We may assume that they will do well, but that is based on presumptions about their backgrounds and personal traits, and in fact they may not do as well as one might speculate. They may end up stumbling into some potential pitfalls that they may not have anticipated in spite of all their planning.

One potential pitfall is social convention, those unspoken "everyone knows" guidelines that tell us all what we're "supposed to" do—and not do. Social convention allows someone retiring at the traditional age of 65 to readily accept leaving the workforce or at least be fairly comfortably resigned to it. Social convention is what pushes many older people out of work with the perspective that one eventually must bow to the inevitable. Additionally, society at large is constructed (literally and figuratively) on the basis of these conventions. On entering retirement, it's easy to assume that older retirees have a more natural fit in the retirement world. They can avail themselves of a variety of services targeted specifically to their age-group and designed with their retirement lifestyles in mind. For example, many urban and suburban areas have senior centers that serve as social hubs for those in this age-group. Many restaurants and other entertainment facilities also cater specifically to this age-group by offering discounts and special privileges.

Early retirees, in contrast, are bucking the norm. Because they are still relatively few in number, they don't have support systems available to meet their specific age-related needs to the same degree as older retirees. Furthermore, because they are younger, early retirees may still have high levels of energy and drive compared to their older counterparts, leading them to seek a more active lifestyle—maybe more active than the retirement world is geared to accommodate. Some may also retain a personal need to continue being productive. In the event that they choose not to take a bridge job or don't find something else engrossing to do, they are likely to experience more boredom on a day-to-day basis than older retirees.

Early retirees may also face more problems than their older counterparts trying to stay socially connected. People who stop working while still in their fifties are not likely to find many of their peers retiring at the same time. Instead, most of an early retiree's friends are likely to be still working, forcing the early retiree to take the retirement journey alone. Yes, there are likely to be some older retirees in their circle with whom they can interact, and they probably have a spouse or significant other as a companion, but neither of these can give the emotional support or companionship best provided by one's peers—those in their age-group who share the same perspective, interests, and possibly drive.

Outside of an intimate partner, early retirees have fewer opportunities for daily social interaction than those who retire at a more conventional age. Some may spend an uncomfortable amount of time alone, and they can come to feel isolated. This is especially apparent if we keep in mind that early retirees lose many of their coworker relationships when they leave the workforce, and the rest of their social network is not readily available. Rob's experiences here are probably typical of many early retirees. In order to eliminate the problems brought on by a lack of daily social contact, he had to come up with some alternative ways of living socially:

> When I retired, my wife owned a small boutique where she worked six days a week, and all of my friends were still working full-time. As a result, I would spend days on end by myself, in my house. Occasionally I would drop by the offices of my former company, but my former coworkers were often so busy they had little time for me. And even if they did, I frankly wasn't very interested in what was happening there day to day, and I certainly didn't want to hear about their work-related problems—those problems were a big part of why I wanted to retire in the first place. So they had little time for me, and I wasn't very interested in what they wanted to discuss—not a good combination for feeling socially connected. So I stayed home, and many days I would just wander around the house, trying to invent things to do.
>
> At the time I was living in a small city in the South, a fine place to live while I was working full-time. But I had only a small circle of friends in the area. So after retiring, I turned back to work, pursuing some new business opportunities. But I didn't want to work too hard, so I still had too much time on my hands and too much time alone. I came to the conclusion that since I'll ultimately always be a New York City boy, a small city could not provide enough stimulation for me if I wasn't working full-time. So I moved back to New York to be closer to friends and family.
>
> But even this wasn't ideal because all of my New York friends were also working, and I faced the prospect of having no social life in two cities. The problem was really an issue of differing priorities. Because all of my friends were working, it was hard for them to commit to doing much socially. On weekends or their days off, they could be backed up with chores and other responsibilities they could not get to during the workweek, and that left them with little free time. As a result I could spend days on end with virtually no social contact at all other than a few email exchanges.
>
> I really had to put in a lot of effort just to come up with a semblance of a social life despite the fact that I knew a lot of people in the area. As one solution, I tried to start off my weeks by setting up a schedule of lunch and dinner plans with friends and acquaintances, just to ensure I would see someone, anyone, each week. Thank the gods people eat, or I probably would not have seen much of my New York friends either. But the reality is I could never get to the point of feeling my social needs were adequately filled.

As can be seen from Rob's experiences, social contact can be cut down quite a bit for early retirees. And even if it is fairly frequent, it is possible that there will also be a distancing from friends because early retirees are likely to have different day-to-day goals and priorities than their working friends. For example, when conversations with friends turn to work, early retirees may lose interest, feel out of touch, or feel they have less to contribute. This is healthy—early retirees can't afford to keep their strong ties to their working role. But the resulting weakening of their social bonds could lead to a dwindling sense of connectedness to the outside world. And early retirees who have most of their friends coming from the workforce may be especially subject to feeling isolated and alone, and that is not healthy.

Again, however, much of this is speculation—reasonable thoughts maybe but still not based on actual evidence. So as part of our own research, we talked to a group of early retirees to get a better handle on what they face as they adjust to retirement and to find out whether their struggles and concerns differ from those of older retirees. Our early retirees are between the ages of 45 and 59, and we compared their attitudes and opinions with those who retired at or close to the more conventional age of 65. The early retirees in our survey averaged 54 years of age, and our conventional retirees were 67 years old on average.

The results of our survey suggest that many early retirees can indeed have a harder time adjusting than their older counterparts. A number of their difficulties were predictable from the issues we already discussed, but there were also a few surprises. To begin, early retirees actually start out well, seeming to get off on the right foot in the initial stages of their retirement. They have a positive mind-set and are optimistic about what the future holds. They come out of the workforce outwardly rejuvenated, excited about the prospect of pursuing new interests. For example, as compared to those retiring at the conventional age, younger retirees are more than twice as likely to retire so they can pursue activities they are passionate about, and they are more likely to put some effort into going out and finding their passions. With such enthusiasm, they feel good about being retired—they are just as happy and adjusted as older retirees, at least for the first couple of years.

But early retirees in our survey part company with their older counterparts after the first two years. Here was a surprise—one would expect that with more and more years of retirement experience, a large proportion should eventually adapt to the retirement lifestyle. And, in fact, that is pretty much what we observed with older retirees. However, younger retirees may actually go in the opposite direction. Many of these retirees appear to become disenchanted, showing less and less enjoyment as they progress deeper into their retirement.

For example, when we looked at their overall feelings about being retired, we found that 74% of younger retirees are happy in their first two years, but this percentage drops to 54% by the time they are retired six or more years. When we asked them how their quality of life has changed since retirement, 62% said they feel it has improved in the first two years, but that figure drops to 42% after six or more years. In contrast, 57% of older retirees feel that their lifestyles have gotten better after two years of retirement, and that percentage stays about the same throughout the two- to six-year time span. In a similar vein, 79% of all older retirees feel adjusted to the retirement lifestyle compared to only 69% of the early retirement group. And here again we see adjustment improves with time for older retirees, from 67% to 85%, but stays at about 69% over the same time span for younger retirees. In other words, we expected to see the same improvement for early retirees over time, but that's not what we observed.

This declining satisfaction with retirement plays into lesser contentment in general. Younger retirees' views of the overall quality of their lives degenerate as well with more time in retirement. Among older retirees, 57% rate their overall quality of life favorably, regardless of how long they have been retired. Younger retirees are just as happy as older retirees at first, but their ratings drop—from 55% to only 37%—by the time they are retired six or more years. We also found that younger retirees are more likely to be taking medications designed to treat depressive symptoms—29% of younger retirees are taking medication for depression and anxiety, and 44% of that group began using them after they retired. In contrast, only 17% of older retirees are taking such medications, regardless of how long they've been retired.

How is it possible that early retirees start out so well and end up not so well? A closer look at their lives reveals the roots of their gradual downturn. In fact, we see quite a few factors that might come into play—living conditions that are known to detract from retirement adjustment and subjective well-being. While we cannot easily assume causality, it would appear that some of these detractors may have resulted from dissatisfaction with their lifestyles. Others may have played a role in creating their unhappiness or, at the minimum, have made their adjustment to retirement more difficult.

For one, early retirees are much more likely to have a working spouse—54% state that their spouses are currently employed, a far higher proportion than the 33% of older retirees in the same situation. Having a working spouse is not really unexpected for those retiring in their fifties. After all, their spouses are still well within the standard working age, too. But that doesn't change the fact that having a working spouse is not without its problems for retirees. As we discussed in other chapters, when a spouse is still in the work force, retirees can be restricted in the types of activities they can take part in. Some may be reluctant, for example, to travel alone or to put themselves in certain social situations without their spouses.

Furthermore, when one spouse retires and the other doesn't, there can be changes in the dynamics of the marriage—how each partner relates to or views the other. If the retiree is a man, for instance, he may feel that his diminished breadwinning role relative to his spouse is a blow to his self-esteem. He may feel a loss of respect, and this in turn could lower his self-esteem. As it turns out, many younger retirees eventually come to dislike this living arrangement, feeling more and more with added years that they do not spend enough time with their spouses. (We will discuss the many issues facing couples when one is working and the other retires in more detail in a later chapter.)

Under such conditions, it's not surprising that the marriages of many early retirees deteriorate—as with other aspects of their lives, not immediately but gradually over time. When just retired, young retirees actually feel good about their marriages—87% describe them positively, well above the 73% found among older retirees. However, as time goes on, their perceived marital quality drops sharply, from 87% to 63% by the time they are retired six or more years. Among older retirees, in comparison, ratings of marital quality stay relatively constant regardless of the number of years retired. Younger retirees are also more likely to feel their marriages have gotten worse with more years in retirement, and they are less and less likely to feel emotionally connected and appreciated by their spouses or to describe the two partners as compatible. Whether these less favorable perceptions are a result of having a working spouse or a result of being disenchanted with retirement is difficult to say, as both can lead to the same unfortunate outcome—an unhappy marriage.

We then examined the broader aspects of their social life. As mentioned earlier, maintaining a sense of social connectedness could be a particular problem for younger retirees. Because many of their peers are unlikely to be retiring with them, they run the risk of spending a good deal of time outside of the company of others, possibly to an unhealthy degree. And indeed that's exactly what we found: younger retirees tend to be unhappy with their social lives, feeling disconnected and out of touch with the rest of the world. In part, this is certainly tied to having less-than-optimal prospects for daily social contact and possibly to having a working spouse.

Here we have to keep in mind that many early retirees take a hit on their social lives when they leave their jobs, losing their regular interactions with coworker friends. Very early on in retirement, both younger and older retirees begin the process of gradually breaking away from their coworker friends—a healthy, if not inevitable, consequence of no longer having daily access when they leave their jobs. As predicted, we found that coworker friends have a diminishing role in all retirees' lives as they move further into retirement. But the breakaway tends to be particularly severe for younger retirees—78% claim to have coworker friendships when retired under two years, but this drops to 35% with six or more years in retirement. In contrast, the coworker friend dropoff is much less—from 71% to 56%—for older retirees in that time frame. So why do older retirees lose fewer friends? Because their peers are also likely to have retired at or near the same time. As such, older retirees are still sharing the same lifestyle with many of their coworker friends and with shared interests may continue to keep their relationship on equal footing.

However, what is more worrisome is that younger retirees also seem to weaken their ties to their friends outside of their jobs—early in their retirement, 92% of younger retirees have friends from outside the workforce, but only 77% report having such friendships six years into retirement. The number of nonworker friends in their social circle also declines, from 8.3 to 5.6, whereas the size of the nonworker friendship circle gradually increases for older retirees, from about 7.4 to 10.5. Younger retirees are also found to be progressively less emotionally connected to their outside friends, while older retirees tend to maintain their closeness to their friends over the years.

To make matters worse, younger retirees feel they have limited opportunities to meet new people—again, this may be tied to the fact that few from their peer group also retire at the same time. With the prospects for establishing new relationships dim and a tendency to loosen ties with their existing relationships, younger retirees gradually become less and less happy with their social lives. In some sense, it appears that early retirees withdraw socially, becoming less and less motivated to interact with others. It is possible that their withdrawal is a natural consequence of a downward spiral from too much time alone—feelings of isolation can lead to weakened self-esteem and perhaps depression. From there, it is not difficult to understand why many early retirees may find themselves preferring to avoid social situations.

Coinciding with their social withdrawal, younger retirees gradually lose interest in the ways they spend their time. As we pointed out, before they left the workforce, they looked forward to retirement as an opportunity to pursue their passions. Their youth provides them with the energy and drive to approach retirement as an opportunity to conquer new worlds. And while they seem to take that direction at first, again we find their interest waning with the years—69% of younger retirees regard their activities as personally rewarding in the first two years of retirement, but this gradually declines to 47% by the time they are retired six or more years. With that decay, more and more develop the perspective that retirement is boring and slow paced, with just too much free time and nothing interesting to do. Note that, as a point of comparison, older retirees are just as interested in their activities six years later as they were on the first day of their retirement.

Tied in with their unfortunate circumstances—less satisfying marriages, unfulfilling social lives, and unrewarding activities—many early retirees also suffer declines in their overall subjective well-being. Over time, they see themselves as unproductive and unvalued, become less self-confident and optimistic, and feel retired life had not turned out as they hoped. From there, it's an easy leap for early retirees to look back fondly on their careers, missing their jobs because they see them as more rewarding, psychologically and otherwise, than what's available to them in retirement. In comparison, older retirees don't miss their jobs nearly as much.

We decided to dig still deeper to find out what's at the core of their problems. In this regard, we looked at the differences between early retirees who have adjusted to retirement versus those who have not. As one major distinction, less adjusted early retirees are much more tied to their past careers. Actually, it's not that they liked their jobs more or found them more personally fulfilling. Rather, it's that they depended more on what they did for a living as a way of defining themselves, and retirement has not offered them acceptable alternative roles.

But their strong ties to their careers are not entirely their own doing—unfortunately, many less adjusted early retirees were forced out of their jobs. Among all early retirees, the proportion claiming to be forced out of their jobs—about 50%—is about the same as we found among older retirees. This is unquestionably a high percentage since we had presumed that early retirees, because they are still of working age, were likely to retire out of their own choice. However, that percentage—high as it is—pales in comparison to that of less adjusted early retirees: roughly 75% of these individuals claim they were forced to retire. In contrast, only 35% of *well-adjusted* early retirees claim to have been pushed out of their jobs. Clearly, the way they reached their retirement certainly has something to do with the difficulties they are facing. Many early retirees are emotionally unprepared for the event.

Further compounding their difficulties, they aren't prepared financially for retirement—less adjusted early retirees have lower annual incomes and have a much harder time making ends meet. Their recourse is to work, but they do so mostly for financial reasons. As we pointed out in an earlier chapter, retirees who take jobs out of necessity are less likely to realize the emotional or psychological benefits that work can provide.

Financial problems and forced retirement are unfortunate events that are beyond the retirees' control. But some of their problems are a result of the choices they make. The way less adjusted early retirees handle their social lives is a good example. Their social circle is not the problem—they have as many friends and spend about as much time interacting with their friends as well adjusted retirees. Instead, it's the quality of their interactions that is questionable. They don't interact in person as much, and they have much weaker emotional bonds to those in their circle. Consequently, they find their social lives much less enjoyable and tend to feel socially disconnected and isolated.

Another issue for less adjusted early retirees revolves around planning and, more to the point, to the quality of their planning efforts. They were actually just as likely to plan their retirement as the well adjusted. However, they fall short relative to the well adjusted in laying out the specific steps of their plans. The result is that they have no plainly designated paths to follow, and without paths, they are not as effective in achieving their goals, and this leaves them feeling that their lives lack direction.

All things considered, our unavoidable conclusion is that retiring young is extremely difficult. There are a lot of issues that can present themselves, many of which are unforeseeable. From the vantage point of one's job, young retirees are just not likely to be aware of how debilitating it can be to retire alone. How can they appreciate that their social lives can be extremely limited, that the things they found interesting may end up less so when compared to the excitement of a job, or that having so much free time could adversely affect their marriages? With no easy way to anticipate these and other obstacles, it seems that younger retirees are especially unprepared for retirement.

From that perspective, the need to plan a retirement lifestyle very carefully becomes even more critical for early retirees. As we discussed, planning leads to goal setting, and this provides young retirees with a constructive way of using time and a path to follow. As it happens, they are not entirely negligent in this area—early retirees are roughly similar to older retirees in planning their retirements. But to our point, many more than the 34% we found in our survey have to take the necessary preparatory steps before leaving their jobs. Note that those who are having particular difficulties adjusting to retirement by their own admission feel their planning was inadequate. It's important to keep in mind that older retirees have retired peers and social systems geared to their needs; early retirees do not have such a safety net to protect their fall in the event retirement is less than they hoped for. Instead, they have to be much more proactive, taking all matters pertaining to day-to-day living in their own hands. And, although they may leave the workforce without a plan of action in place, it's never too late to start, even if already retired.

Knowing what to plan for is important—and a problem—for all retirees and again may be especially so for early retirees. They need to work hard at figuring out how they are going to use all their free time, particularly if they have working spouses. But their planning cannot just be about activities; younger retirees must make detailed plans to ensure a satisfying social life. Here the objective is to maintain a regular schedule of activities with friends, particularly those outside the workforce. Keeping up an active social life may be a difficult task, but it is a critical one, needed to ensure a sense of connectedness to the outside world. And finally, to reiterate, young retirees must be realistic as to what to expect from whatever plans they come up with—it may be hard at first to come up with activities or goals that are as rewarding as their jobs once were. Unfortunately, however, giving up is not a viable option.

If they cannot find leisure goals worth pursuing, early retirees can always consider taking bridge jobs. In actuality, about 43% of younger retirees who are retired two years or less are employed in some capacity, and this may account in part for their tendency to be happier at the start of their retirement. However, this employment proportion gradually drops, reaching a low of 22% by the time they are retired six or more years, the point at which early retirees go through their declines.

As a way of lessening the emotional downturns that might occur down the road, the option to work should stay open, and should be seriously considered as soon as these retirees recognize they have not found their comfort level in retirement. Again, we suggest that the retiree make sure the job itself is interesting and has characteristics that are personally acceptable—in other words, is not stress ridden or overly demanding. For those who unfortunately have to work out of financial necessity, they might as well try to make the best of things. The main goal is to approach their job with a degree of personal commitment. With a more positive attitude, they might realize the psychological and social benefits that work can provide and then feel better about retirement and themselves.

Finally, if at all possible, it is highly recommended that young retirees plan their retirement date to coincide with that of their spouses—that is, of course, if they like each other. Assuming the marriage is a good one, having a spouse who is also retired allows for a greater array of entertaining diversions, helps to reduce some of the loneliness and isolation, and allows the dynamics of the relationship to remain unchanged. However, if partners cannot retire together, then early retirees are advised to pay particular attention in planning how they will spend their time with and without their spouse. Open and frank discussions in this regard are in the best interests of both the retiree and the working spouse and should be carried out either before or very early on in retirement. Such conversations may help to make their marriages progress more smoothly through retirement, lessening the likelihood for resentments to build from both sides, and possibly allowing the retiree to get permission to consider more options to avoid feeling lonely and isolated.

Earlier in this chapter, we mentioned that some early retirees are likely to benefit from their employment histories, where they learned such skills as problem solving and decision making. However, as we found, not everyone's working backgrounds may offer training that is transferable to the retirement lifestyle. Some early retirees who have left jobs where the tasks are mostly routine or repetitive may be more limited in their ability to adapt quickly to lifestyle changes. As such, they may be especially at a loss as to how to feel satisfied or fulfilled in an unstructured setting such as retirement. The nature of one's occupation prior to retirement can dramatically influence the ease and nature of the transition into retirement. This is the subject of our next chapter, not only for early retirees but also for those who wait until the more traditional age.

• 10 •

Ladies, Gents, and Collar Colors

> Preparation for old age should begin no later than one's teens. A life which is empty of purpose until 65 will not suddenly become filled on retirement.
>
> —Arthur E. Morgan

$\mathcal{I}$t should be evident by now that adjustment to retirement depends on many factors. In that light, researchers have found that gender and occupational background can influence how easy or difficult it is to make the transition from work to retirement. Men and women and those who held white-collar or blue-collar jobs tend to have different psychological equipment—different mental tools at their disposal to deal with life's fluctuations. They may also have different resources available to them that can affect their options, and they tend to carry different types of emotional baggage.

In previous chapters, we have touched on some of the findings regarding the ways men and women differ in their adjustment. For example, there is evidence that under many circumstances, women have an easier time making the transition. Their success may in part be due to the kinds of jobs they typically held while in the workforce and to the quality of their social skills and personal relationships. But there are exceptions, events that cause women to have a harder time adjusting than men. One of the few situations that can cause problems for women has to do with how they got to retirement— women who were forced out of their jobs were reported to have a tougher time adjusting than did men.[1] Our survey revealed the same—women forced into retirement find such circumstances to be particularly upsetting as compared to men, which in turn made it harder for them to enjoy their retirement.

However, when retirement is their choice and therefore expected, we found that women are better at retirement than men. As it happens, some of the differences in their workforce experiences can be advantages for women in the early stages of retirement. For starters, their jobs are often less personally involving than those for men, making the break from the workforce a little easier. While still in the workforce, women in our survey worked fewer hours per week on average, held less senior and prestigious positions, and were much less likely than men to describe their jobs as challenging, requiring problem-solving and decision-making skills, or being financially rewarding. Jobs that lack these characteristics are not very fulfilling psychologically and hence are easier to leave.

Jobs that are less psychologically rewarding are also less likely to be a source of one's self-definition. As we discussed in previous chapters, with better jobs, men tend to rely much more—almost exclusively—on their career role to define themselves as people. Women, in contrast, possibly because of the types of jobs they hold, are more likely to hold nonwork identities, including parent, friend, and church member. But it should also be pointed out that working women tend to operate in more worlds at one time than men—for example, maintaining a household and holding down a job. As such, they are more likely to have multiple roles, and in doing so many women can make an easier transition in retirement because they aren't giving up as much of themselves when they leave the workforce.[2]

But it's not solely about the types of jobs they held. Women tend to differ from men in their priorities outside of work. Their approaches to certain aspects of living and certain activities may be especially helpful to them in retirement. For example, we found men and women to be very similar in terms of the ways they spend their time. In fact, we found only one or two differences in their activities—women spend more time doing household chores, while men spend more time just relaxing around the house. These distinctions are not all that surprising and not very substantial except maybe to the wives of those well-rested husbands. But we did find some meaningful differences in the way that women regard their leisure activities—they are much more passionately committed to them and rate them more personally rewarding than men do. Women also put more effort into finding things of personal interest, are more successful in this quest, and generally are more open to new experiences than men.

Along with being more personally committed to the things they do, women tend to be more socially integrated than men, and their better-developed social lives yield considerable enjoyment for them in retirement. They tend to have a broader circle of friends and family members, spend more hours in their company, tend to feel more emotionally connected, and are more motivated to meet new people. As a result, they are more likely to find their social lives personally satisfying and rewarding; this is particularly the case after they retire, when they increase their efforts at maintaining a social life.

In contrast, probably as a result of having weaker social ties, men tend to be more dependent on the company of their wives, especially early in retirement. They are more likely to prefer doing joint activities with their wives and are more likely to complain about not spending enough time with their partners in retirement. But while men appear to enjoy the stronger connection to their spouse that stems from retirement, this dependency appears to put some strain on women when they (women) retire. Perhaps as a consequence of their husband's increased demands for wifely attention, retired women are more likely to feel their marriages have gotten worse since they retired, and the longer they are in retirement, the more they feel that way.

But marriage issues notwithstanding, women's stronger commitment to activities and social life, coupled with their weaker emotional ties to the workforce, allows them to retain more structure and meaning in their lives than men are able to. These, as we've seen, are key elements to success in retirement, and they seem to pay off for women. Right out of the gate, they tend to be more motivated and feel more productive, valued, and socially connected, and this helps them to a happier retirement. But what about later on, after they've been retired for a few years? Do their advantages hold up?

No, they don't. Eventually men catch up—as we hinted above, women enjoy most of their advantages only in the first two years of retirement. And even more interesting: it's not that men necessarily get happier or better at retirement living—their ratings on most measures actually stay fairly flat from year to year, and they show only minor improvements in just a few areas. But women, despite starting off so well, seem to take a noticeable turn for the worse—they get less happy in retirement as time goes on. It might be tempting to argue that some of their lower ratings could be age related, but that's not the case; after all, men are aging just the same as women, and men's ratings do not show the same declines. Here are a few examples of what we uncovered:

- In year 2, 75% of women find their activities to be rewarding as compared to 62% of men. Women's ratings gradually decline to 62% by the time they are retired six or more years; the proportion of men rating their activities as rewarding remains at 62% during that same time span.
- The amount of time men spend with their friends increases from about 10 hours per month in year 2 to about 14 hours once they reach six years in retirement, while women spend the same amount of time with their friends across that span—about 14 hours per month. Men's closeness or emotional connection to their friends stays the same from year 2 to year 6, about 62%, while women's connections decline from 80% to 70% in that period. Relatedly, 44% of men find their social lives satisfying two years into retirement, gradually building to 51% by year

6. In contrast, 61% of women are satisfied with their social lives in year 2 but only 51% by year 6.

- Perceived marriage quality—excellent or very good—also declines for women from year 2 to year 6, from 80% to 69%; for men, about 75% rate their marriages as excellent or very good regardless of number of years retired. Perceptions of their marriage getting better in retirement increase from 40% to 45% for men; for women, ratings of their marriages as better drop from 40% to 31% in that period.

- Up to their second year, 83% of women say they are happy in retirement, but this drops to 71% by year 6. Men's ratings stay at 75% from year 2 to year 6. Similarly, only 23% of men say they are completely adjusted to retirement by year 2 as compared to 39% of women. By year 6, however, 56% of men claim to be completely adjusted as compared to 52% of women—an increase for both but much more so for men.

- Finally, use of antidepressant medications is the same for men and women in year 2, at 16%. By year 6, usage continues at about the same levels for men but doubles to 32% for women.

None of this is meant to suggest that women fail in retirement over the long term; it's more that the retirement playing field seems to level out for men and women by about six or more years into retirement. But it does suggest that women appear to lose their initial enthusiasm over time. They lose, in other words, the thing that gave them an advantage over men in the first place: their zest for the retirement lifestyle. In fact, we observed that about 18% of men feel motivated to pursue new goals regardless of the number of years retired, but for women, this figure drops from a very high 35% in year 2 to only 14% by the time they are six or more years into retirement.

Considering all of the above, our recommendations for men and women are pretty straightforward. For women: find ways to keep your batteries charged. Women do so many things right immediately on leaving the workforce, and there does not appear to be a good reason their momentum has to sink along the way as it seems to. In this respect, continually setting new goals might be helpful. Having enjoyable activities and events to look forward to can be rejuvenating—they provide direction and purpose and a reason to be optimistic about the future, and these help to improve subjective well-being.

As a second issue, many women appear to change the way they socialize as they progress further into retirement. Over time, they have a tendency to rely more and more on their children and other family members as the basis of their social life and in the process become less involved with their friends. In some respects, this has the appearance of a withdrawal from the outside world. As will be discussed in our chapter on social relationships, maintaining friendships is an important means of feeling connected to the outside world and provides avenues for enriching one's life through the interchange of ideas as well as through opportunities to participate in activities and events with one's peers. So, women should try to maintain the vitality and currency of their friendships. Family is wonderful, but it isn't everything—maintaining a balanced social life of family and friends may be a much more effective way to enhance one's subjective well-being.

Our advice for men is to make a faster emotional break from the workforce. Their objective should be to become immersed in roles that are more appropriate for retirement. Since roles are linked to actions, this requires some searching to find things that are personally absorbing—not an easy task, as we've said, but one that can be best achieved through better retirement planning, including more focus on the details as well as the broader picture. Men are actually more likely to plan their retirement than women are, but these plans tend to be almost exclusively tied to finances or how they will spend all the added time with their spouse—and, as we've demonstrated, the latter may be at odds with what their spouses want them to do. Men don't devote much preparation time before they retire to their social lives or to finding activities they would enjoy. Again, they get there eventually, but it would seem that more up-front focus on these aspects of their lives might lead them more quickly to a better place in retirement.

Shifting our focus now to employment history, the type of job held before retirement and the degree of one's personal commitment to it can make a difference in how one feels about retirement. It can also have a substantial influence on how well and quickly a person adjusts to the retirement life change. Some occupations lead retirees to anticipate retirement more positively and to enjoy the event right from the beginning. Others appear to result in some initial discomfort but eventually do better at helping the retiree adapt to the new lifestyle over the long term. Still other jobs are so personally fulfilling that the retirement lifestyle cannot compete, making adaptation a more challenging process.

Typically, researchers have found that white-collar workers and those working in professional fields tend to be less enthusiastic about the idea of retiring than workers in other types of jobs. These men and women often regard their upcoming retirement with some anxiety because they have many reasons to truly enjoy or even love their jobs. Professional occupations are often intellectually stimulating, have considerable flexibility in terms of time and tasks, offer unique challenges requiring the use of creativity and problem-solving skills, and generally don't involve repetitive or otherwise boring tasks. Additionally, many professional jobs are prestigious, conveying considerable status to those fortunate enough to have them. In short, these jobs often contribute greatly to one's emotional well-being; they are personally fulfilling and can easily be a source of confidence and self-esteem. In these kinds of work environments, it's easy to feel as though one is doing something valuable and hard to believe retirement can offer something more.[3]

Since worker roles for professionals tend to be excellent sources of self-worth, it's not surprising that professionals tend to rely more heavily on their worker roles as their primary means of defining themselves.[4] Very often the bond between job and self can be so tight that professionals find their work lives and personal lives blending together, with the boundaries between them blurred or even indiscernible. For many of them, it can even be the basis of a social life. In the course of our conversations with retirees, we have come across many examples of how closely professionals and white-collar employees are tied to their jobs and how for some still in the workforce this blocks their interest in retiring.

With so much to lose, one might also suspect that retiring professionals and executives would have a much harder time adjusting to retirement. Surprisingly, though, this is not the case. Researchers have found that while there is some uneasiness before and immediately after the moment of retirement, white-collar professionals actually tend to adjust well and claim to enjoy their retirement over time.[5]

How does this happen? How do these people manage to love their jobs *and*, afterward, their retirements? As we explored in the previous chapter, what appears to account for their ultimate success in retirement are the same qualities that are required and in some cases learned from their occupations. Professional and many white-collar employees have to apply a variety of skills to their jobs that we've mentioned already: problem solving, functioning in a fluctuating environment, flexibility, and autonomy of thought and action. These skills help individuals adapt to change—like the momentous one that occurs when moving from work to retirement. Furthermore, these employees tend to be very self-confident—and again, this can be partly their own personality but is also likely to be reinforced by the sense of accomplishment engendered by success in what are often challenging and competitive careers. Equipped with such personality traits, these retirees are likely to believe they can also be successful in retirement.

They also have another very important advantage: professionals and white-collar employees generally have higher salaries and pensions than other workers. The importance of the greater financial resources at their disposal cannot be overestimated. These resources can certainly improve the quality of their retirement by allowing these retirees more freedom to pursue interests and participate in a variety of activities that often require a lot of money, such as club membership or travel.

Turning to another side, research has shown that this dynamic unfortunately tends to reverse itself among blue-collar workers and those working in unskilled jobs. These adults are more apt to look forward to retirement and actually hope to retire early.[6] Retirement, they hope, will provide them with a welcome break from heavy, repetitive, and tedious work. Additionally, blue-collar jobs may not be as personally rewarding as white-collar occupations since they tend to be more structured and allow for less autonomy and creative expression. And while blue-collar workers are just as likely to be devoted employees, the quality of their jobs can make them less likely than white-collar workers to develop strong emotional ties to their jobs. As a result, they are not as likely to define themselves in terms of their work and instead may have stronger connections to nonwork roles. This combination of lower satisfaction and reduced emotional investment with their jobs suggests that blue-collar workers would enjoy the initial stage of their retirement since it seems to promise an easier, more relaxing lifestyle, and many are likely to feel less of a role disruption when leaving the workforce.[7]

But for many, the joy doesn't last very long. Past studies have shown that after some time, blue-collar and unskilled workers are likely to become less satisfied with retirement. After the initial euphoria wears off, they describe their days as routine and dull, feeling they have little of interest to occupy their time. Our own survey corroborated what other researchers have discovered, albeit with some differences.

Along with other social scientists, we found that, unfortunately, blue-collar retirees don't fare too well in retirement. In comparison to white-collar retirees, those coming from blue-collar occupations are less happy and less adjusted in retirement, rate their overall quality of life lower, and feel it has declined since retiring. From a psychological perspective, blue-collar retirees tend to have lower self-esteem, feel less productive and useful, and tend to be less optimistic about their futures.

However, despite our expectations that they would at least be happy when first retired, our blue-collar retirees were not very happy right from the start. There was no initial euphoria followed by a decline with the passing of time. Instead, we found their attitudes and perceptions to be negative relative to white-collar retirees within the first year of retiring and generally to stay just as negative over time.

Nevertheless, whether or not they are unhappy from the beginning is not of any real significance—either way, they tend to end up less satisfied in retirement within a relatively short time. Their dissatisfaction can be traced to a number of circumstances, some of which are externally derived. In other words, there are likely to be a few elements in their lives and working backgrounds that may make it harder for them to adjust to the unstructured world of retirement.

For one, blue-collar employees are likely to learn coping skills from their jobs that might not be very conducive to dealing with dramatic lifestyle changes. Our survey revealed that, unlike their white-collar counterparts, the day-to-day work experiences of blue-collar workers are much less likely to require flexibility, creative problem solving, and rapid decision making, the kinds of skills that make it easier to adjust to new situations. After years of working in highly structured environments that include a lot of repetition and routine, the switch into an unstructured environment that requires creating a new lifestyle is likely to be a very challenging undertaking.

To avoid overgeneralizing, we must point out that some blue-collar occupations, such as law enforcement or firefighting, have problem solving and flexibility very much embedded in their job descriptions. The same is true for blue-collar retirees who had risen to supervisory positions—these individuals must know how to deal with new situations whenever they arise. But even these jobs and positions have many standard operating procedures that are in place to protect employees and ensure quality control. That being said, following routines is a requisite of many blue-collar jobs, and those working in such jobs are trained to think along those lines. One can argue that blue-collar workers should actually be better at establishing a daily routine in retirement living since routines were part of their jobs. But unvarying routine does not make for a satisfying retirement, as it did not make for a satisfying career for many of these retirees.

Not surprisingly, we also found that blue-collar workers are at a financial disadvantage. They have much less annual income available to them—about $44,000 per year on average as compared to about $67,000 for white-collar retirees. Consistent with this, blue-collar retirees are much less likely to feel they have enough money to retire comfortably or that their income is adequate to cover their expenses without dipping into their savings. Many are, in effect, continuously worried about their financial futures. Without money, developing a lifestyle that is interesting and includes a number of diversions from the mundane can be a challenge.

To make matters worse, the blue-collar retirees we interviewed tend to suffer more from health problems than their white-collar counterparts. Even though they are the same age, they rate their overall health much lower than white-collar retirees, feel their health has further declined since retiring, and claim that health issues played more of a role in their decision to retire. And to compound their financial concerns, blue-collar retirees are less likely to have private health insurance and as a result worry more about paying their health expenses in the future.

Extenuating circumstances such as these have to be regarded as reasons why many blue-collar retirees run into adjustment difficulties. Less money, poorer health, and possibly less developed coping skills can translate into fewer opportunities to enjoy life in general and certainly can limit one's opportunities in retirement. But unlike these, not all the problems faced by blue-collar retirees are beyond their control. Some may be more a result of how blue-collar workers choose to live. When choice is involved, there are elements under their direct control. So there are some problems blue-collar workers should have the power to fix—that is, as long as they are aware that the problems exist.

For example, one of the areas where blue-collar workers tend to be less effective is in their social lives. Our research clearly demonstrates that blue-collar retirees tend to have fewer friendships and to be much more dependent on their family members for social interaction. They dedicate less time and are less emotionally connected to their friends; furthermore, this tendency worsens with continued years in retirement. And still worse, blue-collar retirees lack the motivation to make new friendships and actually become even less motivated to do so the longer they are retired. As a point of comparison, the reverse is true for white-collar retirees—these retirees are much more invested in their social lives, putting a good deal of effort into maintaining friendships and a sense of connectedness to the outside world. It is then no wonder blue-collar retirees feel more isolated and lonely and are much less satisfied with their social lives since retiring.

All of which begs the question: just how important are friendships to a successful retirement? To answer this question, we looked at blue-collar retirees who are well adjusted and compared their social activities with those blue-collar retirees who are less well adjusted. The results were very clear: well-adjusted retirees tend to have more friends—former coworkers as well as those from outside the workforce—and to spend more time with them than the less adjusted. On the other side of the coin, blue-collar retirees who are less well adjusted spend more time with their family and are much less emotionally connected to their friends. Coinciding with these differences, the well adjusted are much more satisfied with their social lives and feel much more connected to the outside world. These are about the same results we found for white-collar workers (who, coincidentally, are also better adjusted). And, as we mentioned in our discussion of retired women, an overreliance on children and family for one's social life is likely to leave the retiree feeling as though something is missing, and that "something" is likely to be one's peers.

Moving from relationships to activities, we found blue-collar retirees to have problems here as well. They have some habits that frankly are not likely to enhance their satisfaction with retirement or their overall subjective well-being. Blue-collar retirees spend more of their time passively—watching television, reading, or just relaxing. To be sure, some of their passivity might be tied to poorer health and more limited financial resources, but these are not issues for all blue-collar retirees. Rather, for some it may be a matter of perspective—blue-collar retirees are more likely to view retirement as a time to relax, not a time to pursue new goals. Or again it may be a matter of falling into a routine—for example, when nothing else is regularly planned, it is all too easy to rely on television for one's entertainment. But these patterns don't completely work for them, and they seem a little lost—blue-collar retirees are more likely to complain they cannot find interesting things to do and just don't know what to do with their time.

In contrast, white-collar retirees are much more active and passionately committed to the things they do. White-collar retirees are also more likely to regard their activities as rewarding and are constantly searching for new interests to pursue. And sure enough, when we switched our focus back to blue-collar workers and compared the activity patterns of well-adjusted and less adjusted blue-collar retirees, the major difference we found was the greater amount of time the less well adjusted spend doing nothing at all.

The patterns we just laid out suggest that many blue-collar retirees, while acknowledging they don't use their time well, lack the drive to come up with solutions for better ways of living. But low motivation can sometimes be a result of just not knowing what direction to take in order to fix a problem. As we have seen for less well adjusted retirees in general, they know at some level that they have a problem—they even know what it is to some extent—but are often unsure how to change the way they are living. Their lack of direction is understandable in some respects and may be a direct result of having less of an opportunity to develop the coping skills we discussed earlier while still in the workforce.

However, part of the responsibility rests a little more squarely on their shoulders. How these workers approach their upcoming retirement while still working may contribute to their limited activities. We have found, as have other researchers, that employees leaving blue-collar occupations are less likely to make specific plans for their retirement in advance. They tend to neglect the crucial preretirement steps of setting personal goals or seeking activities that have personal value. Note that making plans may be particularly crucial for these retirees since they may have a little more trouble getting started without some amount of preparation.

Unfortunately, they come to realize this to be a part of their problem— as with other groups who run into adjustment issues, blue-collar retirees are much more likely to admit their planning for retirement was inadequate. And, as also found for other less adjusted retirees, it's often the case that they don't know which aspects of their lives they should target for their planning efforts. Consequently, even if they had put more effort into planning, they still may not have come to a better place because in all likelihood their plans would not have covered all their needs.

Along with limited drive and direction, blue-collar retirees suffer from another obstacle—they are less willing to experiment and try new things. Without some open-mindedness, they are restricted to only those relatively few—and often passive—activities already in their repertoire, meaning the same old unsatisfying routines. So they're caught in a double bind; they know they should have planned better, but at the same time they close themselves off from future opportunities to make up for it and so to feel productive. Of course, the limited financial resources that often afflict this segment can restrict experimentation. But not everything a person can do for enjoyment has to cost money, and it may be that blue-collar retirees have to expend more effort and be a little creative and more open-minded in their search for activities that could have some personal value.

But all that being said, it is certainly not the case that white-collar retirees are guaranteed success or that blue-collar retirees are destined to fail despite the seeming advantages held by the former. Whether either retires successfully depends, ultimately, on their course of action *during* retirement. While their work backgrounds may provide white-collar employees with a greater chance of adjusting well over the long term, they may still have some issues—and, as we've seen, not all are completely adjusted. For example, as we've discussed already, they may be more likely to run into an identity crisis. Because they are closely tied to their work, white-collar workers may rely too much on their worker roles when they retire, and this can inhibit their immersion into retirement. A successful transition for these retirees may include developing a strong connection to new roles that are appropriate for the retirement lifestyle, possibly through involvement in nonwork activities and social relationships.

For blue-collar workers, in spite of formidable obstacles, their job histories hardly suggest that failure in retirement is their inevitable fate—they were able to put in the effort to be successful in their work, so they should be able to do the same outside of work. In fact, there are likely to be many in this group who are completely comfortable with their new lifestyle simply through the release from a physically demanding job. But for those experiencing some difficulties adjusting, better planning for a life without work may help in the transition as long as these plans cover all the appropriate dimensions.

For one, planning for blue-collar retirees has to include ways of ensuring a more satisfying social life. In this area, they have to put more effort into their friendships, with particular emphasis on establishing stronger emotional bonds. Through better relationships with peers, these retirees can feel more connected to the outside world and won't feel as isolated and lonely. As one way to be more connected socially, they should try to spend more time with other people in person (we found that well-adjusted blue-collar retirees have more personal contact with their friends but that the less well adjusted interact more by email or telephone—not the best ways to develop emotional connections). Additionally, blue-collar retirees should try to put some effort into developing new friendships. Again, it is easier to stay with what or who you know, but through meeting new people, there is a better chance of expanding horizons, getting exposed to new ideas and things to do.

However, all retirees must keep in mind that success in planning requires motivation and commitment to achieve goals as well as a greater openness to new experiences. Regarding the latter, in one sense some blue-collar retirees can suffer from a different form of identity crisis—they may hold on too tightly to an unbending definition of themselves and their roles. Closed-mindedness can often include a rigid adherence to patterns or habits but also to one's personal identity. Closed-minded people have a hard time changing their beliefs, opinions, and ways of playing out their roles. In this light, they are more likely to see retirement as a time to relax, and this perspective can block their willingness to even consider activities that don't fit within that framework. So, an important first step is to believe retirement can be more than that. While it can be comforting to stay with the old and familiar, there has to be an acknowledgment that the old and familiar has not served their personal needs. From there can begin a search for new ways of using their time, finding events and activities that may not exactly fit with who they are right now.

This will not be easy—you may not have the wherewithal to come up with new ideas on your own, and the urge will be to fall back on old habits. As an alternative, you might consider outside sources, such as the Internet or discussions with friends and family members, as a means of coming up with activities that might not occur to you. Collect these ideas and give each thorough consideration and then pursue those that you feel have some personal merit.

As a final note, retirees must be aware that variety in the types of activities they pursue can go a long way in enhancing adjustment and one's subjective well-being. And they should also know that not all types of activities pay out the kinds of emotional benefits that make them feel better about retirement and themselves. In the next chapter, we get into the details of how retirees can use their time to their best advantage.

· 11 ·

How We Use Our Time

Stay busy [when you retire]. If you are going to sit on the couch and watch TV, you are going to die.

—Bill Chavanne

$\mathcal{T}$hroughout the previous chapters, we have mentioned the generally accepted point of view that staying active and involved is a good thing for retirees. A fair amount of research has already been conducted on this topic, and the consensus is that being active can play an important role in retirees' emotional and psychological health. With the right types of activities, retirees can feel they are using time in a way that is personally meaningful, and that can add to their subjective well-being and make retirement more satisfying.

Fundamentally, the prevailing thinking on the significance of being active holds that a person who retires moves from the role of "producer" to that of "nonproducer." The resulting feeling of being unproductive can threaten one's sense of having purpose in the world. On the other hand, by staying active, that is, by participating in certain kinds of activities, retirees can feel productive and preserve that sense of purpose. In this vein, sociologists have developed activity theory,[1] which claims that maintaining an active lifestyle is important to mental health, especially for older adults and retirees, because such a lifestyle provides a substitute for the benefits they previously obtained from their careers.

This point of view seems reasonable, but there has been some criticism over the years. There are some who argue that activity theory may be overly simplistic. As an example, those with substantial financial resources and good health tend to take part in more activities than poor people or those in poor health. Using that perspective, those who challenge activity theory maintain that while it is often true that people who have more resources are happier and

133

more active, their happiness may in fact derive from their money and health and not from being active.[2] That point of view also seems reasonable and suggests there may be no direct cause-and-effect relationship between becoming more active and being better off psychologically. In other words, the relationship between activity and subjective well-being may be more complex than the straightforward idea that increasing activities leads to a more fulfilling life or a better retirement.[3]

Nevertheless, it's hard to discount the idea that there's at least some positive relationship, even if it's not causal, between involvement in activities and personal well-being. There's lots of evidence that adults who stay active and involved and participate in enjoyable activities are more likely to find their retirements satisfying and fulfilling.[4] So while additional research may be needed to really understand the relationship, it would also seem reasonable to conclude that being active suggests a positive approach to living and at the minimum cannot hurt one's quality of life.

That's a very broad perspective—stay active and you'll be happier. But things are probably not that simple. It's not likely that all types of activities contribute equally to one's quality of life. Researchers have found that the activity itself must be personally meaningful in order to enhance subjective well-being.[5] Activities that tend to be nonengaging or more like chores associated with day-to-day living do little in this regard. It is unlikely, for example, that many retirees get a real sense of fulfillment from housework or raking leaves. On the other hand, activities such as hobbies, writing, photography, or painting may be more psychologically beneficial and can be expected to enhance feelings of productivity and self-worth.

In our survey, we tried to get a better grasp on the value of being active in general as well as whether different types of activities lead to different personal outcomes. We asked retirees about all the things they do each week to occupy their time. Starting from the hypothesis that some activities are better than others in improving one's quality of life, we classified the things they do into a few different categories. Our classifications included the following: activities that are dynamic and home based, meaning they are conducted in the home and require some movement and directed effort, such as exercising, problem-solving games, hobbies, and so on; those that are passive and home based, such as watching television, reading, or just relaxing; those that are social, including any activity other than work that is done outside the home, such as going to clubs, dining out, traveling, and so on; and chores, such as home repairs, cleaning, and so on. Working at a job was kept as a separate category primarily because it did not fit in neatly into the other groupings—work can have social features but also can be seen as a chore or as something that has personal value, depending on one's perceptions and motivations.

Working from this classification, we consider passive home-based activities, such as relaxing or watching television, and chores to be fairly low grade, while social and dynamic home-based activities are regarded as high quality since they are likely to be better at enhancing subjective well-being. Again, a job is a little more complicated and can be either high or low grade, depending on the reasons why the retiree is working (as we discussed earlier).

Beginning with a broad assessment, our results showed that all retirees participate in a variety of activities each week, and the time dedicated to these activities does not vary much among younger and older retirees or as a result of how long one has been retired. But we did find important differences in the way well-adjusted and less adjusted retirees spend their time—those who report a higher quality of life and those who are better adjusted to retirement are more involved in higher-grade activities. And not only do they spend more of their time doing things of personal value, but they also seem to be more emotionally invested in what they are doing. To cite a few examples:

- Well-adjusted retirees spend an average of almost 25 hours per week involved in dynamic home-based activities and about 14 hours per week in social activities as compared to about 20 and 10 hours, respectively, for less well adjusted retirees. When considered together, that means that well-adjusted retirees spend about nine hours more per week—15% of their activity time, or the equivalent of a full working day—engaged in higher-grade activities than their less adjusted counterparts.
- In particular, well-adjusted retirees are much more likely to travel and to be involved in projects of personal interest, such as hobbies or projects around the home. Furthermore, about 30% of well-adjusted retirees say they are passionate about their activities compared to only about 20% for their less adjusted counterparts. The less well adjusted tend to do more of their activities just to fill time and seem to get less satisfaction from them.
- We also looked at retirees in terms of the perceived quality of their lives, and here the differences are even more dramatic. Both spend about the same amount of time doing household chores, but retirees with a high quality of life use much more of their time to do active home-based projects and social activities—45 versus 31 hours per week—while those with a lower quality of life spend much more time in passive home activities, such as just relaxing or watching television—44 versus 33 hours.
- High-quality-of-life retirees are also much more emotionally involved in everything they do but seem to be particularly committed to their hobbies and personal projects and to activities outside the home, such

as dining out and traveling. Again, for retirees reporting a less happy quality of life, their activities serve more to fill time—they don't have the same passionate commitment to the things they do as high-quality-of-life retirees.

We also found that less adjusted retirees spend more hours working than well-adjusted retirees. This is not an indictment of work—we have noted the benefits of bridge jobs in a previous chapter, and nothing here negates the points we made then. But it should be noted that less adjusted retirees are more likely to work out of necessity, for the money, and not for the psychological benefits such jobs can provide. So it's not that working is a problem for them but more that work in this context is not as enjoyable. Considering all the ways they spend their time, less adjusted retirees spend up to 20% more of their time per week in activities that can be regarded as low grade than well-adjusted retirees.

From all these findings, we can conclude that, while having things to occupy one's time is important, it's more important that activities have some personal value—that they fill psychological needs, such as the need to feel productive. Activities that retirees can feel passionate about work in that way—they help them feel good about themselves and let them feel as though they are using their time in a personally constructive manner.

Unfortunately, finding things to ignite a retiree's passions takes time—about 55% of those retired five or more years have found activities they are passionate about, but that figure is considerably lower—about 43%—among those retired four years or less and is only 38% among those less than six months into retirement. On a positive note, these findings suggest that retirees are continually looking for interesting activities, and quite a few are eventually able to add some to their repertoire. But it also suggests that such activities are not readily available—almost half of those retired for five or more years have not yet found their passions. So it's also apparent that the need to keep searching and experimenting for the right activities is an ever-present job in retirement, one that requires as much dedication as retirees put into their careers.

And, sadly, some retirees never get there. The fact that those who are less happy in retirement haven't found things that interest them doesn't seem to result from a lack of desire. When less adjusted retirees are asked directly whether they have tried to find activities they can be passionate about, roughly 45%, the same as found for their happier counterparts, claim they have. But their success in this regard has been relatively poor—only about 6 in 10 reported having found such activities once they tried to as compared to 9 in 10 of those who are well adjusted. From these results, it's really no surprise that we found that less adjusted retirees don't see the things they do for enjoyment to be personally satisfying—only about 47% rate their activities as extremely or very rewarding as compared to about 85% among retirees who are well adjusted. With unsatisfying activities, less adjusted retirees tend to look back on their jobs as a better time—only 18% say the things they do in retirement are more rewarding than their careers as compared with 48% of well-adjusted retirees holding this perspective. Furthermore, while about 54% of the well adjusted admit to missing their jobs, 82% of less adjusted retirees feel this way.

Part of the problem for these less adjusted retirees may lie in their inability to find a solution to their problems. We have often found this same issue with retirees who have adjustment difficulties—they know that what they are doing or how they are living is not working for them, but they just don't know how to make their lives better. For example, those who are less well adjusted admit they don't have enough leisure activities, but they feel they just cannot find things that interest them and often don't know what to do with their time. Yet they are also more likely to acknowledge they need to spend more time trying to find activities they enjoy—and this admission alone suggests they are not doing enough to find activities they would enjoy. They see the problem but are not doing much to fix it.

One would think a relatively straightforward solution would be to keep experimenting, exploring one's options, and looking for new things. But that requires open-mindedness, and not everyone shares that trait. Less adjusted retirees, as we found with some other groups such as blue-collar workers, are not very open to new experiences and trying new things. And, as we pointed out for blue-collar workers, without some experimenting to find new things, less adjusted retirees are stuck with activities that tend to be of low personal value and not very psychologically fulfilling.

As a bit of digression—but still relevant to our topic—it is interesting to see that those still in the workforce rate their leisure activities more personally satisfying than do retirees—76% of employees describe such activities as very or extremely rewarding as compared to only 65% of all retirees. Added to this and falling neatly into the "grass is greener" category, retirees are more likely to believe their careers were more personally satisfying than their leisure activities, while those still working feel their leisure activities are more rewarding than their work. By the time they enter retirement, though, employees are likely to feel the same about their activities as retirees do, and their overly positive expectations about their leisure time are likely to leave some feeling disappointed after they leave the workforce.

It's not that employees and retirees do different things. In fact, they are virtually identical in how they use their leisure time. But they may differ in terms of what leisure time means to them. For those in the workforce, leisure activities are a way of breaking away from the pressures of their jobs. But for retirees, finding good use of their leisure time is their full-time job, and a break from these activities is not something that would have any meaning to retirees. This ties back to something we touched on earlier when Rob talked about how much he enjoyed painting when he was working but much less so after he retired. To him, painting was a diversion from work, and he no longer needed it when he retired.

We should note that many activities available to retirees fall into the nonengaging or low-value categories. They are likely to be routine, provide little exposure to new things, offer limited social involvement, and probably don't involve much, if any, problem solving. When we looked at what retirees do with their time, we found that as much as 65% of it is spent either doing household chores, relaxing, or in passive home-based activities, such as watching television or reading. When this is compared to those who are still working and when we include work as one of their activities, these same low-value activities account for only about 35% of employees' total time. Now, it can be argued that this is to be expected because work takes up a big chunk of time, so their proportion of low-value activity time has to be lower. This is true, of course, but the point still remains that retirees' activities don't offer as much of an opportunity to enhance their well-being as was once provided by work. And if retirees are involved *only* in these low-grade activities, as some undoubtedly are, they are likely to experience a sense of nonproductivity and can come to feel they don't occupy a useful place in the world.

For some, this is not a problem—the well adjusted and those with a high quality of life seem to be happy with their activities. But for others, such as the less well adjusted, who have not been able to find enough engaging activities, retirement is often likely to be dull if not distressing and demeaning. But it's not that routine chores per se lead to psychological distress. They are actually benign in and of themselves, probably because retirees are not too worried about the possibility of failing at such tasks. It is really more the case that retirees are just not getting a lot of joy from many of these activities. There is no stress, but there are also no benefits.

This brings us back to the need for experimenting. Finding activities as psychologically fulfilling as work is no easy undertaking for anyone but may be especially difficult if retirees look at their leisure time as they did before retiring. While still on their jobs, their leisure activities mostly provided a break from work, and even activities of only moderate value were probably effective in this regard. After leaving the workforce, however, these activities take on a greater purpose, and as such retirees may evaluate them with a more critical eye. Unless they have things to do that generate a passionate commitment, retirees are likely to become bored with their old routines because they no longer meet their needs. Those who break out of their boxes and go on a hunt for new activities that have some degree of personal meaningfulness are likely to feel more positive about being retired. That's what well-adjusted retirees tend to do and what the less adjusted are unlikely to do.

However, coming up with just any old bunch of new high-grade activities still might not be enough—some important specifics may be missing. For one, it might be the case that *different types* of higher-grade activities enhance psychological well-being in different ways. For example, activities that are simple yet fun may work differently on retirees' mental outlooks than those that are more serious and have problem-solving components.

Furthermore, as we've alluded to, activities can also be looked at in terms of whether they are conducted alone or with others, and these can offer varied benefits to retirees. While solo activities may make retirees feel productive, it is possible that engaging *only* in solo activities, those that lack a social component, may lead retirees to feel isolated and alone, and this can detract from their subjective well-being. Researchers have demonstrated that participation in social activities, such as sports, and adoption of social roles, such as membership in clubs, organizations, and informal networks, along with volunteer work, can promote psychological and physical health because they strengthen one's sense of connectedness and provide a source of emotional support.[6] They also promote a sense of belonging to a group that is working toward a common goal, a benefit typically found in the workforce.

Along these same lines, there are different types of social activities, and these can vary in terms of the types of emotional and psychological benefits they provide. For example, social activities can be considered to fall into at least two distinct categories—those that are entertainment based, such as membership in a club, and those that are work based, either as a volunteer or a paid job. It is likely that both types are a source of group membership and emotional support, and both contribute to subjective well-being. However, it is possible that work-based social interactions also allow retirees to feel productive, useful to society, and as though they are working toward a common goal. Entertainment-based social activities, in contrast, may not deliver these benefits as well, although at least they do provide a sense of connectedness and a source of enjoyment.

There are also other activities that are altruistic in nature but revolve around one's personal life rather than the community, such as helping friends or family members with projects. It is possible that even routine activities can have added value when conducted within such a social context. For example, painting your own house—even though it may absolutely have to be done—may be boring and of no psychological value, but helping your friend paint his or her house might pay some emotional benefits. Routine tasks or chores performed under these circumstances can strengthen the emotional and social bonds with these friends and family members, along with providing a sense of having done good by someone else, which again might add to one's subjective well-being.

With so many ways to break them down, we felt it could be helpful to take a closer look into the benefit profiles of the various high-grade activities to see how they might affect subjective well-being and retirement adjustment. To explore this issue, we compared well-adjusted to less adjusted retirees in the proportion of time spent in solo activities and those that have some social content. We found that well-adjusted retirees and those who feel they have a high quality life tend to have better balance between their social and nonsocial activities than their comparison groups, and, further, they spend less time in low-value activities, such as chores, watching television, or relaxing around the house—the last of which may also be called doing nothing. It appears that a mix of high-grade activities might be most beneficial—striking a balance is the key. Some should have a social content, providing connectedness and bonding benefits. Others should be conducted alone, allowing retirees some time to pursue their personal interests.

As a final point, we looked at whether the *number* of activities matters. While this probably depends on one's drive and financial resources, it seems probable that a retiree must achieve critical mass in terms of the number of hours spent per week in activities, as well as the number and variety of activities undertaken, to achieve the optimal psychological well-being. To answer this question, we focused specifically on the high-value activities, looking at the number participated in by each of our retirement segments. Again, we found a clear advantage going to well-adjusted and happy retirees—they have more things they do regularly and again show a better balance between their social and personal activities. Well-adjusted retirees have about 6.9 activities—3.8 solo and 3.1 social. In contrast, activities for less well adjusted retirees are 6.0 in total—3.5 done alone and 2.5 with a social context. High-quality-of-life retirees have 7.3 activities on average—3.7 solo and 3.6 social. Lower-quality-of-life retirees average only about 5.7 activities, of which 3.4 are solo and only 2.3 are social.

While the difference in the number of activities between successful retirees and their counterparts is modest, it is in fact meaningful. Keep in mind that each added activity can account for a few hours of time used valuably each week and a few hours less per week doing little or nothing.

When you get right down to it, the activity profiles of successful retirees essentially serve as empirical evidence for variety being the spice of life. This is not to trivialize our findings but rather to remind retirees that adding new and varied activities will likely allow them to feel better about themselves, achieve meaningfulness and fulfillment from their actions, have more fun in retirement, and as a result of all this raise their subjective well-being. And probably the most effective means of achieving a better activity portfolio lies in staying motivated and being willing to experiment. And since it takes some time to find activities that are enjoyable, the key here is to keep looking and be willing to try new things.

Of course, we are fully aware that chores have to be done, and many would argue so does relaxing. Both are a fundamental part of everyday living, and both eat up a lot of time. But these are what retirees should do in their downtime—their uptime should be devoted to higher-value activities, those that pay out personal dividends. That is the work of retirement.

As you strive to compile things to do in your uptime, keep in mind the need for balance between activities you engage in alone and those that have a social component. And within the context of balance, we need to add another albeit somewhat related recommendation—get off the couch and get out of the house. We found successful retirees spend more time in some form of physical activity, such as exercising, playing sports, or gardening. The physical and psychological benefits of these activities have already been discussed and are well documented and can go quite far in building subjective well-being.

Successful retirees are also more likely to travel, even if just on day trips by car. While financial resources can come into play here, they only limit the destinations or the type of transportation used. Day trips are available to all retirees who are mobile, and with just a little effort in planning, you might be surprised how enjoyable your immediate surroundings can be. And to make such trips pay out especially well in personal benefits and provide more balance between your social and personal activities, bring along some friends. That's the subject of the next chapter—the role one's social life plays in retirement adjustment and subjective well-being.

• 12 •

Friends and Family

Without . . . friendship . . . retirement is in most cases found
to be a dead, flat level, a barren waste, and a blank. Neither the
body nor the soul can enjoy health and life in a vacuum.

—Richter

Friendships and social interaction are extremely important for psychological well-being regardless of age and life stage. They contribute to our feelings of personal meaning and value and, by creating a sense of membership in the community, can help to maintain and reinforce our own identities and validate our thoughts and actions. They can be a refuge in time of need, providing emotional support and comfort and a sense of being accepted and loved by others. Additionally, to the extent that social interactions are planned (e.g., things like meetings, functions, and other gatherings that occur at a set time), they provide schedules that can help to add structure and meaningfulness to day-to-day living. Finally, we might also point out that a social life takes on even more importance after leaving one's job, at which point the opportunities to feel good about one's accomplishments may not be so handy.

The results of our survey clearly showed a link between a well-developed social life and better overall quality of life and, more to the point, better adjustment in retirement. Well-adjusted retirees seem to put more effort into developing and maintaining relationships, in terms of both time and emotional attachment, and their efforts have paid off in a greater sense of connectedness to the world. Apparently, it's not just the size of one's social circle that matters but also its composition—well-adjusted retirees tend to be less exclusively reliant on family members for their social needs. Specifically, we found the following concerning well-adjusted retirees as compared to their less well adjusted counterparts:

- Well-adjusted retirees are more likely to have friends outside the workforce and are likely to have more nonwork friends in their social circle. They spend more hours per week interacting with their friends, have increased the time they spend with them since retiring, and tend to be more emotionally close to their friends. In contrast, for the less well adjusted, family members—and especially their children—take up a greater proportion of their socializing time, and they tend to have stronger emotional connections with family members but weaker ones with friends.

- Well-adjusted retirees are more likely to belong to clubs and organizations and spend more hours per week at their clubs. The less adjusted, in contrast, actually spend less time at their clubs in retirement than they did while they were still working.

- Well-adjusted retirees are much more likely to be satisfied with their social lives, more likely to feel connected to the world, and much less likely to say they feel lonely. The less adjusted, on the other hand, feel their social circle is too small, and although they realize they spend too little time interacting with friends, they also acknowledge that they have spent less time with them since retiring. They are also less likely to have made new friends since retiring and are less motivated to do so in the future. These retirees are also more prone to think their social lives have gotten worse since retiring.

The admission by less adjusted retirees that they have put little effort into maintaining their social life, combined with the realization that it has since deteriorated, is highly revealing. This is a problem we find over and over in retirement—retirees know there is a problem with how they approach certain aspects of their lives yet lack either the motivation or the wherewithal to make the appropriate fixes.

We can have some empathy for the position they're in; it's no simple task for any retiree to rebuild a social life, bringing it up to the levels they enjoyed while they were working. Prior to retirement, those who are employed have plenty of opportunities for daily social contact. Indeed, coworkers are many people's primary source of friends and confidants. But in retirement, as one gets older and friends are not so readily available, retirees are basically left to their own devices—they must rely on their own skills and personal drive to develop friendships. But the drive to meet new people tends to diminish—roughly 40% of all retirees say they are not too or not at all motivated to meet new people. This lower drive is compounded by perceptions of reduced opportunities—only about 30% of retirees feel their lifestyles actually afford them the chance to meet people.

Interestingly, the well adjusted are just as unmotivated to meet people as other retirees, but there is a difference between these retirees and the less well adjusted in terms of how they view their chance to meet people—44% feel they have such opportunities compared to only 13% among the less adjusted. We get the sense from the overall patterns in our survey results that the well adjusted put a great deal of effort into many aspects of their lives, the social part being one, as they pursue the big goal of being happy. Both the fact that they are not entirely comfortable meeting new people and the inconvenient fact that visiting their existing friends may require some driving time represent deterrents that are more likely to be overcome by well-adjusted retirees.

And effort is exactly what is required because the changes that take place in one's social life when leaving a job are substantial. There is the quantitative side—retirees are likely to have fewer people within close proximity when they are no longer going to their jobs. But there is also a qualitative piece; the relationships themselves change simply as a result of increased distance. When retirees leave the workforce, they begin a slow process of shedding their coworker relationships, reducing both the number and the quality or depth of those that remain. To be sure, in the initial stages of retirement, many retirees continue to stay in touch to some extent with at least some of their former coworkers—as they should, as that lets them maintain some continuity of their social lives into retirement and that feeling of still being connected as they make the transition helps from an emotional and psychological perspective.

However, retirees' relationships with former coworkers tend to evolve as they get deeper into their retirement. Over time, retirees become less and less reliant on those they used to work with; conversations with former colleagues regarding personal issues, such as problems with retirement, finances, marriage, and so on, become less frequent. The number of coworkers in their circle dwindles, as does, gradually, the frequency of contact with them.[1]

Our survey illustrated the kinds of changes that occur over time in a retiree's social circle. For example, 61% of retirees include coworkers in their social network, which although fairly high, is much lower than the 84% found among those still employed. And this percentage erodes over time—it starts high, with 77% of those retired six months or less having coworkers as friends, but drops to 55% for those retired five years and to 46% for those retired more than 10 years. The size of the coworker social circle also shrinks—from six members among those retired six months or less down to three for those retired six or more years. On a proportionate basis, retirees as a whole say their ratio of nonwork to work friendships is about 80 to 20, but this gradually changes from 74 to 26 for the newly retired to 87 to 13 for those retired more than 10 years. Furthermore, the number of hours spent with coworkers also declines with more time in retirement, and the hours interacting with non-worker friends correspondingly increases. Finally, ratings of their coworker friendships as emotionally close decline after retirement: 32% of retirees have close coworker relationships, much lower than the 48% among those still in the workforce.

Anne, our retired educator, discussed the gradual breakdown of her relationships with her coworkers. While these friendships were important to her while working, the fact that they were no longer working toward a common cause eliminated the bases for many of these relationships:

> Our job was pretty tough, and the school district we worked in was like a war zone without guns. In order to survive, you needed strong support from your fellow workers, a sense of humor and a belief that when the going got tough, your colleagues would be there for you. Under those conditions, we could not have helped but felt a strong bond to the district and to each other.
>
> Those friendships were very important to me when I was working. I depended on each one of them to help get the job done, to keep me aware of problems, to be my support when I needed it, and to help redirect me if I was going off track. I saw these people every day over a 27-year period. They were friends and confidants. I needed them, and they needed me. Together we got the job done.
>
> But things have changed considerably since I retired. Now, while I still feel a bond with many of these people, there is no job for me, and the events and conditions that held us together are no longer there, so the relationships have dissipated. Sad as it is, that is life. I will always think of them with a smile on my face and recall the good times but know that I will never see many of them again. The job brought us together, and the job kept us together. Without the job, there is no glue to bind us.
>
> I have also found that, as time passes, I have less in common and less to talk about with my former coworkers. The "daily rumors" and job-related problems were always a reason to talk for hours, if not days. That stimulus is gone, so when we get together now, we tend to seek out what is common in our lives. I may love to talk about my grandkids and how wonderful they are, but frankly, I'm getting tired of hearing about other people's grandkids—so I guess those bonds are weakening.
>
> The truth is now the number of people I keep in touch with has decreased tremendously. In my position, I saw and worked with hundreds of professionals. Now the ones I keep in touch with are my nearest and dearest, and that is about six to eight people. For the few who were very close, I anticipate keeping their friendship forever. I may not see them as frequently, but they will remain my friends. For those who were not as

close, I expect that chance meetings will not be like the days when I was working, but I will always be happy to see them and to talk with them. Thinking back, I miss the daily conversations, the sense of family, the support, and the fun. These people will always be important to me, but they are in my past, and there are new people and events in my future, so I am transitioning. I am working on a new life with new interests and new friends, so what used to bond me with my former coworkers is really no longer important to me.

As Anne pointed out, though it sounds like a loss, this slow, steady erosion of relationships with former coworkers is not necessarily a bad thing: in fact, it is healthy and in the best interests of the retiree because it is a sign the retiree is coming to accept and become immersed in the retirement lifestyle. As retirees adopt new roles, needs, and interests, they find they have less and less in common with their old friends from the job. We found exactly that among those well adjusted to retirement—a greater proportion of their friendships are from outside the workforce as compared to the less well adjusted. Better-adjusted retirees had made more of a break from their workforce roles and had moved on with their new lives.

The above pattern is a best-case scenario for retirees: initially maintain friendships from the workplace but increasingly build and rely on a social network outside the workplace. This in fact is what happens for retirees who have a variety of non–work-related relationships in place when they retire. With strong emotional ties to family and friends outside of work, they are likely to have an easier time adjusting since their already-existing support system lets them maintain some continuity. It's very possible that these relationships will strengthen further since the retiree is able to spend more time with nonworking friends thanks to the all the free time he or she has in retirement.

But what of retirees who don't follow this pattern? Those unable to make the social transition may run into problems. Some may have too few meaningful bonds outside of work, have not surrendered their worker roles, or lack the skills and drive to create social lives on their own. But even retirees with strong bonds outside of work might find the resulting changes in their social lives to be unsettling. Tony, a retired corporate executive, generally found his retirement a positive experience and did not have issues about leaving the job itself. Instead, he had concerns about the loss of his worker relationships. He also worried about how his retirement was viewed by other people in his social world. Specifically, his issues centered on whether his willingness to stop working would reduce his acceptance by others, thereby weakening his status among those important to him. It's not unusual for some retirees to feel a reduced sense of self-worth if they believe others look down on their decision to retire. This would especially be an issue for those retiring younger, before the conventional age of 65, such as in Tony's case:

> Retirement was actually something I had been looking forward to for quite some time. It was often the subject of daydreams during a particularly difficult day at work. Although I enjoyed my work, I never considered it to be the most important aspect of my life and certainly did not consider myself a workaholic. Only rarely would I bring work home, for instance. So in thinking about retirement, I was never concerned about the sense of loss or feeling of worthlessness that I've heard expressed by some retirees. On the contrary, I considered the relentless pressures of work and the huge portion of my waking hours that it consumed to be, quite frankly, oppressive. Work prevented me from doing things that I wanted to do. I never really had the time to pursue interests like travel, music, and art. I never had the time to really explore and enjoy the fantastic city only 20 miles away. And I actually longed for the freedom to putter around the house and do nothing if I so desired. So I relished the prospect of having time to myself. And the sooner I could swing it, the better off I'd be.
>
> If I had any misgivings at all about the prospect of retirement, they revolved around how it would impact my relationships with family and friends. I was concerned, for instance, about my many friendships with co-workers. How would they evolve, or would they end by virtue of my no longer physically being at work? I was also concerned about how my wife would react to my early retirement. She takes a very traditional view of the role of work in an individual's life. I remember hearing her say on several occasions that she couldn't understand why anyone would want to retire before age 65. In addition, she is also far more financially conservative and frugal than I am, and I fully expected her to deem our financial situation to not be strong enough to support my early retirement. Would she resent the fact that I chose not to look for another job? How would she feel about my being retired while she continued to work? And what about the kids? How would they react to Dad being home all day? And friends? Would they think I am a lazy slacker?

Unfortunately, despite its difficulties, retirees really don't have much choice but to make the social break. Those who remain overly dependent on workplace friendships might not work hard enough on their out of work relationships. They could find themselves slowing their adoption of the retired role, extending the time they operate between roles. That's another way retirees can wind up socially disconnected and roleless—not accepting that they are part of the retired segment but no longer recognized as a full-fledged member of the working segment.[2]

Beyond inhibiting retirees' progression into the retirement role, overreliance on coworker relationships can undermine morale. Here the issue is a change in the nature of their coworker relationships as a result of being an outsider. On the job, workers are members of a working team that has its own specific set of issues, priorities, and immediacies. Once retirees leave their careers, they are no longer part of the team; they become outsiders, no longer sharing in the world of the team that their former colleagues still belong to. This new reality can be painful to accept. Retirees will likely find their ex-coworker friends do not always have time for them, that they are more of an afterthought to be contacted only when their coworkers have downtime. Eventually retirees may then feel they are irrelevant, possibly even an intrusion on their former colleagues' work world. This realization can continually bring retirees face to face with the reality that they have lost their role and whatever prestige their position may have afforded them. Few can face this sense of irrelevance without feeling some erosion of their self-worth along with their relationships.

That being said, the loss in relevance is really two sided. Over time, retirees are likely to find themselves less and less interested in their former coworkers' business issues. Retirees have a very different reality to deal with, and the day-to-day challenges at their prior jobs will eventually lose their luster. With their reduced interest in these problems, the retiree might get fewer benefits from the work relationships and come to believe it is time to move on.

So all things considered, it is in the best interests of retirees to break or at least reduce emotional ties to their coworkers. But that's only part of the equation—these lost relationships need to be replaced by others and not just family members if retirees are going to feel as socially connected as they were when they were working. If their social contact is reduced substantially, retirees are likely to experience feelings of marginality and a diminished sense of self-worth, a consequence of spending too much time alone. The resulting isolation and disconnectedness from the outside world may then interfere in their adjustment and diminish their subjective well-being.

When we explored these issues in our survey, we did indeed find that many retirees go through a process of gradually breaking from their coworkers. Unfortunately, however, we also found that coworker friendships are not replaced—rather, the pool of friends shrinks in retirement. When we compare the size of their social circles, those in the workforce have about 18 friends as compared to 12 among retirees. The difference between the two is in the number of coworker friends—retirees and employees have the same number of friends from outside the workforce (about eight), but retirees only keep about four coworker friendships as compared to about 10 for employees. While these differences are reasonable and wholly expected, the point still stands that retirees have fewer friends to interact with on a regular basis.

With a smaller social circle, it stands to reason that retirees would also spend less time interacting with others. They average about 57 hours per month, which is down from the 68 hours per month they had while in the workforce, a decline of almost 20%. Time spent with friends accounts for most of the difference—this is reduced by almost 50%, from about 32 hours while working to about 17 hours in retirement. This is expected, but again, it doesn't change the fact that retirees have less time with their peers.

Not only is the number of hours reduced, so is the quality of their interactions. Retirees are more likely to communicate with friends and family by email or phone and less so in person as compared to those in the workforce. Although those in the workforce have easier and more frequent opportunities for meeting in person, it is rather surprising that with all the free time available to retirees, they don't spend more personal time together. But this may also be problematic: it's harder to connect emotionally with people if you are not spending time face-to-face.

Considering all of the above, what we notice is a pullback by retirees from the broader social world—not a very good thing for subjective well-being. This brings us to another point about the social life of retirees: they spend as much time with their children and more time with other family members in retirement as they did while working. At first glance, this sounds like a good thing—plenty of time spent with family: what's not to like about that? However, when you consider that the total number hours spent in contact with others is reduced, this means a greater proportion of their socializing time is relatively insular, that is, dedicated to family and not to friends. For example, among retirees, 71% of their social time is spent with family members and 29% with friends. For those in the workforce, in contrast, only 53% is dedicated to family and 47% to friends. Now, some may think this must be age related, that the retirees we interviewed are older than those still working, so they are more likely to be tied to their families. That is not the case: our retirees and employees are virtually identical in age.

When we consider how they split their time, we can conclude that retirees on the whole have a much less balanced social life, which is also not a good thing for subjective well-being. It seems reasonable that the broader and more diverse one's social circle, the more likely it is that a person will be exposed to new ideas and different ways of thinking. And when retirees are interacting directly with friends—people who share the same way of living and have the same issues—they have more opportunities thrown their way to get involved in social activities and the same amount of free time for getting into various forms of healthy mischief.

We are not trying to denigrate the importance of family—this is the sanctuary, the go-to place for comfort and support. But retirees' children are not their peers. They do not share the same lifestyle, so what's important to them may not be what's important to retirees. They have the issues and problems of younger people, trying to build their lives, raise a family, and achieve some level of financial security and success. Retirees, on the other hand, should be much more interested in having fun—or, if that sounds too flippant, in doing the things that matter to people *after* they have achieved the goals their children are still striving toward. So we are talking about balance—a social life that includes equal parts family and friends and less outright dependence on children and other family members.

This point is not based just on our opinion—the data from our survey actually suggest that a more balanced social life is healthier. We looked at those who are well adjusted in retirement and those who rate their social lives very satisfying and compared their social composition to their counterparts. Here is what we found:

- The proportion of time spent with friends is about 32% for those who are well adjusted and have a satisfying social life as compared to about 24% for the less well adjusted and those with an unsatisfying social life.
- Both well-adjusted and socially happy retirees report a greater number of friends in their social circle—about 20 as compared with about 13 who are less adjusted and less happy.
- Retirees who spend more hours with their friends tend to be happier about their social life—62% of these retirees are satisfied as compared to 46% who spend relatively few hours with friends. Those spending more time with their friends also tend to be more satisfied with their retirement—61% as compared to 47% for those spending fewer hours with their friends.

A balanced social life may also pay other dividends. Both the well adjusted and the socially satisfied tend to feel better psychologically. For example, they are much more likely to be confident and productive, feel their lives have been a success and have turned out as they had hoped, are optimistic about the future, and are less likely to be lonely. Again, we cannot imply causality since it may be the case that their positive attitude and self-image lend themselves to being more outgoing and thus more effective at building a rewarding social life. Nevertheless, the linkage found to some of these characteristics, such as not feeling lonely, appear on the face of things to be a direct result of being more social. And feeling more socially involved and having more things to do in turn can help to boost one's confidence and lead to feeling better in general.

So if a balanced social life is healthier emotionally, why don't retirees just take care of the problem? Why don't they, in other words, just go out and spend more time with their friends or find some new ones? For starters, we think retirees actually learn to get by on less. New retirees provide some clues. Among those retired six months or less, 45% complain they don't spend enough time with their friends, but this percentage drops to about 30% for those retired longer. New retirees are also much closer to their friends in and out of the workforce. However, these emotional connections gradually weaken as they spend more time in retirement.

New retirees seem to experience something of a culture shock. They feel the pinch of a much diminished social life immediately on retiring, when daily contact with coworkers is abruptly cut off. It takes some time—about six to nine months—for them to realize that their coworker friendships will diminish and their social worlds will become smaller. Eventually, they seem to settle into the less socially rich world of retirement—to come to accept it or at least to be convinced that this is, for them, the new normal. Unfortunately, there is also the likelihood that retirees are just now—once they accept it—becoming aware that such a social separation can hurt their subjective well-being in the long run.

Then there is the problem of motivation. As we have already pointed out, nobody seems to be particularly comfortable with the idea of making new friends. Among both retirees and those in the workforce, only about 20% are interested in meeting new people, and about 4 in 10 are just not interested in doing so at all. Now this is not much of an issue for those in the workforce—being surrounded by coworkers, they have a social life thrust on them.

But retirees, with their reduced circle of friends, cannot afford to hold on to this "friends are all around me all the time" perspective. Meeting new people is essential to reestablishing the balance in time spent with family and friends. We found that those who report a satisfying social life are much more motivated to meet new people and have made more friends since retiring than those who are socially unhappy. If retirees persist in not putting some effort into maintaining an adequate circle of friends, they are likely to feel the loss as they move further into their retirement. We found that, when asked how their social life compares to when they were still working, mentions of having gotten worse since retiring start to increase six or more years into retirement.

As we have mentioned already, finding new friends is no easy task. We must keep in mind that a deteriorating social life is not their own doing—retirees are victims of circumstances. They don't have the ready-made social world provided by a job, so they are required to make their own opportunities. At some point, as baby boomers swell the retirement ranks, somebody somewhere will come up with a retireematch.com as an online way for retirees to meet other retirees. But until that day comes, retirees have to help themselves.

In this regard, they should consider committing time each day, as part of their daily routine, to seek out the ways and places to meet other retirees.

Joining clubs and senior organizations is one option, but if this is not to your taste, starting your own retiree club may be something to consider. This may initially sound silly, but if each retiree knows another retiree who knows another, soon a great many retirees will be connected—enough to meet most anyone's social needs. Such "clubs" can be established on a theme basis, such as dining, wine tasting, or golf, allowing retirees to meet others who share the same interests.

As another option, retirees can consider taking on some kind of work, either salaried or as a volunteer, specifically for the social benefits. That means, of course, that such a job should not be one that is worked from home. We have found that, while those with a satisfying social life are no more likely to hold a salaried job, they are more likely to work as volunteers, and they are more likely to have taken a salaried or volunteer job specifically for the social opportunities it provides. But whatever path is chosen, the key is to stay motivated and do something on your own to find people who share your lifestyle and your interests.

· 13 ·

Love and Marriage

When a man retires, his wife gets twice the husband but only half the income.

—Chi Chi Rodriguez

*M*ost of us would probably agree that being married or having a significant other in one's life is a good thing that adds to subjective well-being. (For the sake of brevity, we will refer to all of these relationships as "marriages" in this chapter, but our observations can be assumed to apply equally to couples who aren't married but have a loving relationship.) Intimate relationships provide regular companionship and emotional support. For retirees, they serve an additional purpose: they help in the adjustment process by providing some continuity in an otherwise disrupted life.[1] Additionally, although it can be overdone, researchers find that couples tend to welcome the greater opportunity to participate in activities together.[2]

Of course, that's as long as the marriage is a good one, but, unfortunately, not all are. Retirement and marriage are what might be called "mutual influencers." In other words, research has shown that intimate relationships can either help (if good) or hinder (if bad) retirees' adjustment, and the act of retiring itself can either strengthen or weaken a marriage. The emotional ups and downs that can accompany the retirement adjustment process can make their presence strongly felt in retirees' relationships. Furthermore, with the change in roles and the added amount of time spent together, there is a good chance that some aspects of the relationship will be altered, perhaps substantially.[3]

On the positive side, retirement can make a happy marriage even better. For these couples, more time together lets them be involved in more joint activities and pursuits and allows more sharing of household chores and responsibilities. Additionally, the elimination of work-related pressure—which can often spill over into the home—means that there may be fewer stress points of the sort that can lead to arguments and disagreements. As a result, happily married couples tend to feel their home environment has become more comfortable, especially if the retiree has left a high-stress job.[4] Over time, these couples are likely to look at their marriage as more and more enjoyable, especially if there are added opportunities to bond over additional shared activities and adventures afforded by retirement.

Turning to our survey, we found that about 7 in 10 retirees are either married or have a significant other in their lives, which is not too shocking given that estimates of divorce rates hover somewhere around 50%. Roughly three-quarters of retirees who are intimately involved claim their relationships are happy ones. Although this may seem like a rather high proportion, it probably reflects the tendency for divorce to have weeded out the unhappy marriages.

On the other hand, the relatively low percentage of intimate relationships is unfortunate since we have also found that, consistent with other research, such relationships do contribute to overall quality of life and adjustment to retirement. For example, 72% of those who say they are completely adjusted to retirement have a significant other in their lives compared to 65% of those less well adjusted. We cannot know which one causes the other, meaning whether better adjustment leads to happier marriages or whether happy marriages lead to better adjustment. But we can know that the two go hand in hand: retirees who are better adjusted to retirement also have happy marriages. When we compared those in happy marriages to those in less blissful relationships, our survey showed the following:

- Happily married retirees tend to spend more time doing things together and have more active sex lives. They also had much more positive in-going perceptions about retirement but were also more accurate in their expectations. They were better at planning their retirement, particularly in terms of how they would spend time with each other, and report a much more positive quality of life overall.
- In contrast, those in unhappy marriages are much less likely to describe their relationships as intimate, connected, or comfortable and more likely to feel their relationships had gotten worse since retiring. They are unhappy in retirement, feel the quality of their life has worsened, and wish they were back at work. They are much more likely to feel depressed and feel their sex life is poor and has gotten worse since retiring and are less satisfied with how their lives have turned out.

Even before retiring, good marriages make the idea of retirement more appealing and can work to "pull" individuals out of the workforce. We found that those planning to retire in the near future have better marriages and believe that retirement would further improve their relationships. On the other hand, those who do not plan to retire are less happily married—they tend to feel unappreciated and disconnected from their spouses and don't think their interests are compatible. The quality of their relationships may be one reason why they remain at their jobs and probably would like to do so for as long as they can.

But those wanting to retire may also run into some snags, good marriages notwithstanding. Would-be retirees—more so than those already retired—put a lot of stock in carrying out shared activities with their spouses. Of course, it's entirely possible that their marriages really are *that* good. But we suspect it is equally likely, if not more so, that those planning to retire have unrealistic expectations about how the two will spend their time together in retirement. That's especially true if a retiree's spouse had not been in the workforce and therefore had established a way of spending time that did not include the retiree. If and when these expectations are not met, there may be some emotional letdown, at least until the retiree learns the rules of engagement—retirees with nonworking spouses may have to find a way to wiggle into their spouses' schedules.

That may not be how things first start out—interesting things happen to a marriage in the early stages of retirement, that is, within the first six months. In many respects, couples behave just like they are on their honeymoon when they first leave the workforce. It is likely that, when both are first at home together without the interruptions of a job, there is some real enjoyment of the stress-free time they can spend together. We found that rookie retirees rate their marriages more favorably in general, have better sex lives, and feel their relationships benefit from retirement. In describing their relationship, they are more likely to use words and phrases like "compatibility," "connectedness," "friendliness," and "a sharing of interests." They are also more likely to prefer doing things as a couple rather than separately and wish they could spend more time together. And this is not a matter of new retirees being younger—the average age of those retired six months or less is 62, virtually identical to those retired more than six months (63 on average).

Unfortunately, as with marriages in general, pretty soon the honeymoon ends for many couples. Retirees settle into their new lifestyles, and the mundane aspects of daily living take over. We found that the honeymoon phase can actually come to an end fairly quickly—a little after six months into retirement. It is at that point that there are likely to be some pitfalls. While this is especially true for those in unsatisfying marriages, problems can emerge even for those in happy relationships, particularly in the early to middle stages of retirement, right after the end of the honeymoon.

For one thing, couples are likely to have a lot more time together under the same roof. This forces more frequent direct interaction, and that can be harmful even to good marriages. Conflicts are particularly likely for couples who are too dependent on each other for their social needs; that is, they have few friends outside their marriage. Researchers have found that marriages work better when spouses have lots of potential for outside social contact and suffer when there aren't many outside relationships.[5] Our own survey supports these findings—happily married retired couples have more friends, spend more time with their friends, and have stronger emotional bonds with their friends than less happy couples, probably because there is less pressure on both partners to fill the other's needs.

Actually, there are quite a few ways too much time together can lead to marital discord. For example, non-working wives can face problems when their husbands retire. Societal changes of the past 40 years or so notwithstanding, there are still many households where the husbands are the only breadwinners and are typically the retirees, particularly in the upcoming class of retirees, the baby boomers. These husbands have two adjustments to make: First they must leave the workforce, often a source of personal fulfillment and identification; and second, they have to figure out what to do and how to think as they grapple with full time home living. Regarding the latter, very often wives are the household bosses, and that leaves their husbands struggling to find ways to fit into an established way of doing things. For their part, wives may have to learn how to cope with an invader. That may be a strong term, but it is very often literally the case.

As a case in point, there is the strong possibility that when a husband retires, his partner will feel an invasion of her personal space and time. Some researchers, for example, have found that conflicts occur when newly retired husbands interfere with their wives' daily routines, or cut into their privacy and personal time.[6] For their part, our survey has shown that husbands, when they first retire, expect their wives to alter their daily patterns to satisfy their personal needs. Our survey further showed that wives often did no such thing—these men tended to complain that their wives didn't spend enough time with them. To some extent this may be tied to the tendency for men to be less socially connected; that is, they are less likely to have a well-developed social life independent of their work and of their wives. As we have mentioned previously, women in general are more socially integrated, putting in the time and effort to maintain fairly regular contact with family and friends. But many men are less prone to maintain such strong social connections, preferring to rely more on their wives to ensure they have a satisfying social life with lots to do. Unfortunately, men who take this approach to their social lives generally have no one other than their wives to turn to for some company, especially in the early stages of their retirement.

Of course, the expectation that a wife will drop everything to service the attention needs of her newly retired husband is not at all realistic for many marriages, and the resulting backlash is not hard to predict. In fact, under such circumstances it would probably be unrealistic to expect a wife to feel anything but pressure, and very often anger and resentment, at the prospect of husband-sitting, especially if her husband is overly demanding in his time and attention needs.

As we have pointed out in an earlier chapter, this is in fact one of the more common fears that wives have even before their husbands retire. In our interview with Lynne, she pointed out that her friends who have working but someday-to-retire husbands are already anticipating how their lives might change once their husbands leave work and have nothing to do—and not one of these wives felt the changes would be for the better. Some worry that their husbands will be constantly looking over their shoulders, questioning where they are going, when they will back, and so forth. For each of these women, their husbands' upcoming retirements are unpleasant clouds hanging over their heads.

But all is not doom, ladies, at least not forever. In fact, as a positive, we also found that eventually husbands become less demanding of their wives' time. After they've been retired for a while, most men get better at retirement. As they come to adapt to the lifestyle, husbands learn to either establish their own personal interests, or just to accept that their wives have their own lifestyles. Of course, there is also the possibility that husbands become less demanding of their wives' time and attention because the wives have succumbed to the pressure and made adjustments to their own lives, giving up a lunch here, an activity there. In all likelihood it's probably a combination of the two—husbands expect less and wives give more. After all, compromise is what good relationships are all about.

As another potential type of invasion, there is the issue of what might be called domestic management consulting. Newly retired husbands, now spending more time at home, may be inclined at times to turn a critical eye toward their wife's management of household affairs. But, to be fair to these men, their need to interject a perspective on how to run a household is in some ways understandable. By the time they retire, many men have risen to supervisory positions in their careers and are used to directing and controlling people and events. In retirement, they lose that supervisory role but some may retain the habit of being the boss, so they turn their attention to managing what is left to them—their home. In other words, some just may not be able to help themselves. However, that need to be in control may not matter much to their spouses. When husbands express dissatisfaction or suggest alternative ways of handling things around the house, many wives, who have successfully managed the home front without much help for years, may not take too kindly to what they see as an exasperating encroachment on their territory.

Gerry provides some insight as to how, on entering retirement, he became too engrossed in the running of household affairs. In his career, Gerry was a high-level executive for a major corporation with a large staff under him. When he left his job, he tried to hold on to his management role; his wife, to no one's surprise except perhaps his own, objected. However, over time, both he and his wife came to a solution, one that required Gerry to make some adjustments:

When I first retired, some 11 years ago, it was the first time in almost 30 years of marriage that I did not have a focal point in my life other than my "home" life. It was also the first time that my wife and I were spending 24/7 together. For most of my career, I managed things and people, and it wasn't until I no longer had that as a formal part of my life that there was an emptiness that needed to be filled. So, I started managing the only thing—and person—available to me—my home and my wife. At that time, neither I nor my wife was immediately aware of this phenomenon and how it would challenge our relationship as never before.

To say that this created friction in our lives that had not existed before would be an understatement. As I said, we were initially unaware of my "management creep," but it became clear fairly quickly that I was interfering with the normal ebb and flow of my wife's daily routines. She had always managed our home and her personal activities. Now, I was becoming an unexpected and unwanted dominating presence in a part of her life that previously had been solely her domain. Arguments became more frequent and disturbing. But there is a very important point here—prior to this time, honestly I have to say that we never argued. That was just never a part of our relationship. But it was that way now.

Within a few months, the unsettling realities of this new existence began to crystallize for both of us, and we were determined to address them. Neither of us could have anticipated how annoying I would become in those early days of retirement—we were totally unprepared. We talked about what was happening to us and to our relationship and worked at righting the ship before things got out of control. I focused on backing off and giving her the space she was accustomed to. I had to bite my lip and shut my mouth when I saw her doing things that I would have done differently. I had to adjust—me, not her. With time, it worked and continues to work these 11 years later. Sure, I backslid (and still do) sometimes—I am who and what I am. But being aware of and sensitive to the consequences of my behavior, thankfully, has helped to keep my backsliding to an acceptably reasonable level.

Sometimes couples can run into problems if their expectations are out of sync. Both partners are likely to have their own preconceived notions about how they will live together in retirement. For example, on her husband retiring, a wife might presume more assistance in household chores than her husband expects to give, or either spouse may expect more involvement from the other in leisure activities. Feelings of disenchantment resulting from unmet expectations are most likely to crop up at the start of retirement, when both partners are still trying to settle into a new and relatively unfamiliar living arrangement. The conflicts may dissipate over time as the two partners get used to their nonworking lifestyle and establish their own patterns separately and together. But they can also lead to further problems if resentment builds from either partner, leaving the conflicts to fester unresolved.[7]

Compatibility is yet another issue. It is possible, for example, that some husbands and wives will find, after they are no longer distracted by full-time jobs or raising a family, that they do not have as much in common with each other as they once thought. While still in the workforce, different perspectives regarding living styles can be masked because so much time and effort is taken up by work. However, even in what may appear to be good marriages, these differences are likely to come to the forefront when couples are more focused on each other. There may be an emerging and uncomfortable sense from each partner that they don't really know the person they are married to. One of the individuals we talked to, Michael, a midlevel manager in a corporation, retired about a year ago, but his wife continued to work. Michael found his wife's continued employment to be acceptable since it allowed him to use his time to satisfy his own needs. However, since his own retirement, he started to acknowledge to himself that he and his wife might not be marching to the same tune. Their disparate interests have Michael concerned as to how they will live together once they are both retired:

> Looking ahead, I have some trepidation about the time when my wife does decide to retire. Although being able to travel with her is certainly a positive, I wonder how things will change for me on a day-to-day basis. Will I miss my solitude? Will we get on each other's nerves? Even though my wife's motives were not related to concern for our relationship but rather to her desire to maintain a fulfilling career, as well as a self-imposed concern about our finances, I'm happy that things happened the way they did.
>
> In particular, I have come to realize fairly recently that my wife and I are very different from each other—more so, I suspect, than the average couple in their late fifties. So we're both liberal Democrats, but the similarities pretty much end there. For instance, she loves the big house in the suburbs

and wants to stay indefinitely. I, on the other hand, would love to move to a smaller place, preferably an apartment in the city. She's extremely frugal, while I've never had an issue with spending money, within reason. I love all types of music and am a big fan of NPR and PBS; she's indifferent to music, listens to books on tape while driving, and is addicted to crime shows on TV. My ideal retirement has European travel as its centerpiece; hers, I suspect, is centered around grandchildren (if and when we have any) and home improvement projects.

Don't get me wrong. I love my wife and like being married, but it's fair to say that I view the time when we're both retired with some consternation. Since my own retirement, I've settled into a comfortable routine that may change, fairly dramatically I think, when she is retired as well. I've been perfectly happy being alone for a good portion of each day but suspect that the freedom that I've come to take for granted may very well be curtailed. My fear is that she will question how I choose to spend my time and pressure me to spend more time doing the things that she considers productive and necessary. Another concern is that the differences between the two of us might become magnified and a source of tension in a situation in which we're together all of the time.

I'm trying to be optimistic, though, about what happens post her retirement. The positive side of me says that, after 35 years of living with me, my wife knows me pretty well. She knows I'm reasonably independent, that I enjoy my solitude, and that home maintenance, shopping, and gardening are not high on my list of fun activities. I think she'll also realize that when she hits retirement, I will have already been at it for quite some time and that she'll have at least some respect for the patterns I've established. On a day-to-day basis, if we settle into a pattern of peaceful coexistence where mostly I do my things, she does hers, and we do together some things that we both enjoy, that would be great. Just as there are some battles I know I won't win (like selling the house and moving to Manhattan), so I won't even try to fight them, I would hope that she relents on some of the things she would like for me/us to be doing. As clichéd as it sounds, I guess marriage really is about compromise. Also on the positive side, I know that she is as interested in travel as I am (although probably not on as grand a scale), so that is something we will happily do together. A big wild card, though, is whether there will be grandchildren in the picture. Of course, we'd both be pleased if that does come to pass, but I'd also be concerned that it might become too central a focus of her life postretirement. I'm certainly not interested in the house becoming a day care center, for instance, even for my own grandkids.

Of course I certainly don't want my wife to work forever, and I don't have a burning desire to continue my solo retirement for much longer, happy as I have been in it. Although she's still very much into her career, there will come a time, I'm sure, when she's had enough of work. But, by the same token, I fervently hope that when it becomes a dual retirement situation, a second stage of retirement for me, my own happiness will continue, if not be enhanced, and that she will be as happy as I am.

Michael is hopeful that he and his wife will be able to cope with their differences through compromise. His wish is that each will respect the other's need to pursue their individual interests and that they will participate together in those interests they have in common. However, when interests are too disparate or if one or the other partner is unwilling to compromise, what appeared to be intact or happy marriages may suffer, at least until the appropriate adjustments are made.

The loss of a steady paycheck can also disrupt a relationship. Adults still in the workforce can, of course, count on regular income, but for retirees, the only way to make additional money is to go back to work. Conflicts arising from money can stem from difficulty meeting essential needs but also from unfulfilled expectations relating to leisure, such as reduced travel opportunities.[8]

Additionally, regardless of the degree of real financial security, financial concerns may be especially prevalent in the early stages of retirement since at that point neither partner may have a realistic idea how much their retirement really costs. (As we've pointed out previously, financial security is in part perceptual, and even when there are adequate funds, retirees have to believe they have enough money.) However, as long as their finances are adequate, retirees are likely to become more comfortable over time, and the stress of financial worries on a marriage should eventually fade away.

Then there is the issue of dual-worker households. When both husband and wife work, whether they retire simultaneously or at different times can also affect the relationship. Researchers have found that when spouses retire together, the marriage is seldom affected by their joint decision; good marriages will stay good and bad marriages bad.

But problems can occur when only half of a two-income couple retires. For some couples, of course, joint retirement is not possible. Adverse circumstances can get in the way, such as the need to hold on to health benefits or the need for additional income or if one partner has to retire to care for another family member.[9] Other researchers have found that husbands and wives react differently if one retires and the other continues to work. If the husband retires first, he may become dissatisfied with the marriage but still like the idea of being retired. Wives retiring first, on the other hand, have been found to be less happy with both their retirements *and* their marriages.[10]

We found the same from our survey. Retired men tended to rate their marriages equally positive whether or not their wives were working. Retired women, on the other hand, rated their marriages the same as men if their husbands were retired but rate them less favorably if their husbands were still working. Michael provided a case in point from a man's perspective. He was actually comfortable with the fact that he retired and his wife didn't; actually, his concerns have more to do with what may happen when she *does* retire.

Some researchers have looked at nonsynchronized retirements from the perspective of changes in balance of power. Here we are talking about the amount of influence or status each partner has in the marriage. In some marriages, the husband has the dominant role; in others, the wife is dominant; and in still others, the two partners have equal status. If the two retire together, then as long as both had equal say in their own decision to do so, the status of each partner will remain unaffected. The structure of the relationship, the position held by each partner, should stay the same because the decision to retire affects both equally.

But the balance of power can be upset if one partner retires and the other continues working. For example, if the main breadwinner retires and the other spouse keeps working, the retired breadwinner may feel threatened because he or she has lost that status. This situation is most likely to occur in households that have more traditional gender roles where the husband is the main provider. When he loses the breadwinner role, he may feel less valued in the household, and the resulting hit to his self-confidence will weaken his subjective well-being.[11]

So does that mean the wife should retire first in that sort of marriage? If only it were that simple: if the wife retires first and the husband is already dominant before retirement, this can lead to even greater dominance on his part, undermining *her* feelings about the marriage and her retirement.

There is actually one circumstance that according to most researchers does not seem to be problematic—the wife holds a dominant role and retires before her husband. When she retires, his status is enhanced because he becomes the primary breadwinner. The resulting changes in relative status actually have a positive effect on the quality of the marriage and do not detract from either party's feelings about retirement.

Michael noticed a change in the dynamics of his marriage when he retired. Michael and his wife were more or less equal throughout their marriage while they were both working. But his relationship changed when he retired and his wife kept working. Michael felt this had to do with his diminished role in the household, as he was no longer the primary breadwinner. Michael noticed these changes through his wife's expectations as to how he should use his time and energy in retirement. Michael felt some (but not all) of her expectations were acceptable, and his objections and concerns had more to do with her tone than her requests, which he felt undermined his prestige in the relationship:

Since my retirement, there have also been subtle, nonformalized shifts in the marital balance of power. They've focused in two key areas: household responsibilities and money. Because she's still working, she clearly feels I should shoulder a larger share of the housework. I happen to agree, at least to an extent. So I'm now doing more of the grocery shopping, laundry, vacuuming, and other everyday types of chores. She also initially had expected me to do a lot of the bigger stuff as well (painting, plumbing repairs, gardening, etcetera). That's where I've drawn the line. I've never been a do-it-yourselfer: don't have the knowledge or the interest. My response has always been to pay to have someone else do that stuff.

But because we no longer have my income and she is the sole wage earner, she also clearly feels that she should have a greater say in how we spend money, and, unlike myself, she always comes down on the side of financial conservatism. But I have to say I feel less important to her than I did while I was working.

Beyond the balance of power, other elements come into play when couples retire at separate times—some have good and some have bad effects on the marriage and a retiree's well-being. On the positive side, a working partner provides income for the household. As we've noted, the loss of a paycheck can be a source of concern for retirees, especially the newly retired, until they become familiar with their expenses. Having a working spouse also allows retirees their own time to pursue their individual interests or develop new interests without impinging on their spouses' time.

On the downside, a working spouse can restrict the plans and activities of the retiree, such as limiting travel and social opportunities. And if the retiree is too restricted in his or her individual pursuits, the large blocks of time spent alone while the spouse is at work can reduce his or her subjective well-being. Michael has experienced some of these restrictions as a result of his wife's continued working. Although he felt he could pursue his own personal interests, he was limited in traveling, something that he perceived to be important:

> I find myself feeling a little ambivalent about [the fact that my wife is still working now that I'm retired]. On the one hand, as someone who doesn't mind being alone and having the ability to pursue my own interests at my own speed, I'm okay with her being away during the day. But on the other hand, I feel that one of my key goals in retirement, travel, is stymied by the fact that her work greatly limits her free time. As a self-employed realtor, it's difficult for her to get away for more than three or four days at a time. She's says she's not ready for retirement and is unsure about how long she wants to continue working, and I feel as if we're missing out on the opportunity to travel while we're still relatively young and healthy. I've

actually given some thought to doing some travel on my own but haven't quite gotten to that point yet.

So synchronized retirement is looked on by social scientists as a good thing, and our research has demonstrated the same. But is it a realistic expectation? Not necessarily—the tendency for retirement to include work these days, having one spouse working and the other retired, has become fairly typical. Among our retirees, only about half reported their spouses retired at the same time, and 4 in 10 note that their spouses are still currently employed. The percentages of having a working spouse are particularly high for the newly retired—55% among those retired six months or less. While this percentage drops off with more years into retirement, even after eight or more years one in three retirees have a spouse who is still working.

However, despite the high employment rates of spouses, our survey supports the view that couples are better off retiring together. Couples may be doing themselves a disservice when one works and the other doesn't. In fact, it is possible that some of the difficulties retirees face in adjustment may be a direct result of desynchronized retirements. Some of the more important differences we found can be summarized as follows:

- When spouses retire together, they are more likely to plan their retirements, particularly in terms of how they will spend their time together, and are more likely to have achieved the goals they set for themselves.
- Simultaneous retirees are happier and better adjusted in retirement, report a better overall quality of life and happier marriages, and are more prone to think their marriages have improved with retirement. They are also more socially involved and connected, feel they have direction in their lives, and are better able to find interesting things to do.
- In contrast, those with a working spouse spend less time in joint activities and are more likely to complain they do not spend enough time with their spouses. They are more likely to feel lonely and to be less involved with other people, are less happy overall, and are less committed to stay in their marriages in the future.

Up to this point, our focus has been on how husbands and wives fare as a couple, mostly based on the impact of added time together as a result of retirement. But there is another side to this issue: how the retiree's reactions to retirement can affect the quality of both good and not-so-good marriages. There is considerable evidence that if the retiree likes being retired, those feelings can translate into positive feelings at home, possibly strengthening the marriage. On the other hand, if the retiree is dissatisfied with this new lifestyle, the resulting unhappiness can spill over into the marriage itself. Even couples with sound and fulfilling marriages can have problems if one spouse is not adjusting to retirement easily.[12]

To find out how one's adjustment to retirement is linked to marital quality, we compared the relationships of those who are completely adjusted to retirement to those who are less well adjusted. Again, we cannot imply causality since it may be the case that the poorly adjusted had less happy marriages from the onset or that unfulfilled expectations regarding their relationship interfered with their retirement adjustment. But it is nevertheless worthwhile to take a look at how their relationships differ. And it is interesting to note that emotional support seems to emerge as a particular problem among the less adjusted; this could suggest they feel their spouses have not been helpful in their time of need. Specifically, we found the following:

- Those who are less well adjusted tend to have spouses who did not retire at the same time and to feel they do not spend enough time with their spouses. They tend to rate their marriages less favorably overall, are less likely to have sex regularly, are much less likely to feel emotionally connected or to feel appreciated, are more likely to feel their marriages have gotten worse since retiring.
- They are less committed to staying together in the future, primarily because they feel a lack of emotional support, a lack of trust, and an inconsistency in their personal needs and goals.

We have made some passing references to sex in this chapter, so it's time to explore the issue of intimacy in more detail. One might assume that, with all the free time alone, the lack of job-related pressures, and the tendency to view their relationships positively, the sex lives of retirees would blossom, if for no other reason than to add some excitement to those days when there is little else to do. But we actually found the reverse—retirees have sex less often in comparison to their counterparts still in the workforce. We didn't see much difference among the younger group, those 45 to 54 years of age. These retirees are about as active as their working counterparts (although one could argue retirees should be more active). But among retirees 55 and older, the dropoff is substantial. And not only does the frequency decline, but retirees rate their sex life less favorably overall and feel it has suffered since they retired. We compared the intimacy of retirees age 55 and older who have a significant other and describe themselves as healthy to that same group of people still in the workforce and found the following:

- Only about 75% of those retired have sex regularly (i.e., at least once per month) versus 90% among those employed. The average frequency is 4.9 times per month among retirees as compared to 8.8 times for those still in the workforce. (Note: The absolute numbers here may be exaggerated by self-reporting, but the frequencies can be compared from group to group with confidence.)

- And this is *not* solely a matter of "older people don't have sex as often" (although our findings do show that to be the case); it seems to be a function of retirement itself. Among those 55 to 64 years of age, sexual intimacy occurs 5.9 times per month among retirees versus 9.6 times among those still working; for those 65 and older, it occurs 3.6 times per month for retirees versus 5.7 times among employees.

- Only 39% of these retirees rate their sex lives as excellent or very good, while 36% rate it as fair or poor. In comparison, among those still in the workforce, 50% rate their sex lives as excellent or very good and 24% as fair or poor. In total, approximately 3 of 10 of all retirees say their sex lives got worse after they retired, but only 13% say they have gotten better.

Sexual intimacy isn't affected by retirement adjustment—the average monthly frequency of sex among completely adjusted retirees is about 5.0 times as compared to 4.6 times among those less well adjusted (both are much lower than the 7.2 times among those still working). But the frequency of having sex is associated with overall quality of life. Retirees with a high quality of life have sex 6.5 times per month as compared to 3.4 times for those with a lower quality. Half of those with a high quality of life rate their sex lives as favorable as compared to only 7% of those who consider their quality of life low. We found the same results among those still in the workforce, further suggesting an active sex life contributes to overall happiness.

We are uncertain why there is a downturn in sexuality among retirees. In truth, their relationships seem generally sound—retirees as a group rate their relationships about as favorably as do people who are still working. Nevertheless, if we are to hazard a guess, possibly the increased amount of time together plays a role. This would be in the sense that too much familiarity breeds contempt or at least disinterest. Or possibly, retirees, being constantly in such close quarters with their spouses, have a lot more skirmishes than they have been willing to admit to in a survey, putting more emotional distance between them.

Another possible explanation may lie in self-image. There is a tendency for retirees to rate themselves much lower than those still in the workforce on characteristics that are tied to self-esteem—feeling useful, productive, and in control of their lives and believing their best days are ahead of them. Additionally, retirees are less likely to feel energetic. It is possible that, with a weaker sense of self-worth and lower overall drive, many retirees have a reduced inclination to have or want sex.

Whatever the reasons, this is not an ideal situation since the importance of sexual intimacy in a marriage is well documented. While we do not proclaim to be sex therapists, our recommendation to retirees would be to have more sex—this is one thing that should not be easier said than done, after all. An active sex life will make retirees feel more connected with their partners and feel better emotionally and psychologically, improve their motivation to do other things, and provide the less physically active with some much-needed exercise. We suggest that you and your partner start to look at sex as a health treatment, one that you can devote your time and effort to without much chance of getting injured. Those who cannot find their way to a more interesting and satisfying sex life can even consider a visit to a sex therapist. The results of doing so might be surprisingly helpful and, if not, will likely give you and your partner a good laugh.

Returning to more mundane issues, how can married people maintain a relationship in the absence of distractions provided by work? There are a number of ways couples can avoid some of the skirmishes that can arise during retirement and ways to overcome conflicts that turn out to be unavoidable. For starters, if circumstances permit, both spouses in dual-worker households should retire simultaneously or as close to that as they can so that they avoid such problems as changes in the dynamics of the relationship or interference with the retired partner's ability to participate in certain types of activities or social events. Retiring together also provides each partner with some emotional support as they try to adjust to their new living arrangements.

As the same time, couples should focus on building their social lives to avoid becoming too dependent on each other or spending too much time together. In addition to maintaining and strengthening existing friendships, retirees can consider joining clubs and organizations that cater to their personal interests and that provide opportunities for developing new independent relationships.

Exploration and pursuit of separate interests and activities is important for all couples. The time devoted to these can provide each partner with his or her own space, along with a contribution to personal development. Such separate pursuits may be particularly beneficial for those in unhappy marriages, assuming the participants plan to stay together. Since the added time together brought on by leaving the workforce can exacerbate the potential for conflicts, these couples would probably benefit greatly from activities or social networks that allow them a good deal of time apart, very much the way their jobs did.

The loss of personal pursuits can be especially problematic for nonworking wives, if retiring husbands interfere with their personal lifestyle developed over the years of being outside the workforce. Husbands have to realize that their wives cannot drop their daily patterns completely to satisfy their needs.

Such expectations are not realistic and can lead to resentments if husbands are overly demanding of their wives' time. These retirees would probably help themselves and their marriages by developing some of their own patterns, finding things to do that do not include their wives and thereby creating personal space for each partner.

Probably the most crucial point for all couples, regardless of marital quality, is to talk to each other, both before and after retiring, about the full range of topics. As a dramatic change in lifestyle, retirement's pitfalls can sneak up on both good and bad marriages. But talking about the issues allows each partner to establish the ground rules for what is likely to be a much more intrusive coexistence. Conversations can help to manage expectations, allowing partners to understand what each expects of the other, thereby helping to head off disappointments or resentments. Topics can include what each will do with their time together and apart, how much they can afford to spend, how the division of household responsibilities will be shared, and how to handle incompatible interests, if they exist.

Some couples may also need to discuss the issue of space invasion within the household, a situation particularly relevant to nonworking wives with retiring husbands. In the event they feel the need to offer unsought-after advice, these husbands might first want to consider that their wives had run the household for years on their own and have developed their own way of doing things. Instructing or commenting on her style is not only an intrusion on her space but can also undermine her sense of competence, and this is likely to lead to anger or resentment. For their part, wives in this predicament should try to understand that their newly retired husbands have only just surrendered a role of responsibility, and that role may still be in their mind-set—in other words, they can't help themselves. Talking out the problem as soon as it becomes noticeable would be helpful for avoiding such problems.

• *14* •

How We See Ourselves

Happiness is when what you think, what you say, and what you
do are in harmony.

—Mohandas K. Gandhi

*W*e've seen the importance of roles as a recurring theme throughout this
book, and this chapter is intended to focus on them in some detail. People use
various roles—more than one at a time—to define themselves. Roles come
from their involvement with career, family, friends, religious organizations,
and the like throughout their lives. Roles give us the identities that connect
us to other people and to groups or organizations; each role we take on has a
specific set of benefits and responsibilities connected to it.

Roles are neither rigid nor permanent. Different roles can have varying
importance for different people and can also vary in importance at different
times in a person's life. To cite an obvious example, the role of parent is
dominant for most people when their children are young but often changes as
their children become adults. The dominance of the parental role versus other
roles can diminish, and the nature of the parental role can morph from raising
a child to more of a unique variety of adult friendship.

As we've noted, one of the more dominant roles throughout adulthood
is that of the worker. It's almost inevitable that this role should be firmly embedded in our psyche if for no other reason than the sheer number of years
it's held. But it is also unquestionably a useful role. The worker identity, in
conjunction with other identities, helps people develop a sense of self-worth
and feelings of connectedness to a group and keeps them focused on worker
responsibilities. Its presence is reinforced by the positive experiences obtained
on the job, such as a sense of being productive, easy access to enjoyable social
experiences, and the like.

That's the primary identity that people take into retirement. With so many responsibilities and so much history, the worker role is too deeply ingrained to be switched off the day someone retires. Rather, is almost certain to remain a key part of one's self-definition.[1]

That said, though, the strength of the worker role can vary depending on how an employee feels about his or her job and the extent to which he or she finds it personally rewarding. The more satisfying or ego gratifying one's job, the more one will use one's worker role as the primary or even sole means of self-definition. In the chapter on occupational background, we noted that professionals and white-collar employees tend to have very strong identity bonds with their occupations because their jobs often are a boost to their self-esteem.[2] On the other hand, employees whose jobs are tedious, routine, or unrewarding are less likely to establish strong emotional connections to those jobs and so are less likely to singularly define themselves by their occupation.

But again, roles are neither rigid nor permanent, and regardless of one's past job, the worker identity weakens over time. For those who have already retired, this is a slow decay as they move further away from their careers. But there is evidence that the breakaway process actually begins for many adults even before retirement. Research suggests that at some point in middle age, adults start to loosen their ties to their careers and their worker identity diminishes. As they do so, people gradually come to define themselves more by the new roles they occupy.

In one important way, the fact that most people can't immediately switch off the worker role when they retire is a good thing. Holding on to the worker identity in the early stages of retirement is psychologically healthy because it helps combat feelings of "rolelessness." Retirees can use their worker identity to help get their bearings, providing a self-identity reference point until they become adjusted to their new lifestyle.[3]

But keep in mind they are also holding on to other roles while they are still thinking of themselves in terms of what they used to do for a living. These other roles, such as friend or parent, provide continuity as they make the switch from working to retirement. Dropping the worker role immediately, even if it could be done, would be a mistake: those who are able to do so would walk into retirement with a radically diminished sense of who they are, without a basis for self-esteem. A major psychological disruption like that could result not only in a loss of personal identity but also in a diminished sense of control over one's life, and this would work 'against one's subjective well-being.

So it's not about "switching off" the worker identity; instead, retirement is a catalyst for a gradual self-definition makeover. When people leave their jobs, work-related issues are no longer relevant to their new lifestyle. The changeover can be a slow process, particularly for those who had strong emotional connections to their careers. For some, the change in identity can take longer than they might wish, and for others their worker identity may stay with them indefinitely. Many of us have known retired people who, despite many years outside the workforce, still define themselves in terms of their careers; they are often incapable of holding a conversation without mentioning their former roles somewhere along the way.

If retirees don't eventually replace their worker identities, it's probably because they have not found a role that provides them with the same benefits they once got from their jobs. For example, if one's job was prestigious, it might be hard to find another role in retirement that feeds his or her self-esteem as well as the job did. If the worker identity retains too much prominence, chances are it will interfere with a retiree's ability to transition. They can run into problems adopting their new lifestyle. Their lack of enthusiasm and commitment may inhibit their ability to develop new interests which are personally meaningful. Without new activities, they have fewer ways of maintaining their sense of productivity and self-worth.

Retirees who have not adequately adopted their retirement role may also feel out of place socially. They may experience difficulties relating to their peers who have adopted other roles or be unable to reap the emotional rewards from other roles because they are not absorbed in them. In essence, these retirees can become caught between two worlds, no longer a member of one but not committed to or absorbed by the other. The result is a sense of disconnectedness and alienation, and that can lead to weakened subjective well-being.[4]

Rob discovered how much he defined himself by his career and how disruptive that role was in acclimating to retirement:

> I always knew that how I looked at myself was almost entirely wrapped up in what I did for a living. I become particularly aware of this when, on meeting new people, I always found a way early on in the conversation to find out what kind of job they had. By knowing their occupation, I felt I could understand who that person was and whether or not I could relate to him or her. This is not to say I liked or disliked a person based on his job, but it was my way of looking for common ground and finding a basis for conversation. Even to this day, the first thing I ask people I know is how work is going. At least now I try to catch myself and move the conversation away from work.
>
> When I gave up my position and retired, my self-image as a business owner and market researcher was so much a part of me that I had really had no other way of seeing myself. I'm sure this was obvious and a source of annoyance to my partners who were still working and running the company.

Whenever I tried to have conversations with them that revolved around work, I sensed their hesitancy to discuss business issues too deeply with me and a resistance to my comments or recommendations.

For my part, I tended to resent what I perceived to be their indifference, thinking that all I was trying to do was help. On their part, they were simply holding on to their turf, letting me know the company was now their responsibility. This was all very subtle—I just didn't consciously realize what was really happening. I still wanted to feel I was head of the company, and I had not started to look at myself in terms of my present circumstances, that is, as a retiree. I just had not found anything so meaningful to me that it could replace the sense of value and purpose I had while running my company. Coming to this realization was important—while I still don't have a well-developed retiree role, I also know I cannot continue to hold on to my former role. Well, at least it's a start.

Charlie had a similar all-pervading reliance on his role as police chief and talked about his struggles in trying to change how he defined himself. Rob and Charlie held positions of some prestige, and as such both viewed their careers as ego gratifying. And as with Rob, Charlie felt that his career identity interfered with his ability to occupy other roles in retirement. But making a role change was uniquely difficult for Charlie because people in his town knew him as "Chief." Each time people addressed him this way, the role was constantly being reinforced, which in turn forced Charlie to retain it. Eventually, he found the only way to achieve his redefinition was to build connections with people and organizations that were not tied to his work history:

Looking back, I have to say that I enjoyed my position of authority. Being a police chief is an important role in any town. People came to me for help, and I always did what I could for them. I took all their problems seriously. I felt like Don Corleone in the scene when he was in his office at his daughter's wedding. I know that sounds arrogant, but I always humbly assisted anyone who needed my help. I always told my officers that people in need should get the same treatment as if they were family.

With that kind of power and prestige given to me, I was always the police chief, and I seldom came out of that role. All my experiences related in some way or another to my job. Somewhere in here, I have to point out that being a father was very important to me. I always had very strong feelings about that, and my kids were always there on my mind. But *I was the chief!* That mattered to me more than anything else.

As rewarding as it was, I would never want to return to my job even if I could. I have come a long way in retirement, and going back I would eventually have to retire all over again—*no way*. But even though I no longer have that job, I had a hard time escaping from seeing myself as something else. Even today, 10 years into retirement, anything I do, organizations I join, or people I meet on the street address me as "Chief."

The only way to get away from that to some degree was to be with those who knew me before my job or be around people who don't know me at all. I am always invited to social functions out of respect for who I was, but I tend to avoid them because they make me feel uncomfortable. In some ways, I have become withdrawn, and I don't go to any function that is police related—if it were something I would have done as the chief, I run and hide.

I had to find my worth and self-esteem as Charlie again. I am almost there after 10 years, and I feel good being Charlie most of the time. But there really should be some kind of exorcism you can go through right after you retire.

Earlier we mentioned that men and women relate differently to their careers from an emotional perspective. As a general rule, women tend to be more socially integrated and to occupy multiple roles, even while they are working—mother, homemaker, and so on. They tend not to rely on their jobs as a means of defining themselves to the singular degree that many men do. Because many women have weaker emotional reliance on their worker roles, they often can enter retirement with less of a "roleless" problem and with a greater degree of continuity in their daily lives. So at least from the perspective of self-definition, women might have an easier time moving forward when they exit the workforce. Jeanette provides a fairly typical example of how women tend to view themselves in and out of their jobs. While she obviously took a lot of pride in her work as a special education teacher, Jeanette did not leave that role with much regret. We should mention here that Jeanette is married to Charlie, and it is interesting that two people sharing a life together have such completely different experiences of how their careers impact their self-perceptions:

My 32-year career as a special education high school teacher is one role in my life that I am especially proud of. Although this may sound like a cliché, I know I made a difference in the lives of many of my students. My strong relationship with parents, the community, administration, and fellow colleagues gave me deep pride. My job was always very high on my list of priorities, and I demanded excellence of myself in the classroom.

Did I define myself as a teacher? Yes, of course I did. Today, when asked what I did for a living, I proudly state that I was a teacher. I am proud of the success I accomplished with my students and appreciated the many thanks that came with that success.

But when I retired, I did not let the title of teacher define me. I knew I wore many hats—I was first and foremost a mom to my incredible daughter. I knew this time would be our time where I could slow down from my hectic schedule and savor each and every moment of our lives together. I am a wife who wants to enjoy all the things I ever dreamed of enjoying with my husband—a lunch along the shore, a house project, visits with old friends and travel to places I never thought I would! I am a daughter of an 88-year-old mom who is in phenomenal health and I'm now able to see her more often and spoil her as much as I can. I am a devoted sister and a good friend to wonderful people who have been in my life for over 30 years. My roles are many—an aunt who adores her nieces and nephew, a cousin who loves her family, and a neighbor who is willing to help.

I find it difficult to say that I felt a loss of the teacher role when I retired because I am able to apply that role in my relationships outside the classroom, in other ways. I will always be a teacher, but now that role is defined in a different way. Endearing grandchildren look to me to teach them new and exciting things. As a mother, the role of teaching never ends. Just the other day, an extremely concerned grandmother of a special needs child asked for my professional opinion as to how she could best help her grandchild. Living in a small community, I often run into students who update me on their careers and families. Former students phone me, ask for my personal advice, and stay in touch with me. I am even teaching my husband to dump the garbage and empty the dishwasher! In all seriousness, when I retired, I never looked back. I had many personal reasons to say good-bye to a phenomenal career. What the future holds, I am very much looking forward to.

Keep in mind that this is a general observation, not a universal one. As we have mentioned before, many women are just as wrapped up in their jobs as men and just as reliant as men on their careers as a way to define themselves as people. Anne, the retired educator, is a clear case in point. Her story about the difficulties she faced in adjusting to retirement had much to do with losing a prestigious job. But the point still holds that women tend to be more socially integrated in general and as a result have more roles they occupy at any one time than men. Many women could, therefore, have an easier time walking into retirement.

In any event, for men and women, the perspective that the worker role could interfere with retirement adjustment seems to make sense. We explored this issue in our own research, asking retirees about the relative importance of various roles they use to define themselves, such as parent, friend, club member, employee, and so on. We also looked into whether the importance of the worker role changes with more time in retirement.

Consistent with the findings of other social scientists, we found that the worker identity is a key element in many retirees' self-definitions. However, we were somewhat surprised as to how fast this role weakens. Like the new car that loses half its value as soon as it leaves the showroom, it appears that reliance on the worker role diminishes almost immediately on leaving the workforce. For example, about 85% of those still in the workforce rank their worker role in the top three of all roles they occupy, but that percentage drops to 71% for retirees well within their first year of retiring. In fact, as soon as retirees leave work, that role drops to third in importance, behind being a parent and a friend. As a point of comparison, those still working rank their worker role equal in importance to any other role they hold.

But although the worker role may not stay at the very top of the list, we did find that it stays at relatively high levels for quite a long while. Indeed, it never disappears completely, and years into retirement there is still a good deal of reliance on that role as a means of self-definition. For example, as we mentioned, once out of the workforce, 71% of all retirees rank this role in the top three of all their roles, but this only drops to 59% for those who are retired 10 years or more.

Some of our other findings were similar to that of other researchers. For example, women were found to be less dependent on their worker roles than men. Roles such as parent, friend, or church member hold much more prominence for women, and these roles seem to help them make a faster adjustment—39% of women who are retired less than two years say they are completely adjusted as compared with only 23% of men. While men eventually catch up, their stronger dependence on their worker identity is likely to slow their adjustment right out of the gate.

Additionally, we also found some retirees are more dependent on their worker identity than others. As other researchers have pointed out, the more rewarding the job, the more employees will rely on its role for their self-definition. White-collar and prestigious positions tend to be in this category. But the question remains—do retirees who relied heavily on their careers for their personal identities have a harder time adjusting?

On this point our results were somewhat surprising. We found retirees whose self-definition is derived from their careers have few problems adjusting to retirement. And whatever difficulties they ran into, they largely go away after a few years. Here are a few examples:

- Among those who define themselves by their work, 27% claim to be well adjusted to retirement in their first two years, only slightly below the 31% among those who depend less on their worker roles. After six or more years in retirement, 57% of retirees who are defined by their worker roles say they are well adjusted, just slightly above the 54% of those who depend less on these roles.
- In their first two years, 74% of career-oriented retirees are happy they're retired, below the 81% we found for their counterparts. But by the third year of retirement, the two groups are equally happy in retirement. Similarly, only 14% of those who rely on their worker

identities describe their adjustment as easy compared to 22% who rely more on other identities; but again, by their fourth year, ratings on ease of adjusting are the same for the two.

That's how they feel about being retired. When it comes to how they feel *about themselves*, those who are more reliant on their worker role are just as self-confident, active, socially connected, goal directed, optimistic about the future, and in control of their destiny as those who rely primarily on other roles. As such, holding on to the worker role did not detract from their subjective well-being, even if it does slow retirement adjustment a bit.

At first blush, this seems counterintuitive—and at odds with existing research. But a closer inspection shows that for many of these retirees, other factors may have come into play, including characteristics about the type of people they are and the resources available to them. And these could help them adjust to retirement and overcome any problems that would be caused by their slower breakaway from their worker identity.

But there turns out to be a compelling reason why these retirees avoid adjustment problems. They have a sort of smoke and mirrors way of coping with retirement: they keep working! Roughly 34% hold a job as compared to only 21% who rely less on careers for defining themselves. And they are especially likely to work early on in retirement—43% of those retired less than two years are working.

In some ways, this sounds like cheating: they are okay in retirement because they really aren't completely retired. In fact, they may be more tied to their worker identity because they are still working. Whatever the reason, they don't find retirement to be as interesting as their jobs were. As a positive, they recognize that retirement isn't cutting it for them, so they find a way to make their lives better. And they work for the right reasons—social contact, feel productive, and feel good about themselves—and not primarily for money or because they are bored.

But this is a two-edged sword. On the one hand, they reap the psychological and social benefits that jobs can provide. They in fact have closer emotional ties to their coworkers and maintain these relationships longer in retirement. In the short term, this gives them an expanded social life, helping them feel socially connected. On the other hand, working reinforces their already strong worker roles, and this may make it more difficult to become absorbed into the retirement world in the long term.

But they are not the only socially vulnerable group. Retirees who are not career oriented may also run into difficulties—they tend to become more and more dependent on family, especially their children, as they go further into retirement. As we pointed out in a previous chapter, a social life without a balance of family and friends can lead to feelings of isolation and disconnectedness over time, just as will staying too connected to coworker friends.

In view of all this, at this point we weren't sure whether overreliance on one's worker role hurts adjustment. For a more definitive answer, we divided retirees who defined themselves by their careers into two groups—those who are working versus those not working. We found those who are not working are doing quite well as retirees—53% say they are completely adjusted as compared to only 32% of working retirees. These nonworking retirees also felt the adjustment process was easy and are much happier in retirement. From these results, it's not as simple as just saying that the worker self-definition interferes with adjustment. Rather, it depends on the individual—some have no problems in retirement, while others find it difficult. As we mentioned, those who have difficulties fix the problem by getting a job. In the short term, this eases their transition, but in the long term, it just prolongs the inevitable.

Considering all of the above, we would conclude that it's probably in the best interests of retirees to lessen their dependence on their worker role. While some retirees might not find the role too disruptive, others may find it problematic. In any event, sooner or later all retirees will need to come to terms with the fact that such a role is not relevant and must be discarded.

In this regard and as a potential first step, take a good honest look at yourself and how important your career is to your self-definition. If being a worker is predominant, make the admission that you are no longer a worker. You won't be able to drop the role immediately, but be vigilant as to how much it pervades your life, and when you feel it emerges too strongly, try to focus your attention on other roles you occupy.

Remember that you can't discard the worker role without replacing it with other roles. As we have mentioned throughout, it's worthwhile for retirees to increase their involvement with non–work-related activities or environments or strengthen relationships with people outside the workforce. However, for a redefinition to truly take place, there must be some perceived personal value to these new activities and relationships. Retirees have to search continuously for things that can be personally meaningful outside of work. Throughout this exploration, it's important to acknowledge the sometimes painful truth that it may be difficult to find a replacement role as rewarding as a career. To minimize the pain of this common reality, focus on the positives of these new activities or relationships on their own terms rather than trying to make a direct comparison to a career.

If retirees feel a bridge job is their best option for a more comfortable retirement, this should not be seen as an escape from the need to switch roles. It's more of a delaying action. There will come a time when many coworker relationships will end as friends stop working and those with bridge jobs will eventually no longer be able to work. At that point, those who have continued to rely too much on their worker identity may be ill prepared for a "full retirement" (i.e., no bridge job at all). While the worker role will probably grow weaker on its own, just through the passage of time, this can take years. Rather than wait for time to do its healing thing, it is recommended that retirees put some focused effort to change their self-definition to other nonworker roles.

· *15* ·

The Good and Bad in Each of Us

I enjoy waking up and not having to go to work. So I do it three
or four times a day.

—Gene Perret

*S*ome people handle things better than others. They have a particular blend
of personality characteristics that helps them cope with change. Some of these
traits can be very useful in handling a variety of situations, and some are particularly suited for coping with life stage changes and other catastrophic events.[1]

By now, most of these traits will be familiar to you, as we have referred
to each of them repeatedly as elements that work either for or against the
transition process. In this chapter, we're going to explore these characteristics
in more detail, how they may be helpful during the retirement adjustment
process, and how to make the best use of whichever of these traits you happen to possess. We'll also look at the traits that can hinder one's transition to
retirement and how retirees can work around them to improve their odds of
success.

Some of the characteristics we're talking about are inherent in a person's
makeup and are not readily learned or eliminated. Those who possess the good
traits may have an advantage in transitioning to retirement, and those with
the bad traits might seem likely to struggle or fail. But of course it's not that
cut and dried. Lacking the desirable personality characteristics does not auto-
matically lead to failure, nor does having the good ones necessarily produce a
smooth transition. They represent one more piece of the adjustment puzzle,
along with the other factors we discussed in earlier chapters. They can either
help or hinder but offer no guarantees in either direction.

We'll begin with traits that can work against an easy adjustment. Researchers have found that people who are easily stressed, who are introverted,

and who are not conscientious (i.e., are not deliberate and well organized) are more likely to have problems making the transition to retirement.[2]

High stress can be debilitating. Not only can it impair one's physical health, but it can affect one's mood and mental outlook and inhibit the ability to focus and make decisions. Retirees with low stress thresholds can have a hard time dealing with a life stage transition as dramatic as retirement, especially in the initial stages when they first feel that loss of continuity.

Our survey clearly showed the same results. High stress retirees, representing about one-quarter of our sample, describe themselves as chronically tense and worried. They have serious problems with self-confidence and have bouts of depression and sleeplessness—32% of these retirees are taking antidepressant medication compared to only 12% among those with low stress levels. Most important, they have a very hard time coping with change—a major concern for a person ending one life stage and beginning another.

With such a profile, it's no surprise they have trouble with retirement—only 34% of high-stress retirees say they are completely adjusted as compared to 57% with low stress. In fact, high-stress retirees seem to reject the retirement lifestyle; they miss their jobs and wish they were back at work. However, the work environment is not likely to be their salvation—reducing stress was one of the primary reasons they retired in the first place. The stress experienced by this group—or, more accurately, their reaction to it—has put them in an intractable "damned if you do and damned if you don't" dilemma.

In truth, they seem trapped and maybe a little housebound. Their emotional baggage can also include low motivation levels, possibly brought on by pessimism, inadequate decision-making skills, and a sense they are not in control of their lives. As a result, they are much less active, preferring instead to just relax around the house. But that's not working for them—they know they spend too much time doing nothing and wish they could find activities that interest them. And while they haven't been successful, they know it's partially their own fault—high-stress retirees acknowledge they don't put enough effort into finding activities of interest. Yet, possibly because the unknown can raise their stress levels, they are not open to new experiences, so they have little opportunity to find new activities. And they have problems socially—they have fewer friends in and out of the workforce and are less emotionally connected with both friends and family members. For that reason, they experience more loneliness and isolation and feel their social lives are extremely unsatisfying.

Despite all their issues, it's not as hopeless as it sounds. Retirees who have problems managing stress might make things easier on themselves by preparing for retirement while still in the workforce. In fact, our survey showed that high-stress retirees are much less likely to plan their retirement than are low-stress retirees. Planning is a good idea for anyone, but it's particularly important for poor stress managers since it allows them to take on the role of retiree vicariously, before they have to live it. Mentally, they will get used to the idea of the lifestyle change they will be facing, and this may make it lose some of its disconcerting newness. With the right approach and effort, these retirees can reinsert some direction and purpose into their lives.

Their preparation has some essential pieces. For one, they need to be aware of the importance of a social life and focus on maintaining their relationships in and out of the workforce. These provide emotional support, help eliminate feelings of isolation and disconnectedness, and, most important, provide continuity from work to retirement. Second, in making plans for what to do, the details are critical. Having just a general idea of how they will spend their time would not work for high-stress retirees. If their plans include the specific steps, they can take some of the guesswork out of day-to-day living. Establishing routines also works in this regard, so they might consider keeping a "to do" calendar, showing their schedule of activities and events—this will force structure and purpose into their lifestyle.

Moving on to another incapacitating trait, the difficulties faced by introverted people obviously focus on social issues. When retirees leave the workforce, they lose the associated friendships and social connections as well as membership in a group that has work as its collective purpose. That sums up their problem—retirees who are introverted enter a world where new relationships must be developed and membership in alternative groups outside of work must be sought.

About 25% of retirees in our survey describe themselves as introverts, who prefer to avoid social interaction and the company of others. Most of their time is spent around the home and rarely includes other people, and that leaves them feeling especially disconnected and isolated. Generally, though, they don't seem to have many interests (even solitary ones), tending to find most activities personally unrewarding. And, while they're not really sure what to do with all their free time, they're also not interested in finding things to do. But this is not a new pattern for them—they weren't very much in love with their jobs either.

Predictably, they have a very small social circle and are much less emotionally connected to their friends and family members. Not that they don't see this as a problem—they find their social lives extremely unrewarding and believe they have gotten worse since retiring. However, as they are not motivated to meet new people, they have little means of getting out of their predicament. Unfortunately, they are also less likely to be married. In theory, at least, marriage could be a way to alleviate their loneliness or a means of building social contacts. But introverts just don't work that way—those who *are* married tend to have unhappy relationships, to the point where they prefer time away from their partners.

Retirement is not working out well for many of these folks and certainly not as well as they hoped—in fact, their expectations about retirement were as positive as other retirees while they were still in the workforce. But reality fell well short of their expectations, reflected in how they feel in retirement—only 39% of introverts feel they have adjusted well as compared to 53% of extroverts; other measures of subjective well-being, such as overall happiness and perceived quality of life, show the same pattern: much lower ratings than for other retirees.

Recommendations for introverted retirees are hard to come by since they have to focus on greater social involvement—something they prefer to avoid. Nevertheless, their admission that their social lives are lacking suggests they are at least aware that improvements are needed. On the other hand, they may not be aware of the importance of social interaction to their overall subjective well-being, and if that's the case, our recommendations have to start with that point.

While we would further suggest that introverts consider activities that have a social component, they may lack the wherewithal or motivation to seek these out on their own. But taking a job is an option—at the minimum, working practically forces you to meet people. Fortunately, these retirees are not averse to working—about a quarter hold a job, similar to the levels of other retirees, and they like their job as much as other retirees. However, they don't seek work's social benefits, which should be their primary reason for working. As such, a change in perspective toward a stronger focus on coworker friendships should be considered.

Another option for introverted retirees can include finding organizations that focus on their specific interests. Getting involved in these organizations may be an easier task since it's based on their interests rather than on meeting people, but shared interests still provide a ready-made basis for striking up friendships. If they are not interested in making new friends even in such environments, then at least they will have placed themselves outside of their homes, and this alone will provide some social benefits.

Finally, they certainly can get more involved with their already existing friendships and family relationships. Or they might consider using the various Internet services that are available to track down old friends they might have lost touch with over the years, those with whom a relationship might have been particularly meaningful or comfortable. Obviously, any change won't be easy—they're introverts, after all—but there's little question that they could benefit greatly from even a moderate increase in their social involvement.

Turning to a third trait, retirees who are not actively conscientious face problems stemming from inadequate planning. These retirees, about 15% to 20% of our sample, describe themselves as somewhat unfocused and disorganized and lacking in deliberateness to their actions—in effect, they are procrastinators. Consequently, it's no great shock to find they were much less likely to plan their retirement, especially in terms of the key issues of their social lives and how they would use their leisure time.

A look at their work backgrounds reveals their jobs were less flexible and offered fewer opportunities for problem solving, skills that are needed for focusing efforts and achieving goals. That being said, they are not at all goal oriented. As far as their other characteristics, they share many with high-stress retirees and introverts—the unconscientious are less active and more home based, are less socially involved and committed, and view their leisure time as unrewarding, certainly not as satisfying as their jobs were.

The fact is they don't enjoy retirement; they miss their jobs and feel the quality of their lives has declined since they left their jobs. Getting accustomed to the lifestyle has been difficult—only 23% describe themselves as well adjusted as compared to 44% for retirees in general. Their biggest problems, as they see them, revolve around not having enough direction in their day-to-day living or enough goals to pursue. With such discontent, they tend to have lower self-esteem and feel unproductive. And, as so often happens, these emotional states are accompanied by feelings of stress, pessimism, and lack of energy.

A recommendation for these retirees must begin and end with plan, plan, and plan some more. These are not the type of people who can easily wing it. However, such a proposition is tricky and at worst may be doomed from the start. Suggesting they plan and establish goals for retirement amounts to telling someone who isn't conscientious that they should be—not terribly helpful.

However, all is not lost. These retirees should first recognize that their approach to retirement is not helping them. At that point, if they can also admit that they lack the drive and organizational skills to plan well on their own, they can consider some outside assistance. This is not an attempt to be flip; rather, we want to point out that retirees who lack conscientiousness must realize that they need to work around this characteristic. One way around it may be to find some help. They can, for example, talk to other retirees or search retiree websites or blogs about activities or social events. In other words, use the resources around them to come up with ideas that might lead to a better retirement and subjective well-being.

Our focus will now turn to the personality traits that can help smooth the transition into retirement (and along the way, we'll look at what happens to those lacking these characteristics, too). People who are energetic, goal directed, self-confident, and open minded can have an easier time navigating retirement's obstacles and building a lifestyle that is fulfilling and enjoyable.[3] Again, we've touched on many of these already because they are typically part of the makeup of well-adjusted retirees.

Our research suggests these traits are often a package deal, meaning those who possess one generally possess all or most of the others. This is understandable since emotional and psychological states can feed off each other—for example, goal-oriented retirees are confident because pursuing goals gives direction to their lives, allowing them to feel good about themselves and so on.

We also found that retirees with these personality traits have similar backgrounds and a common approach to living. For example, they are more likely to feel in control of their lives and have the wherewithal to deal with issues as they arise, and that allows them to keep moving in a positive direction. They held higher-paying and more prestigious positions at work, and these jobs taught them (or took advantage of) some of the skills that help them be successful in other aspects of living, such as problem solving and constantly facing new challenges.

While they enjoyed their jobs, they are not overly dependent on their worker roles for their self-identity, and they don't miss being in the workforce—in truth, they retired by their own choice, very often to pursue their own interests. There is the sense from these retirees that working was fine when it was the primary element in their lives, but that role is no longer quite as relevant, and retirement is their time to move on. Nevertheless, roughly 3 in 10 hold a job—a higher percentage than for other retiree segments. But more than others, they do it for psychologically beneficial reasons, to feel productive and reap the social benefits.

Not that they need much help in the social sphere. These retirees have more friends, spend many more hours in their company, and have stronger emotional ties to those in their circle than other retirees. Understandably, they find their social lives very rewarding as they are, yet they are still much more interested in meeting new people, which their lifestyle allows for. Importantly, they are also less dependent on their children and other family members, looking more instead to their friends both in and out of the workforce for social contact. As a result, they are more likely to feel connected to and involved in the outside world and less subject to isolation and loneliness.

Another important characteristic of these retirees is that they embrace the retirement lifestyle. They use their time to pursue personal interests and have little desire for rest and relaxation. They feel a sense of rejuvenation in retirement and are highly motivated to travel down new paths and take on new goals. Despite having a full plate, they have the combination of openness to new experiences and willingness to seek them out—they still are constantly on the lookout for new worlds to conquer. We also found these retirees tend to have solid marriages. Good relationships can contribute to success in all areas of life.

With their proactive approach, these retirees believe, more so than other retirees, that their quality of life has actually improved after leaving the workforce. Their adjustment ratings reflect their contentment—for those possessing one or more of these beneficial psychological features, approximately 6 in 10 are completely adjusted; in contrast, less than 40% of those who do not have any of these psychological traits feel that comfortable in retirement. Interestingly, those with the right psychological underpinnings also claim to have had very high expectations about what it would be like to be retired—and were more likely to feel their expectations were satisfied. In all likelihood, this is a result of the efforts they made to build an enjoyable way of living: they are very good at dictating their own destinies.

Along with their common elements, each of these positive traits has some unique associated features. For example, energetic retirees, as the name suggests, are highly active; they act with speed and energy.[4] They tend to bring a lot of passion to whatever catches their attention, continually creating new roles for themselves. They put a lot of effort into planning and are good at achieving their goals. And they plan well—they are more likely to pay attention to elements often missed by other, less successful retirees, such as their social lives and finding activities of interest. Retirees with this trait are also excellent at coping with change and are more likely to experiment and explore the variety of options available to them to meet their personal needs and goals.

Highly energetic retirees don't need assistance in getting to a successful retirement. But what are the options for low-energy retirees? To come up with some recommendations, we took a look at their weaknesses relative to energetic counterparts. We worked from the perspective that low energy can result from other psychological issues. We found that, in comparison to those who are energetic, low-energy retirees have much weaker self-esteem, are much less optimistic about their futures, feel unproductive, and can't find ways to spend their time meaningfully. All of these, and particularly not knowing what to do with one's time, can be demotivating. It's easy from there to feel one's energy level is drained.

It's important to realize that low-energy retirees hold two perspectives that might be at the heart of their other emotional issues. They tend to view retirement as a time to relax and do nothing, and they are not very open to new experiences. Such attitudes are inappropriate for retirement and in fact are the reverse of the thought processes required for rebuilding one's life. If we are to venture an opinion, it's possible these retirees are not aware their quest for inactivity can lead to lowered self-esteem and feelings of unproductivity, and that can leave them discontented in retirement. The obvious solution is to drop the relax/do nothing viewpoint and go on a search for pastimes of personal interest. All the while they must also try to keep an open mind since the unexpected can be surprising in its ability to make life enjoyable.

Moving next to the subject of self-esteem, retirees who are self-confident believe they can take on most problems with a good chance of success. They tend to view retirement as a challenge, feeling that they can overcome any difficulties involved in the transition. Their self-assurance makes them better equipped to create and organize new opportunities for themselves and to implement a course of action that gives them a pretty good chance of meeting their goals.[5] Additionally, highly confident people approach the world with a positive attitude, and with that they expect retirement to be a rewarding experience—or they would make it so. An interesting distinction for these retirees versus other successful segments is their lack of planning. However, this is one group for whom plans were not required—they have an innate ability to wing it and a can-do attitude that lets them achieve what they set out to do.

For those on the low-self-esteem side of the spectrum, boosts in self-esteem can lead to enhanced subjective well-being and hopefully yield the mind-set needed to make retirement a more positive experience. The tough question is how to get there. They might begin by taking a good honest look at themselves, recalling their accomplishments throughout their lives. For example, you worked once, you might have raised a family, you survived some tough times, or people depended on you and you came through. You might not be working now, but you can still give yourself a lot of credit.

If that doesn't get you there, then keep in mind that nothing feels quite as good as success. Your goal should be to seek out opportunities to achieve that outcome. Activities that can lead to feelings of being productive or a member of a group might be effective in this regard. Another approach focuses on strengthening your social role, including stronger emotional ties to those in your existing social circle, or expanding that circle by joining various clubs and organizations. Acceptance by others can go a long way in making us feel good about ourselves.

Two more "good" traits are more appropriately described as mental strategies and have been found by researchers to help in the retirement transition: open-mindedness and goal directedness. Some retirees possess these traits in their arsenal of everyday coping mechanisms; that is, it is their nature to be goal directed or open minded. But these are also skills that can be learned, at least to some extent, with sufficient effort and mental discipline—so all is not lost for those who aren't goal directed or open minded as a basic part of who they are.

Psychologists characterize keeping an open mind—the willingness to consider new ideas, values, feelings, and experiences—as an adaptive trait. It is one of a number of characteristics that help us cope with day-to-day events and achieve enjoyment in life. Adaptive traits are important because they help people achieve their personal goals and fulfill their basic psychological needs. For retirees, adaptive traits contribute to their ability to handle not only the changes that come up as one adjusts to retirement but also the physical and social challenges that are tied to aging in general.[6]

The advantages of open-mindedness are linked to flexibility—the ability to roll with the punches. Open-minded people are not locked into an unbending set of beliefs and values and don't see themselves as having a strict set of rules to live by. People who are open to new experiences have been found to adjust more quickly and effectively to changes in their environment.[7] They are better able to revise their attitudes and behaviors in the face of new ideas or situations, and this is obviously a huge benefit for retirees as they go through the process of building a new life. Although they were below average in planning their retirement, they are still highly goal oriented, and with their adaptability and goal directedness, up-front planning was probably not as essential for them—actually, they are probably the rare type who is better off *without* the structure of planning, as it is easier for them to study a situation and make adjustments from there.

There is another key aspect to this trait—open-minded people do more than just roll with the punches; they seem to *benefit* from new experiences and actually enjoy bringing change into their lives. Research suggests that these people have a deep-seated need to build up their set of experiences as a means of enhancing their personal growth and development. They seem to relish the idea of reinventing themselves.

With their tendency to take advantage of new opportunities and their desire to be enriched through experimenting, retirees who maintain openness are likely to pursue new hobbies, get involved in new activities, and entertain new ideas and ways of thinking. They also show a tendency to become involved in activities that help them maintain their physical and mental health and level of functioning. These help improve their overall life satisfaction, and that lets them get the most out of retirement.

In contrast, those who are more closed minded can have a hard time adjusting to retirement as they would to any lifestyle change. All retirees face the elimination or at least radical shrinkage of the structure and patterns that once directed their lives. Since closed-minded people tend to rely primarily on established habits and patterns, it is easy to see how they might have difficulty creating a new lifestyle that requires experimentation and a consideration of the broad variety of things to do that might be outside their comfort zone.

Beyond their unwillingness to experiment, closed-minded retirees approach retirement in a way that cannot possibly help them. When we compare their attitudes to those of other retirees, closed-minded retirees are one of the weakest segments in preretirement planning. Because they are unwilling or unable to adjust on the fly, up-front planning is more critical for these retirees than for others. Furthermore, with their difficulty coping with change, walking into an unstructured world without a prespecified course of action would be especially challenging for these retirees. They may be much better off in dealing with retirement's lifestyle change if they can anticipate and prepare for it.

Along with better planning, our first recommendation would be to try to open up at least a little. Consider things you haven't in the past. For example, if you don't know how to dance, take some dance lessons; you might find it more fun than you thought. For these retirees, we know this is a long shot, but if they can try one new thing, they might find they're more open to other new things. (Provided, of course, their new experience was a good one; if not, then there's an equal likelihood they will walk away feeling even more committed to things they already know.) And for those who won't consider new ideas or activities in their plans, still there may be enough old, familiar activities that they can pursue—hobbies or personal interests from their youth they might have dropped after taking on other responsibilities.

Turning now to goal directedness, this is defined as the propensity to set personal goals and to use these goals to direct one's behaviors. The value of this characteristic in creating a sense of well-being and life satisfaction for retirees cannot be overstated and has already been discussed in detail. But just to review, the beneficial features of goal setting represent one of the most consistent findings in the field of psychology. In fact, social scientists point out that goal directedness and its tendency to guide people to add purpose to their lives is a critical element for adjustment in *all* life stages.[8]

Researchers have found that goal-directed people have a number of corollary attitudes and behaviors that are extremely helpful in transitioning to retirement. For example, they tend to use time in a personally meaningful manner and continuously make plans for their futures. Additionally, goal-oriented people tend to be more energetic and optimistic and retain a more positive attitude in retirement. Their positive energy helps them stay motivated to achieve their personal aims.

Goal-directed retirees are the epitome of planners, entering this life stage with a precise course of action in place. But even if they had not developed plans prior to retirement, by nature they could be expected to do so when they get there. Furthermore, through their self-initiative, resourcefulness, and persistence, these retirees are not likely to give up if a chosen path does not yield the results they wanted. Rather, they will just change their direction as often as they need to until a desired outcome is achieved. These people feel in control of their lives, and that is linked to better adjustment and subjective well-being.[9]

In contrast, those who don't set personal goals for themselves can lack a sense of direction to their lives, and that can leave them feeling unsure about their futures and unadjusted in retirement.[10] Without a sense of direction, it's hard to feel one's life has purpose, and that may be one reason why these retirees tend to be more pessimistic, more withdrawn, more anxious, and more cautious.

Retirees who are not goal oriented by nature are not likely to develop this trait at this stage of their lives. Nevertheless, they can still achieve the benefits associated with goal directedness simply by focusing on a plan of action. In other words, they identify things to make their day-to-day living meaningful, come up with a specific step by step process for putting these elements in place, and then actually carry out those plans. And if at first these elements are not as useful as they were thought to be, it pays to remember that it's almost impossible to get it completely right the first time, so experiment with other ideas and keep moving forward.

We've painted a rosy retirement picture for those who have the right psychological stuff. Indeed, when we looked at the psychological profiles of those who are well adjusted, their major psychological strengths over the less well adjusted include the elements we have been discussing—they have much greater self-confidence, energy levels, and goal directedness and much lower stress levels.

So, if you have the right stuff, successful retirement must be a lock, right? Not so fast. Our study showed us that retirees who have the aforementioned characteristics are in fact not perfect in retirement—only 60% or so say they are completely adjusted, and about 10% to 15% are actually having a rough time getting used to the lifestyle. Furthermore, even though we found sizable percentages of retirees having each trait, there is evidence that most of these traits may actually deteriorate in retirement.

When we compare retirees to those still in the workforce, retirees tend to be less confident, less motivated, less energetic, less optimistic about the future, less socially involved, less goal oriented, and less open to new experiences. As one example, self-confidence, at 54%, is one of the strongest traits claimed by retirees, but that pales in comparison to the 68% confidence ratings among those still working. And we also found that many of these attributes tend to have a declining presence with more time in retirement. As examples, being able to cope with change gradually declines from about 48% in the first year of retirement to 39% for those retired more than 10 years; similarly, openness to new experiences declines from 50% to 35% across the same years. Conversely, with more time in retirement, retirees are more likely to feel disconnected, feel they have too much free time, and are more anxious and depressed. While much of these declines may be age related and possibly exacerbated by declining health, it is possible that the loss of structure and direction in retirement contributes to less positive feelings about oneself and life in general over time.

So although there are innate psychological characteristics that make adapting to retirement easier, possessing any or even all of these doesn't guarantee success. And, fortunately, having some of the negative qualities that work counter to a smooth adjustment does not inevitably doom you to retirement hell. There are, as we have discussed throughout in previous chapters, a multitude of other factors that play into success, of which personality characteristics are only one. Many of these fall into the class of attitudes and behaviors. As such, they are under the direct control of and available to all retirees to help them in the transition. Every retiree can choose how they feel about being retired or decide how active or socially involved they want to be.

Regardless, although few retirees are likely to have all the tools and skills needed for an easy transition, almost all retirees are likely to have at least a few. But some factors are likely to play a dominant role in adjustment, some may be of only limited importance, while some, even if important, may be compensated for if a retiree possesses other important traits or characteristics. If they indeed vary in importance, then it would be helpful to understand how the factors we have been talking about compare to each other in driving overall happiness in retirement. We turn our attention to that question in the next chapter.

· *16* ·

Where to Go from Here

When one door closes, another one opens, but we often look so
long and regretfully at the closed door that we fail to see the one
that has opened for us.

—Alexander Graham Bell

*T*he best stories, or at least the ones that people like most, have happy
endings. And so it can be with retirement. But like every story in which the
good guy wins, there are trials and tribulations to suffer before reaching that
"happily ever after" conclusion, what we have been calling adjustment and
subjective well-being. We have tried to provide a road map for navigating the
maze, pointing out the pitfalls and ambushes so you stay on the path to a successful retirement. And for each potential problem, we have tried to provide
solutions that can make your way smoother and easier.

At this point, you might have gotten the sense that retiring successfully
is a difficult and rare accomplishment. Difficult it can be but certainly not impossible; most people eventually settle into and even enjoy their retirement,
achieving a comfort level they can live with and arriving at a feeling of acceptance of their new life. Even for those who don't work at it, meaningfulness
and structure seem—eventually— to become part of their lives through a sort
of osmosis. The simple act of living day to day seems to be enough for patterns
to become established and specific paths to be discovered. Some retirees simply come to accept what retirement living is all about—a slower pace, maybe
less exciting, certainly less focused and directed, but also less stressful. This is
not to say they become unhappily resigned to the lifestyle; although for a few
that may be the case, for others it may be more a matter of adjusting their
thinking about how to live and what to expect from day to day.

In truth, even when things seem to be less than ideal, there are enough good things about retirement to make it a better alternative than working for lots of people. But these positives may be hard to see while you're going through the emotional ups and downs of the adjustment process. Rob came to the realization that retirement wasn't as bad as he thought quite by accident:

> Here is an incident which sums up how I felt about being retired without even knowing it. One evening I walked into a bar and ordered a martini, straight up, with plenty of olives, preferably stuffed with blue cheese—a good martini is a beverage and a meal all in one. Anyway, after I placed my order, the bartender said to me, "Rough day, huh?" My response to her came without any hesitation whatsoever: "Sweetie, nobody's got it better than me. I just like martinis."
>
> Honestly, at that moment I realized that, despite all the emotional turmoil I felt I was going through, I loved being retired. Not once throughout all the nonsense of trying to adjust did going back to my job full time seem a better way to go. I loved my freedom, the ability to come and go as I please. I had to answer to no one, no more hoops to jump through. I actually got to a point where I wanted no responsibilities at all, including household chores. So I sold my house and moved into an apartment.
>
> I also developed a greater appreciation of a slower pace. Throughout my career I rushed through my leisure time because work was always beckoning. I could not tolerate traffic, bad weather, anything that placed added stress on me beyond my job. When I retired, I stopped worrying about things like weather or traffic because I have no place I have to get to. I didn't care what day it was because I always had the next day off too. And every day began with the hope and anticipation of some new idea to pursue, a new adventure to plan. I found that retirement really is very much like being a kid again, during the summer when school is out. Sure, there are boring and lonely days. But when I realized that I wasn't really unhappy in retirement, I tried to look back on what my days were like while I was working. There were dull and boring days on my job too, so work wasn't the cure for boredom that I thought it was.

Of course, Rob spent the last two years working on this book, so his retirement was anything but just relaxation and leisure. And although he was not as displeased with retirement as he once thought he was, he still knew at some level that pieces were still missing from his life. He came to the realization that he did not miss working so much as he missed the structure to his days and the feeling of being productive—things provided by his career. This was the real issue behind his struggles to create a new life. Ultimately, through experimentation with different types of activities, he was able to find things that were of value to him. In the end, he returned to his original field of research but not the business end. Instead, he went back to the social sciences, but he did it on his own terms and in a way that still allowed him to feel retired.

There's a crucial lesson in Rob's determination to keep experimenting. He felt enough discomfort to know he had to keep working at it if he was going to enjoy his retirement. The fact that he found out that he was happier about retirement than he first believed does not negate the fact that various factors can complicate how one adjusts to retirement. Instead, it points to the need to deal with the issues as they arise and keep moving forward. The real trick is to become adjusted as early in retirement as possible rather than relying on it to happen slowly over a period of years. Time becomes more precious as we get older, and it should not be wasted by just waiting for subjective well-being to improve on its own.

We've said it before, but it surely bears repeating—successful retirement is essentially about rebuilding your life, replacing the structure and sense of purpose that is lost when leaving the workforce. To speed this process, our broad advice begins with two rules—keep vigilant and stay motivated. Retirees must be aware of their feelings and prepared to act on them. If you feel unhappy or uncomfortable, then trust those feelings: they're telling you something is not quite right. Through introspection, try to discover the source of your uneasiness. By keeping in touch with your feelings, you may be better at handling certain issues before they become major problems. At the same time, vigilance about your emotions will help you come to a better understanding of your own needs. From there, you have a better chance of establishing a lifestyle that meets these needs.

Staying motivated is critical to a successful retirement. There's always the threat that the lack of structure can lead to lethargy, and laziness can beget more laziness. There are no mandatory schedules to follow, no time constraints for completing specific tasks. Without deadlines, it's all too easy to keep putting things off until tomorrow, which, of course, never comes when you're retired. There's nothing and no one forcing you to do anything, so it's all too easy to just shrug and say, "Why bother?" However, retirees who are driven to put some structure and purpose to their lives are likely to achieve a forward momentum, and momentum also tends to feed on itself.

Staying motivated can be a daunting task. As discussed, our research shows that many retirees lose their drive shortly after going into retirement, and this declines further with the years as aging becomes more of a factor. However, it's probably not only about getting older. It may also have something to do with how we think about retirement, possibly social mores passed down to us, that retirement is a time to do nothing. In fact, when we asked retirees what being retired is all about, 6 in 10 said it is a time for rest and relaxation.

In our opinion, seeing retirement as a time to relax is an antiquated thought, one more appropriate when people retired older and lived shorter lives. In this day and age, people can live 30 years outside the workforce—you may live as long in retirement as you did working at your career. Our research bears out that a "just relax and enjoy it" attitude just doesn't work today. When we looked at those who feel retirement is for resting, we found them less satisfied with their lives and their retirement, less happy with their social lives, and making less rewarding use of their time. Psychologically, they feel less socially connected, less productive and valued, less confident, less optimistic about the future—and much less motivated—compared to those who consider retirement to be a time to pursue new goals. None of this is to say that you need to move at a frenetic pace; rather, it's a matter of perspective and a realization of how much time you may have. After all, 30 years is a very long time to do nothing.

We feel a successful retirement must begin with reeducation. Broadly speaking, retirees need to come to understand that in retirement you must be reborn or else wither away. Further, the learning process must also include a greater awareness of the particulars. Retirees just don't know about the specific kinds of problems they could face in each of the various aspects of day-to-day living. For example, when asked about retirement planning prior to leaving their jobs, fewer than 4 in 10 put in even a moderate amount of effort, and only 2 in 10 made plans that included a step-by-step plan of action. And those who tried to plan focused almost exclusively on finances—fewer than 5% had the foresight to make specific plans for handling other aspects of living, such as their social lives or how to use time constructively.

But planning is only part of it. The truth is that the number of factors that can help or hinder adjustment is astounding. It would be impossible for anyone to make all the changes we've recommended—and probably not a good idea. Not all recommendations, for example, will pay the same dividends. Some may have a major impact, while others may contribute only a little to one's happiness. As such, knowing how personal background, personality, activity level, social life, finances, and so on stack up against each other can direct retirees to the best ways to focus their efforts.

So, as a next step, we tried to prioritize the "to do" list. We looked at the relative ability of all things we talked about to improve adjustment and subjective well-being. We utilized a statistical procedure (don't worry, we won't bore you with the math) that illustrates the correlation, or degree of association, between all the questions we asked retirees about their lives and their overall ratings of retirement adjustment. Through this technique, we are able to prioritize factors in terms of how much each contributes to retirees' overall levels of adjustment.

Our results show five elements fall into the top tier, that is, have the most impact on whether retirees feel adjusted. These five are ranked so close to each other that it's impossible to say whether one is more important than the others. Nevertheless, we can still use these findings to set some priorities. So if you feel you need to make improvements to your retirement lifestyle, then your attention should focus first on the following "big five."

PUT BACK STRUCTURE, PURPOSE, AND DIRECTION

As was mentioned often, direction and structure are elements most surrendered in retirement. After leaving the workforce, many retirees lose the regular schedules and routines that make up a job. Without structure, retirees my feel a loss of focus and a lack of direction to their lives, and this can lead them to feel unproductive, disconnected, and without a sense of personal control. We have attempted to convey the importance of this issue: each time we presented problems, the solutions we posed were generally couched in terms of putting structure and direction into day-to-day living.

As we have discussed, one means of putting direction and structure into your life is through planning and goal setting. These guide your actions so you can achieve personally meaningful outcomes, and that leads to better subjective well-being. Prior to retirement, begin to make plans for your future, setting goals you would like to accomplish to meet your personal needs. And if you haven't made any plans while still working, you can start at any point—in fact, goal setting and planning should be a continuous process throughout your retirement.

There are some retirees for whom planning is especially important, notably those who have problems managing stress, those who tend to procrastinate, those who are not goal directed, and those who are less open minded. These retirees are especially unlikely to make detailed plans but also tend to have difficulty coping with change and have less of the needed tenacity to adapt as they go. Going through the process of mapping out their course of action might help to reduce some of the stress caused by the prospect of change and may give them a better chance of coping with their new lifestyle if they can anticipate and prepare for it.

But again, such plans must be made in detail, not in just a general sense. Set up the specific steps you must take to reach these goals and make sure these goals are realistic, that is, require only the amount of energy you want to expend, and are truly achievable—overreaching can lead to failure, which can be demotivating. Another key point about planning and goals is seemingly self-evident but often not done: follow through on the plans you make either before or after you've retired. Achieving your goals is closely tied to feeling adjusted and to subjective well-being, and, of course, without follow-through, planning is just a waste of time.

Structure and direction also come from setting up schedules and routines. These are more with respect to everyday living and less in terms of planning long-term goals. For such schedules, it is important that you pay attention to those parts of living often missed by retirees in their planning stages. As we have pointed out, retirees' planning tends to focus almost exclusively on financial matters, and few retirees plan out their social lives and activities. Creating schedules for seeing friends or attending social engagements, as well as for activities that are of personal interest, will go a long way in making you feel you're using your time in a meaningful and constructive way. At the same time, through regular participation in social events and activities, you can reap the benefits of connectedness and productivity, both of which are also important to retirement adjustment and subjective well-being.

MANAGE YOUR EXPECTATIONS

The expectations you bring into retirement are strongly tied to how well you will adjust. The objective here is to be realistic—if your expectations are overly optimistic or aggressive, you run the risk of being disappointed, and if they are too pessimistic, you may start your retirement in an unfavorable state of mind. Either of these can be demotivating, with the end result being poor adjustment and weakened subjective well-being.

Ideally, retirees should try to leave the workforce with as few expectations as possible. However, such an idea in itself is unrealistic; expectations cannot be avoided any more than it's possible to think about nothing. And it's hard to be accurate because it's difficult to know how it feels not to work without the actual experience of not working. But if you have to err in this regard, it is best to err in the direction of expecting too little rather than too much. It may be more difficult to overcome disenchantment due to overoptimism than to live with the pleasant surprise that it's not as bad as you thought it would be.

To arrive at realistic expectations, first it would be wise to acknowledge that retirement may not be as exciting or fulfilling as your career. A simple mental exercise may help you get a better grasp. Try to imagine living a lifestyle in which you are not going to work every day, avoiding the thought that it is a holiday or a vacation. Instead, think about living day after unstructured day—no workplace to go to, no daily contact with coworkers, and no assignments you are responsible for completing. If you go far enough into the future—not just weeks or months but years—you will get a sense of just how much free time you will have. You should also sense quite a few gaps in your days that need to be filled with something to do. From there, hopefully you can start the process of planning how to use those many, many years in a way that will be meaningful to you.

STAY SOCIALLY CONNECTED

Enjoying retirement is unquestionably tied to the quality of your social life. A satisfying one lets retirees feel connected to the outside world and results from having a sufficient number of people in your social circle and spending ample amounts of time with them. So what's the right amount? The simple answer is, if you think you don't have enough friends or you feel you don't devote enough hours to socializing, then you probably don't, and you need to fix that.

Friendships are important for a satisfying social life, at least as important as family and children. Your friends are your peers—they share the same life-style and more likely than not have the same issues and concerns. Time with your friends can help you feel connected to the outside world and provide avenues for enriching your life through sharing of ideas. They also provide opportunities to participate in activities and events more appropriate for your age and lifestyle. In contrast, your children's priorities are about building their lives, raising families, and working, which are not relevant to your stage of life. Not that you should ignore your kids, but you should avoid becoming overly dependent on your children and family for your social life. Instead, put your efforts toward making friends and strive for balance in the time you devote to family and your friends. You will likely feel more connected to the outside world and feel better about yourself.

Some retirees who limit their social contacts, such as introverts, may not be aware of the importance of relationships and social interaction for their sub-jective well-being. And even if they can come to that realization, some may lack the wherewithal to create and maintain a social life. To these retirees, tak-ing a job or joining organizations geared to their interests may be worthwhile since doing so forces them into social situations, and the shared objectives of their members serve as a basis for establishing relationships. As another means of gaining social connectivity, they can increase their involvement and emo-tional commitment to already existing friendships and family relationships, or they can try using the various Internet services to track down old friends with whom they might have had a meaningful relationship in the past.

We must also emphasize once again the need for all retirees to focus on developing relationships outside the workplace. In the initial stages of retirement, friendships from work can serve you well by allowing you to keep some continuity into your new life stage. However, over time, you may find many of these relationships less fulfilling since you no longer share the bond of working toward a common goal. Building nonwork relationships, on the other hand, will help strengthen your own role as a retiree, along with providing the emotional benefits of social contact.

GET YOUR FINANCES IN ORDER

Surprisingly, money issues or, more to the point, the feeling that you have enough to live comfortably did not emerge as the number one factor for adjustment. Nevertheless, any reasonable person must admit that one's finances have to be adequate to even contemplate retirement. Furthermore, even if your funds are adequate, money is likely to stay a concern for quite a while into your retirement. The absence of a regular paycheck can be nerve wracking, especially in the early stages of retirement. Have a thorough understanding of your income and expenses, making sure you have enough to cover both basic living costs and discretionary spending.

If you're worried about money, there are a few steps you can take to help. For one, discuss your situation with your accountant or financial adviser before you retire. These professionals can help you understand the lifestyle you can safely afford. You should also consider keeping a running ledger of income and expenses so you can track your finances precisely. Putting the numbers down on paper can help to clarify retirees' thinking as to whether they are truly operating in the black or red. If, over time, you find yourself in the black, that is, your income is equal to or surpasses your expenses, you can relax: you can afford the lifestyle you have adopted. And if at times you again start to worry about money, you can always refer back to your financial records to again achieve a comfort level—or, perhaps, discover that your situation has changed and you need to revisit how you live.

KEEP SEARCHING AND EXPERIMENTING

Having activities that are rewarding helps you feel good about retirement. However, what actually seems to be more important than your specific activities is your motivation to continually look for things that meet your personal needs. Well-adjusted retirees are constantly on the lookout for new and interesting things to do and view retirement as an opportunity for new experiences. Those who are able to sustain their curiosity not only enjoy retirement more but also tend to feel younger, rejuvenated, and productive, all of which also contribute to positive feelings about retirement and to subjective well-being.

The search for new interests and activities has two essential attitudinal components—keep an open mind and be willing to experiment to discover your passions. An open mind prevents you from being locked into old patterns and allows you to adopt new ways of thinking and acting. Only through experimenting can you have an opportunity to discover interests you didn't know you had. You just never know what you might find out there if you keep looking. We old dogs have no choice but to learn new tricks.

As you experiment, keep in mind that this is trial and error and that you are bound to fail at times. Do not let your failures discourage you. Discouragement can be demotivating and get in the way of moving forward. It might be useful to remember some advice you've probably heard before: if you never try and fail, you'll never learn. So expect some failures along the way, and when they occur, drop the activity, not the pursuit of new ones.

Another piece of old-fashioned advice is relevant here: variety is the spice of life. A broad range of activities—some personal and some social—will likely let you feel productive, achieve meaningfulness and fulfillment from your actions, have more fun, and raise your subjective well-being.

So that's "the big five": is it enough? Unfortunately, not by a long shot. As helpful as these five points might be, as was found so often throughout our analysis, things are just never that simple. None of the five points we just discussed has a perfect relationship with adjustment. In other words, just because your social life is exactly the way you want it, you may not feel completely adjusted. In fact, even if you completely satisfied all five criteria, there's a chance you will still have some adjustment issues. But this shouldn't be surprising—there are so many elements that make for a happy retirement—and a happy life for that matter—that a few rules just can't capture it all.

So what else can be done to feel adjusted and happy? We've pointed out a multitude of other steps and courses of action available to retirees that could help speed the adjustment process. For the sake of review, as well as to provide an easy-to-find reference, these are summarized below. Some can be implemented while still in the workforce, and others should await retirement. Focusing first on the former, here are a few thoughts to keep in mind before you retire:

- Want to just chuck it all and retire in the hopes of greener pastures? Bad idea. You need to know where you are going, and you have to see retirement as a destination. That's the only way you can be prepared to develop your retirement lifestyle.

- While you are making every effort to have realistic expectations, at the same time be hopeful and positive about the future. It is important that you move into retirement in a positive state of mind. The right mental attitude can make retirement your end goal—a destination—which can give you the motivation to build a new lifestyle.
- A crucial point for married couples—talk to each other both before and after retiring about the full range of topics. Talking allows each partner to establish the ground rules to maintain a peaceful coexistence, making it easier to manage expectations about how to live together in retirement and helping to head off disappointments or resentments. Such conversations might also help couples develop goals and plans for the future, both of which will be carried out together and separately. Topics can include what each will do with time together and apart, how much they can afford to spend, how the division of household responsibilities will be shared, and how to handle any incompatible interests that may exist.
- For working couples, try to synchronize your retirement so you can avoid such problems as changes in the dynamics of the relationship or interference with the retired partner's participation in certain types of activities or social events. And both partners should have input into the decision to retire. This may be particularly a problem for some wives— if working women have to base their decision on their husbands' plans, they may not be fully prepared mentally for retirement and as a result be less happy in the event. Wives also tend to be happier if they have input into the retirement decision for their husbands since it allows them to be better prepared for his being home all the time.
- If you are being forced into retirement, embrace the inevitable—you *are* going to be a retiree. Do not dwell on wishing you could remain in the workforce since such thoughts are likely to contribute to negative feelings about retirement and may prevent you from adopting your retirement role. Once you have fully accepted your new reality, make every effort to adopt a positive mind-set and get to work on planning how you will live in retirement.
- Start to break your emotional connection to the workplace while still on your job and begin the process of defining yourself as a retiree, not as a worker. As a new perspective, view your retirement as the next logical step in your life: not the termination of a career but rather a movement into a new life stage. In this way, you may be less likely to look back to your working days with longing or to define yourself

solely by what you did for a living. You will also prime yourself to adopt other roles that are more appropriate for retirement.

Once you've left the workforce and begun your retirement, there are a few points to keep in mind in your quest for a better lifestyle. Some are proactive, steps you can take on your own to hasten your adjustment and subjective well-being. Others are more reactive, meant as guidance for nipping problems in the bud as soon as they arise:

- First of all, in the initial stages of retirement—the first six months or so—you will be elated. This will probably not last, so don't be fooled into thinking that things will just get easier as you go. By the time you hit 18 months or so, you are likely to be disenchanted. So never forget you have work ahead of you if you plan to enjoy your retirement.
- Keep a positive attitude and an eye to the future. As we've said, your life will lack structure, so it may be tempting to look at retirement as boring and to look back on work through a veil of sentimentality that is far from accurate. Don't ruminate on what you gave up; remind yourself that your job also had plenty of boring and less-than-satisfying moments. You may find you don't miss work as much as you miss the structure and routine it provided. Ideally, this will free you to focus on the positive features of retirement, the freedom from worry and the realization that you can mold your life according to your needs. But also be aware that, as you build a new life, it is important that you know who you are and what your interests and needs are. Self-exploration and personal honesty are essential for your ongoing life-building process.
- Many retirees work in retirement and still consider themselves retired. These bridge jobs can help in adjustment but only if taken on for the right reasons—to feel socially connected, to feel productive, or to achieve emotional benefits, such as enhanced self-esteem. Work in and of itself is not essential to a happy retirement, so work only if that works for you, meaning you like working or it fills a social or psychological need. However, the job has to be the right one to avoid the potential problems of feeling stressed, overworked, or even unretired.
- And what if you simply need the money? That's a reason that some retirees *have to* go back to work. However, if that's the only reason you do so, the odds are high that you will not be happy with yourself or your job. Instead, try to recognize the positives of working the social contact, feelings of productivity, and so on. In that way, you will have taken a job for positive rather than negative reasons, and that can help you feel better about things.

- And again, if you're working, keep an eye on how strongly you are tied to the worker role. Try to build your reliance on roles of personal value outside the workforce as a means of self-definition. As part of this effort, focus attention on non–work-related activities or environments and build relationships with people outside the workforce.
- Some retirees are particularly good candidates for bridge jobs, such as those who have a working spouse or have retired at a young age. For the latter, they still have a good deal of energy, tend to have a working spouse, and often have few peers who have retired with them. The resulting overabundance of free time can create problems for some younger retirees. Working in some reduced capacity can be a way of moderating potential emotional downturns, and the option to work should stay open and be seriously considered if young retirees recognize they cannot reach a comfort level in retirement.
- Retiring young, ahead of most or all of one's peers, can be difficult, so the need to plan and set goals is even more crucial than for those retiring at a more conventional age. Younger retirees should establish detailed schedules regarding use of their personal time, paying particular attention to their social lives. If at all possible, young retirees should also plan their retirement to coincide with that of their spouse. Having a spouse who is also retired allows for a greater array of entertaining diversions and helps to reduce some of the loneliness and isolation.
- Retired men whose wives have been full-time homemakers need to figure out and accept their place in the home and should avoid turning an overly critical eye on the way the household is run. Remember: your wife has managed the household quite nicely on her own for years, and odds are she neither wants nor needs your advice after you retire. But even if she does seek your advice, realize the price you may be paying in terms of invading her space and, as a result, building resentments. On the other side, wives in this predicament should understand their husbands have only just surrendered a role of responsibility and may require some time to let that role go completely. Talking out the problem as soon as it becomes noticeable would be helpful for avoiding bigger problems later.
- Relatedly, a retiring husband must acknowledge that his spouse has established her own patterns and ways to spend personal time, and his retirement does not put an end to that. Rather, husbands should develop and pursue their own interests so that they are not completely dependent on their wives for their entertainment. Husbands should also consider that when they retire from their job, their wives are likely

to expect some of the household burdens to shift from them to their husbands—and rightly so.

- In that vein, couples should focus on establishing a broad social life to avoid becoming too dependent on each other or spending too much time together. In addition to maintaining and strengthening existing friendships, retirees can consider joining clubs and organizations that cater to their personal interests and provide opportunities for developing new independent relationships.

- While you're out socializing, talk to other retirees. Only they can understand the difficulties you face in the transition, so you can empathize and maybe sympathize with each other. More important, you can trade war stories and possibly exchange ideas as to what has worked and not worked on your path to adjustment.

- Get out of the house as often as possible. We found successful retirees are particularly likely to travel. It's not just grand adventures; "travel" also includes simple day trips by car. While financial resources might limit destinations or types of transportation, day trips are available to all retirees who are mobile. And to make such trips help bring balance between your social and personal activities, bring along some friends.

- Even some typically home-based activities can be conducted in a social environment. For example, if you like to read, join a book club or start one on your own. And if you're not into joining groups, there are plenty of public spaces, such as cafes, where you can read and have an opportunity to feel part of the world. If you prefer going online, some even offer free Wi-Fi connections.

- Exploration and pursuit of each partner's separate interests and activities is important. The time devoted to these can provide each partner with their own space, along with opportunities for each one's personal development. Too much time together can lead to feelings of isolation, alienation, and disconnectedness from the community at large. However, there should also be some shared activities and relationships since these help to maintain the bonds between you and your spouse. Balance is the key here.

- For whatever reasons, retirees have been found to have sex less often than those still in the workforce. An active sex life is important and healthy for a relationship—partners feel more connected with each other, feel better personally, may have increased motivation to do other things, and have an opportunity for some enjoyable exercise. Make room for some fun time with your partner. You may find it a wonderful way to break up the monotony of the day when you have nothing else planned, even if you have built up a very busy schedule.

- But don't forget the less exciting types of exercise—even the most active sex life might not eliminate the need for a full exercise regimen. Well-adjusted retirees are much more active physically, exercising regularly, playing sports, and so on, and regular exercise has been proven to provide all kinds of psychological and emotional benefits to its participants.
- As one means of building a regular routine (and avoiding the trap of losing your motivation), consider keeping a calendar or the ever popular "to do" list. In this way, you treat your retirement very much like a job, keeping track of the personally meaningful things you want to pursue, social engagements, and the more mundane chores and responsibilities. A calendar may be the better option since it more clearly illustrates what you have planned for each day and points out the gaps when nothing is planned. Each morning should start off with a review of your calendar or list so that you know what the day ahead holds for you. If it's nothing, then you can fill in the blanks.

As one final, very important point—get selfish. You have raised a family, fought your way through your career, and suffered the trials and tribulations of just plain living, so you've earned it. It's time to focus on yourself and your needs.

As we stated way back in our opening paragraph, retirement is a full-time job, as demanding as any you have held in the past. That job is about filling a void—the gaping holes that are left in one's life after departing the workforce. Unfortunately, you won't get paid for retirement, but that does not diminish the importance of this job. It is the unavoidable job of living, and each of us has a personal responsibility to live as well as we can. So be aware: you have work ahead of you. If retirement is attacked with the same gusto that you applied to your job, there is a good chance that you can achieve the high levels of inner peace and subjective well-being we all strive for. It will not be easy, but if you stay focused, a happy ending may be reached sooner than you think.

Notes

CHAPTER 2

1. Melissa A. Hardy, The transformation of retirement in twentieth-century America: From discontent to satisfaction, *Generations* 26, no. 2 (2002): 9–16.

2. Anne-Marie Guillemard and Martin Rein, Comparative patterns of retirement: Recent trends in developed societies, *Annual Review of Sociology* 19 (1993): 469–503.

3. K. Abraham, Restructuring the employment relationship: The growth of market mediated work relationships, in *New developments in the labor market*, ed. K. Abraham and R. McKersie (Cambridge, MA: MIT Press, 1990), 185–220.

CHAPTER 3

1. Steven B. Robbins, E. Christopher Payne, and Judy M. Chartrand, Goal instability and later life adjustment, *Psychology and Aging* 5, no. 3 (September 1990): 447–50.

2. Gordon F. Streib, Morale of the retired, *Social Problems* 3, no. 4 (April 1956): 270–76.

3. Julienne Garland, *Making the most of retirement for dummies* (Hoboken, NJ: Wiley, 2009); Elizabeth Kuball, ed., *Retirement for dummies* (Hoboken, NJ: Wiley, 2009).

4. V. Richardson and K. M. Kilty, Adjustment to retirement: Continuity vs. discontinuity, *International Journal of Aging and Human Development* 33 (1991): 151–69, cited in Martin Pinquart and Ines Schindler, Changes of life satisfaction in the transition to retirement: A latent-class approach, *Psychology and Aging* 22, no. 3 (September 2007): 442–55.

5. D. J. Ekerdt, R. Bosse, and J. S. LoCastro, Claims that retirement improves health, *Journal of Gerontology* 38 (1983): 231–36, cited in Mo Wang, Profiling retirees in the retirement transition and adjustment process: Examining the longitudinal change

patterns of retirees' psychological well-being, *Journal of Applied Psychology* 92, no. 2 (March 2007): 455–74.

6. K. Seccombe and G. R. Lee, Gender differences in retirement satisfaction and its antecedents, *Research on Aging* 8 (1986): 426–40.

7. Martin Pinquart and Ines Schindler, Changes of life satisfaction in the transition to retirement: A latent-class approach, *Psychology and Aging* 22, no. 3 (September 2007): 442–55.

8. N. T. Feather and M. J. Bond, Time structure and purposeful activity among employed and unemployed university graduates, *Journal of Occupational Psychology* 56 (1983): 241–54.

9. A. Regula Herzog, James S. House, and James N. Morgan, Relation of work and retirement to health and well-being in older age, *Psychology and Aging* 6, no. 2 (June 1991): 202–11.

10. R. C. Atchley, Continuity theory, self, and social structure, in *Families and retirement*, ed. C. D. Ryff and V. W. Marshall (Newbury Park, CA: Sage, 1999), 145–58.

11. Donald C. Reitzes and Elizabeth J. Mutran, The transition to retirement: Stages and factors that influence retirement adjustment, *International Journal of Aging and Human Development* 59, no. 1 (2004): 63–84; Martin Pinquart and Ines Schindler, Changes of life satisfaction in the transition to retirement: A latent-class approach, *Psychology and Aging* 22, no. 3 (September 2007): 442–55; Mo Wang, Profiling retirees in the retirement transition and adjustment process: Examining the longitudinal change patterns of retirees' psychological well-being, *Journal of Applied Psychology* 92, no. 2 (March 2007): 455–74.

12. Monika E. von Bonsdorff, Kenneth S. Shultz, Esko Leskinen, and Judith Tansky, The choice between retirement and bridge employment: A continuity theory and life course perspective, *International Journal of Aging and Human Development* 69, no. 2 (2009): 79–100.

13. R. C. Atchley, *The sociology of retirement* (New York: Wiley, 1976).

14. Mo Wang, Yujie Zhan, Songqi Liu, and Kenneth S. Shultz, Antecedents of bridge employment: A longitudinal investigation, *Journal of Applied Psychology* 7 (2008): 818–30.

15. B. Ashforth, *Role transitions in organizational life: An identity-based perspective* (Mahwah, NJ: Lawrence Erlbaum Associates, 2001); Daniel C. Feldman, The decision to retire early: A review and conceptualization, *Academy of Management Review* 29, no. 2 (April 1994): 285–311.

16. P. Moen, D. Dempster-McClain, and R. W. Williams Jr., Successful aging: A life course perspective on women's multiple roles and health, *American Journal of Sociology* 97 (1992): 1612–38.

17. P. A. Thoits, Identity structure and psychological well-being: Gender and marital status comparisons, *Social Psychology Quarterly* 55 (1992): 236–56.

18. Heather E. Quick and Phyllis Moen, Gender, employment and retirement quality: A life course approach to the differential experiences of men and women, *Journal of Occupational Health Psychology* 3, no. 1 (January 1998): 44–64; J. E. Kim and P. Moen, Moving into retirement: Preparations and transitions in late midlife, in *Handbook of midlife development*, ed. M. E. Lachman (New York: Wiley, 2001), 487–527.

19. G. H. Elder Jr., The life course paradigm: Social change and individual development, in *Examining lives in context: Perspectives on the ecology of human development*, ed. P. Moen, G. H. Elder Jr., and K. Lüscher (Washington, DC: American Psychological Association, 1995) 101–40; L. K. George, Sociological perspectives on life transitions, *Annual Review of Sociology* 19 (1993): 353–73.

20. Robert Crosnoe and Glen H. Elder, Successful adaptation in the later years: A life course approach to aging, *Social Psychology Quarterly* 65, no. 4 (December 2002): 309–28; Phyllis Moen, A life course perspective on retirement, gender, and well-being, *Journal of Occupational Health Psychology* 1, no. 2 (April 1996): 131–44.

CHAPTER 4

1. Anne-Marie Guillemard and Martin Rein, Comparative patterns of retirement: Recent trends in developed societies, *Annual Review of Sociology* 19 (1993): 469–503.

2. Mark D. Hayward, The influence of occupational characteristics on men's early retirement, *Social Forces* 64, no. 4 (June 1986): 1032–45.

3. Daniel C. Feldman, The decision to retire early: A review and conceptualization, *Academy of Management Review* 19, no. 2 (April 1994): 285–311.

4. Guillemard and Rein, Comparative patterns of retirement.

5. L. K. George, Sociological perspectives on life transitions, *Annual Review of Sociology* 19 (1993): 353–73; R. C. Williamson, A. D. Rinehart, and T. O. Blank, *Early retirement: Promises and pitfalls* (New York: Insight Books Plenum, 1992).

6. S. Kim and Daniel C. Feldman, Working in retirement: The antecedents of bridge employment and its consequences for quality of life in retirement, *Academy of Management Journal* 6 (2000): 1195–210; J. E. Kim and P. Moen, Moving into retirement: Preparations and transitions in late midlife, in *Handbook of midlife development*, ed. M. E. Lachman (New York: Wiley, 2001), 487–527.

7. T. L. Gall and David R. Evans, Preretirement expectations and the quality of life of male retirees in later retirement, *Canadian Journal of Behavioural Science* 32, no. 3 (July 2000): 187–97.

8. A. Regula Herzog, James S. House, and James N. Morgan, Relation of work and retirement to health and well-being in older age, *Psychology and Aging* 6, no. 2 (June 1991): 202–11.

9. Donald C. Reitzes and Elizabeth J. Mutran, Lingering identities in retirement, *Sociological Quarterly* 2 (2006): 333–59.

10. John C. Henretta and Angela M. O'Rand, Joint retirement in the dual worker family, *Social Forces* 62, no. 2 (December 1983): 504–20.

11. Donald C. Reitzes, Elizabeth J. Mutran, and Maria E. Fernandez, The decision to retire: A career perspective, *Social Science Quarterly* 3 (1998): 607–19.

12. Deborah B. Smith and Phyllis Moen, Spousal influence on retirement: His, her, and their perceptions, *Journal of Marriage and Family* 60, no. 3 (August 1998): 734–44; Maximillane E. Szinovacz and Stanley DeViney, Marital characteristics and retirement decisions, *Research on Aging* 22, no. 5 (September 2000): 470–98.

13. Smith and Moen, Spousal influence on retirement; Szinovacz and DeViney, Marital characteristics and retirement decisions.

CHAPTER 5

1. Mo Wang, Profiling retirees in the retirement transition and adjustment process: Examining the longitudinal change patterns of retirees' psychological well-being, *Journal of Applied Psychology* 92, no. 2 (March 2007): 455–74.

2. Shigehiro Oishi, Erin Whitchurch, Felicity F. Miao, Jaime Kurtz, and Jina Park, "Would I be happier if I moved?" Retirement status and cultural variations in the anticipated and actual levels of happiness, *Journal of Positive Psychology* 4, no. 6 (November 2009): 437–46.

3. G. Perry, The need for retirement planning and counseling, *Canadian Counsellor* 14 (1980): 97–98, cited in T. L. Gall and David R. Evans, Preretirement expectations and the quality of life of male retirees in later retirement, *Canadian Journal of Behavioural Science* 32, no. 3 (July 2000): 187–97.

4. Phyllis Moen, A life course perspective on retirement, gender, and well-being, *Journal of Occupational Health Psychology* 1, no. 2 (April 1996): 131–44; Gall and Evans, Preretirement expectations and the quality of life of male retirees in later retirement.

CHAPTER 6

1. Donald C. Reitzes and Elizabeth J. Mutran, The transition to retirement: Stages and factors that influence retirement adjustment, *International Journal of Aging and Human Development* 59, no. 1 (2004): 63–84; Steven B. Robbins, Richard M. Lee, and Thomas T. H. Wan, Goal continuity as a mediator of early retirement adjustment: Testing a multidimensional model, *Journal of Counseling Psychology* 41, no. 1 (January 1994): 18–26.

2. Daniel C. Feldman, The decision to retire early: a review and conceptualization, *Academy of Management Review* 19, no. 2 (April 1994): 285–311.

3. Reitzes and Mutran, The transition to retirement; E. J. Mutran, D. C. Reitzes, and M. E. Fernandez, Factors that influence attitudes toward retirement, *Research on Aging* 19 (1997): 251–73.

CHAPTER 7

1. Raymond Bossé, Carolyn M. Aldwin, Michael R. Levenson, and David J. Ekerdt, Mental health differences among retirees and workers: Findings from the normative aging study, *Psychology and Aging* 2, no. 4 (December 1987): 383–89.

2. Ed Diener and Robert Biswas-Diener, Will money increase subjective well-being? A literature review and guide to needed research, *Social Indicators Research* 57, no. 2 (February 2002): 119–69.

3. Susan F. Higginbottom, Julian Barling, and E. Kevin Kelloway, Linking retirement experiences and marital satisfaction: A mediational model, *Psychology and Aging* 8, no. 4 (December 1993): 508–16; S. Kim and Daniel C. Feldman, Working in retirement: The antecedents of bridge employment and its consequences for quality of life in retirement, *Academy of Management Journal* 6 (2000): 1195–210.

4. E. J. Mutran, D. C. Reitzes, and M. E. Fernandez, Factors that influence attitudes toward retirement, *Research on Aging* 19 (1997): 251–73.

CHAPTER 8

1. K. S. Shultz, Bridge employment: Work after retirement, in *Retirement: Reasons, processes, and results,* ed. G. A. Adams and T. A. Beehr (New York: Springer, 2003), 215–41.

2. Daniel C. Feldman, The decision to retire early: A review and conceptualization, *Academy of Management Review* 19, no. 2 (April 1994): 285–311.

3. Shultz, Bridge employment; Kevin E. Cahill, Michael D. Giandrea, and Joseph F. Quinn, Retirement patterns from career employment, *The Gerontologist* 46, no. 4 (2006): 514–23.

4. K. L. Fiori, T. C. Antonucci, and K. S. Cortina, Social network typologies and mental health among older adults, *Journal of Gerontology: Psychological Sciences* 61B (2006): 25–32.

5. L. R. Berkman and L. Breslow, *Health and ways of living: The Alameda County study* (New York: Oxford University Press, 1983); J. S. House, K. R. Landis, and D. Umberson, Social relationships and health, *Science* 241 (1988): 540–45.

6. S. K. Han and P. Moen, Clocking out: Temporal patterning of retirement, *American Journal of Sociology* 105 (1999): 191–236. Yujie Zhan, Mo Wang, Songqi Liu, and Kenneth S. Shultz, Bridge employment and retirees' health: A longitudinal investigation, *Journal of Occupational Health Psychology* 14, no. 4 (October 2009): 374–89.

7. Shultz, Bridge employment; Zhan et al., Bridge employment and retirees' health; Monika E. von Bonsdorff, Kenneth S. Shultz, Esko Leskinen, and Judith Tansky, The choice between retirement and bridge employment: A continuity theory and life course perspective, *International Journal of Aging and Human Development* 69, no. 2 (2009): 79–100.

CHAPTER 9

1. Anne-Marie Guillemard and Martin Rein, Comparative patterns of retirement: Recent trends in developed societies, *Annual Review of Sociology* 19 (1993): 469–503;

Melissa A. Hardy, The transformation of retirement in twentieth-century America: From discontent to satisfaction, *Generations* 26, no. 2 (2002): 9–16. Daniel C. Feldman, The decision to retire early: A review and conceptualization, *Academy of Management Review* 19, no. 2 (April 1994): 285–311.

2. Mark D. Hayward, The influence of occupational characteristics on men's early retirement, *Social Forces* 64, no. 4 (June 1986): 1032–45; Feldman, The decision to retire early.

CHAPTER 10

1. Heather E. Quick and Phyllis Moen, Gender, employment and retirement quality: A life course approach to the differential experiences of men and women, *Journal of Occupational Health Psychology* 3, no. 1 (January 1998): 44–64.

2. Quick and Moen, Gender, employment and retirement quality; J. S. House, K. R. Landis, and D. Umberson, Social relationships and health, *Science* 241 (1988): 540–45.

3. A. Regula Herzog, James S. House, and James N. Morgan, Relation of work and retirement to health and well-being in older age, *Psychology and Aging* 6, no. 2 (June 1991): 202–11.

4. Donald C. Reitzes and Elizabeth J. Mutran, Lingering identities in retirement, *Sociological Quarterly* 2 (2006): 333–59.

5. Robert S. Weiss, The experience of retirement, *Contemporary Sociology* 35, no. 4 (July 2006): 382–83.

6. Gordon F. Streib and Clement J. Schneider, *Retirement in American society* (Ithaca, NY: Cornell University Press, 1971).

7. Weiss, The experience of retirement.

CHAPTER 11

1. R. J. Havighurst, Successful aging, in *Processes of aging*, ed. R. Williams, C. Tibbitts, and W. Donahue (New York: Atherton Press, 1963), 299–320.

2. F. R. Lang, N. Riekmann, and M. M. Baltes, Adapting to aging losses: Do resources facilitate strategies of selection, compensation and optimization in everyday functioning?, *Journals of Gerontology Series B: Psychological Sciences and Social Sciences* 57 (2002): 501–9; S. Burnett-Wolle and G. Godbey, Refining research on older adults' leisure: Implications of selection, optimization and socio-emotional selectivity theories, *Journal of Leisure Research* 39, no. 3 (2007): 496–513.

3. Galit Nimrod, Megan C. Janke, and Douglas A. Kleiber, Expanding, reducing, concentrating and diffusing: Activity patterns of recent retirees in the United States, *Leisure Sciences* 31 (2009): 37–52.

4. Galit Nimrod, Retirees' leisure: Activities, benefits, and their contribution to life satisfaction, *Leisure Studies* 26, no. 1 (January 2007): 65–80; Susan F. Higginbottom, Julian Barling, and E. Kevin Kelloway, Linking retirement experiences and marital satisfaction: A mediational model, *Psychology and Aging* 8. no. 4 (December 1993): 508–16.

5. Nimrod, Retirees' leisure.

6. Phyllis Moen, A life course perspective on retirement, gender, and well-being, *Journal of Occupational Health Psychology* 1, no. 2 (April 1996): 131–44.

CHAPTER 12

1. R. L. Kahn and T. C. Antonucci, Convoys over the life course: Attachment, roles, and social support, in *Life-span development and behavior*, ed. P. B. Baltes and O. G. Brim (New York: Academic Press, 1980), 253–86; Raymond Bossé, Carolyn M. Aldwin, Michael R. Levenson, Kathryn Workman-Daniels, and David J. Ekerdt, Differences in social support among retirees and workers: Findings from the Normative Aging Study, *Psychology and Aging* 5, no. 1 (March 1990): 41–47.

2. M. Jahoda, *Employment and unemployment* (Cambridge: Cambridge University Press, 1982); Corinna E. Löckenhoff, Antonio Terracciano, and Paul T. Costa Jr., Five-factor model personality traits and the retirement transition: Longitudinal and cross-sectional associations, *Psychology and Aging* 24, no. 3 (September 2009): 722–28; Martin Pinquart and Ines Schindler, Changes of life satisfaction in the transition to retirement: A latent-class approach, *Psychology and Aging* 22, no. 3 (September 2007): 442–55; Wesla L. Fletcher and Robert O. Hansson, Assessing the social components of retirement anxiety, *Psychology and Aging* 6, no. 1 (March 1991): 76–85; E. J. Mutran, D. C. Reitzes, and M. E. Fernandez, Factors that influence attitudes toward retirement., *Research on Aging* 19 (1997): 251–73.

CHAPTER 13

1. Scott M. Myers and Alan Booth, Men's retirement and marital quality, *Journal of Family Issues* 17, no. 3 (May 1996): 336–57; J. E. Kim and P. Moen, Moving into retirement: Preparations and transitions in late midlife, in *Handbook of midlife development*, ed. M. E. Lachman (New York: Wiley, 2001), 487–527.

2. Tanya R. Fitzpatrick and Barbara Vinick, The impact of husbands' retirement on wives' marital quality, *Journal of Family Social Work* 7, no. 1 (2003): 83–100.

3. Myers and Booth, Men's retirement and marital quality.

4. Maximiliane E. Szinovacz, Female retirement: Effects on spousal roles and marital adjustment, *Journal of Family Issues* 1 no. 3 (September 1980): 423–40.

5. Myers and Booth, Men's retirement and marital quality.

6. E. A. Hill and L. T. Dorfman, Reaction of housewives to the retirement of their husbands, *Family Relations* 31 (1982): 195–200; David J. Ekerdt and Barbara H. Vinick, Marital complaints in husband-working and husband-retired couples, *Research on Aging* 13, no. 3 (September 1991): 364–83.

7. M. Szinovacz and A. M. Schaffer, Effects of retirement on marital conflict tactics, *Journal of Family Issues* 21 (2000): 367–89; M. Szinovacz and P. Harpster, Employment status, gender roles and marital dependence in later life, *Journal of Marriage and Family* 55 (1993): 927–40; Ekerdt and Vinick, Marital complaints in husband-working and husband-retired couples.

8. Jeffrey Dew and Jeremy Yorgason, Economic pressure and marital conflict in retirement-aged couples, *Journal of Family Issues* 31, no. 2 (February 2010): 164–88.

9. D. M. Blau, Labor force dynamics of older married couples, *Journal of Labor Economics* 16 (1998): 595–629; K. Henkens, Retirement intentions and spousal support: A multifactor approach, *Journal of Gerontology: Social Sciences* 54B (1999): S63–S74.

10. Maximiliane Szinovacz, Couples' employment/retirement patterns and perceptions of marital quality, *Research on Aging* 18, no. 2 (June 1996): 243–68; P. Moen, J. E. Kim, and H. Hofmeister, The interaction between marital relationships and retirement, *Social Psychology Quarterly* 64 (2001): 55–71; Kim and Moen, Moving into retirement.

11. Adam Davey and Maximiliane E. Szinovacz, Dimensions of marital quality and retirement, *Journal of Family Issues* 25, no. 4 (May 2004): 431–64. Myers and Booth, Men's retirement and marital quality; Moen et al., The interaction between marital relationships and retirement; Szinovacz and Schaffer, Effects of retirement on marital conflict tactics; Szinovacz and Harpster, Employment status, gender roles and marital dependence in later life.

12. M. Jahoda, *Employment and unemployment* (Cambridge: Cambridge University Press, 1982); Susan F. Higginbottom, Julian Barling, and E. Kevin Kelloway, Linking retirement experiences and marital satisfaction: A mediational model, *Psychology and Aging* 8, no. 4 (December 1993): 508–16.

CHAPTER 14

1. Donald C. Reitzes and Elizabeth J. Mutran, Lingering identities in retirement, *Sociological Quarterly* 2 (2006): 333–59.

2. Robert S. Weiss, The experience of retirement, *Contemporary Sociology* 35, no. 4 (July 2006): 382–83.

3. Reitzes and Mutran, Lingering identities in retirement.

4. V. Richardson and K. M. Kilty, Adjustment to retirement: Continuity vs. discontinuity, *International Journal of Aging and Human Development* 33 (1991): 151–69, cited in Martin Pinquart and Ines Schindler, Changes of life satisfaction in the transition to retirement: A latent-class approach, *Psychology and Aging* 22, no. 3 (September 2007): 442–55.

CHAPTER 15

1. M. A. Lieberman, Adaptive processes in late life, in *Life-span developmental psychology: Normative life crises*, ed. N. Datan and L. H. Ginzberg (New York: Academic Press, 1975), 135–59; N. K. Schlossberg, A model for analyzing human adaptation to transition, *Counseling Psychologist* 9 (1981): 2–36.

2. Corinna E. Löckenhoff, Antonio Terracciano, and Paul T. Costa Jr., Five-factor model personality traits and the retirement transition: Longitudinal and cross-sectional associations. *Psychology and Aging* 24, no. 3 (September 2009): 722–28.

3. Löckenhoff et al., Five-factor model personality traits and the retirement transition.

4. Löckenhoff et al., Five-factor model personality traits and the retirement transition.

5. E. J. Mutran, D.C. Reitzes, and M. E. Fernandez, Factors that influence attitudes toward retirement, *Research on Aging* 19 (1997): 251–73; Donald C. Reitzes and Elizabeth J. Mutran, The transition to retirement: Stages and factors that influence retirement adjustment, *International Journal of Aging and Human Development* 59, no. 1 (2004): 63–84.

6. Duane S. Bishop, Nathan B. Epstein, Lawrence M. Baldwin, Ivan W. Miller, and Gabor I. Keitner, Older couples: The effect of health, retirement, and family functioning on morale, *Family Systems Medicine* 6, no. 2 (1988): 238–47. Lieberman, Adaptive processes in late life.

7. Yannick Stephan, Openness to experience and active adults' life satisfaction: A trait and facet level analysis, *Personality and Individual Differences* 47, no. 6 (October 2009): 637–41.

8. E. Christopher Payne, Steven B. Robbins, and Linda Dougherty, Goal directedness and older-adult adjustment, *Journal of Counseling Psychology* 38, no. 3 (July 1991): 302–8.

9. R V. Russell, The importance of recreation satisfaction and activity participation to the life satisfaction of age-segregated retirees, *Journal of Leisure Research* 19 (1987): 273–83; Steven B. Robbins, Richard M. Lee, and Thomas T. H. Wan, Goal continuity as a mediator of early retirement adjustment: Testing a multidimensional model, *Journal of Counseling Psychology* 41, no. 1 (January 1994): 18–26. Payne et al., Goal directedness and older-adult adjustment.

10. Steven B. Robbins, E. Christopher Payne, and Judy M. Chartrand, Goal instability and later life adjustment, *Psychology and Aging* 5, no. 3 (September 1990): 447–50.

Bibliography

Abraham, K. Restructuring the employment relationship: The growth of market-mediated work relationships. In *New developments in the labor market*, edited by K. Abraham and R. McKersie, 185–220. Cambridge, MA: MIT Press, 1990.

Ashforth, B. *Role transitions in organizational life: An identity-based perspective.* Mahwah, NJ: Lawrence Erlbaum Associates, 2001.

Atchley, R. C. *The sociology of retirement.* New York: Wiley, 1976.

Atchley, R. C. Continuity theory, self, and social structure. In *Families and retirement*, edited by C. D. Ryff and V. W. Marshall, 145–58. Newbury Park, CA: Sage, 1999.

Barnes-Farrell, J. L. Beyond health and wealth: Attitudinal and other influences on retirement decision-making. In *Retirement: Reasons, processes, and results*, edited by G. A. Adams and T. A. Beehr, 159–87. New York: Springer, 2003.

Berkman, L. R., and L. Breslow. *Health and ways of living: The Alameda County study.* New York: Oxford University Press, 1983.

Bishop, Duane S., Nathan B. Epstein, Lawrence M. Baldwin, Ivan W. Miller, and Gabor I. Keitner. Older couples: The effect of health, retirement, and family functioning on morale. *Family Systems Medicine* 6, no. 2 (1988): 238–47.

Blau, D. M. Labor force dynamics of older married couples. *Journal of Labor Economics* 16 (1998): 595–629.

Bossé, Raymond, Carolyn M. Aldwin, Michael R. Levenson, and David J. Ekerdt. Mental health differences among retirees and workers: Findings from the normative aging study. *Psychology and Aging* 2, no. 4 (December 1987): 383–89.

Bossé, Raymond, Carolyn M. Aldwin, Michael R. Levenson, Kathryn Workman-Daniels, and David J. Ekerdt. Differences in social support among retirees and workers: Findings from the Normative Aging Study. *Psychology and Aging* 5, no. 1 (March 1990): 41–47.

Burnett-Wolle, S., and G. Godbey. Refining research on older adults' leisure: Implications of selection, optimization and socio-emotional selectivity theories. *Journal of Leisure Research* 39, no. 3 (2007): 496–513.

Cahill, Kevin E., Michael D. Giandrea, and Joseph F. Quinn. Retirement patterns from career employment. *The Gerontologist* 46, no. 4 (2006): 514–23.

Crosnoe, Robert, and Glen H. Elder. Successful adaptation in the later years: A life course approach to aging. *Social Psychology Quarterly* 65, no. 4 (December 2002): 309–28.

Davey, Adam, and Maximiliane E. Szinovacz. Dimensions of marital quality and retirement. *Journal of Family Issues* 25, no. 4 (May 2004): 431–64.

Dew, Jeffrey, and Jeremy Yorgason. Economic pressure and marital conflict in retirement-aged couples. *Journal of Family Issues* 31, no. 2 (February 2010): 164–88.

Diener, Ed, and Robert Biswas-Diener. Will money increase subjective well-being? A literature review and guide to needed research. *Social Indicators Research* 57, no. 2 (February 2002): 119–69.

Drentea, P. Retirement and mental health. *Journal of Aging and Health* 14 (2007): 167–94.

Ekerdt, D. J., R. Bosse, and J. S. LoCastro. Claims that retirement improves health. *Journal of Gerontology* 38 (1983):231–36.

Ekerdt, David J., and Barbara H. Vinick. Marital complaints in husband-working and husband-retired couples. *Research on Aging* 13, no. 3 (September 1991): 364–83.

Elder, G. H., Jr. The life course paradigm: Social change and individual development. In *Examining lives in context: Perspectives on the ecology of human development*, edited by P. Moen, G. H. Elder Jr., and K. Lüscher, 101–40. Washington, DC: American Psychological Association, 1995.

Feather, N. T., and M. J. Bond. Time structure and purposeful activity among employed and unemployed university graduates. *Journal of Occupational Psychology* 56 (1983): 241–54.

Feldman, Daniel C. The decision to retire early: A review and conceptualization. *Academy of Management Review* 19, no. 2 (April 1994): 285–311.

Fiori, K. L., T. C. Antonucci, and K. S. Cortina. Social network typologies and mental health among older adults. *Journal of Gerontology: Psychological Sciences* 61B (2006): 25–32.

Fitzpatrick, Tanya R., and Barbara Vinick. The impact of husbands' retirement on wives' marital quality. *Journal of Family Social Work* 7, no. 1 (2003): 83–100.

Fletcher, Wesla L., and Robert O. Hansson. Assessing the social components of retirement anxiety. *Psychology and Aging* 6, no. 1 (March 1991): 76–85.

Gall, T. L., and David R. Evans. Preretirement expectations and the quality of life of male retirees in later retirement. *Canadian Journal of Behavioural Science* 32, no. 3 (July 2000): 187–97.

Garland, Julienne. *Making the most of retirement for dummies.* Hoboken, NJ: Wiley, 2009.

George, L. K. Sociological perspectives on life transitions. *Annual Review of Sociology* 19 (1993): 353–73.

Guillemard, Anne-Marie, and Martin Rein. Comparative patterns of retirement: Recent trends in developed societies. *Annual Review of Sociology* 19 (1993): 469–503.

Han, S. K., and P. Moen. Clocking out: Temporal patterning of retirement. *American Journal of Sociology* 105 (1999): 191–236.

Hardy, Melissa A. The transformation of retirement in twentieth-century America: From discontent to satisfaction. *Generations* 26, no. 2 (2002): 9–16.

Harlow, Robert E., and Nancy Cantor. Still participating after all these years: A study of life task participation in later life. *Journal of Personality and Social Psychology* 71, no. 6 (December 1996): 1235–49.

Havighurst, R. J. Successful aging. In *Processes of aging*, edited by R. Williams, C. Tibbitts, and W. Donahue, 299–320. New York: Atherton Press, 1963.

Hayward, Mark D. The influence of occupational characteristics on men's early retirement. *Social Forces* 64, no. 4 (June 1986): 1032–45.

Henkens, K. Retirement intentions and spousal support: A multifactor approach. *Journal of Gerontology: Social Sciences* 54B (1999): S63–S74.

Henretta, John C., and Angela M. O'Rand. Joint retirement in the dual worker family. *Social Forces* 62, no. 2 (December 1983): 504–20.

Henretta, John C., Angela M. O'Rand, and Christopher G. Chan. Joint role investments and synchronization of retirement: A sequential approach to couples retirement timing. *Social Forces* 71 (1993): 981–1000.

Herzog, A. Regula, James S. House, and James M. Morgan. Relation of work and retirement to health and well-being in older age. *Psychology and Aging* 6, no. 2 (June 1991): 202–11.

Higginbottom, Susan F., Julian Barling, and E. Kevin Kelloway. Linking retirement experiences and marital satisfaction: A mediational model. *Psychology and Aging* 8, no. 4 (December 1993): 508–16.

Hill, E. A., and L. T. Dorfman. Reaction of housewives to the retirement of their husbands. *Family Relations* 31 (1982): 195–200.

House, J. S., K. R. Landis, and D. Umberson. Social relationships and health. *Science* 241 (1988): 540–45.

Jahoda, M. *Employment and unemployment*. Cambridge: Cambridge University Press, 1982.

Kahn, R. L., and T. C. Antonucci. Convoys over the life course: Attachment, roles, and social support. In *Life-span development and behavior*, edited by P. B. Baltes and O. G. Brim, 253–86. New York: Academic Press, 1980.

Kim, J. E., and P. Moen. Moving into retirement: Preparations and transitions in late midlife. In *Handbook of midlife development*, edited by M. E. Lachman, 487–527. New York: Wiley, 2001.

Kim, J. E., and P. Moen. Is retirement good or bad for subjective well-being? *Current Directions in Psychological Science* 3 (2001): 83–86.

Kim, S., and Daniel C. Feldman. Working in retirement: The antecedents of bridge employment and its consequences for quality of life in retirement. *Academy of Management Journal* 6 (2000). 1195–210.

Kuball, Elizabeth, ed. *Retirement for dummies*. Hoboken, NJ: Wiley, 2009.

Lang, F. R., N. Riekmann, and M. M. Baltes. Adapting to aging losses: Do resources facilitate strategies of selection, compensation and optimization in everyday functioning? *Journals of Gerontology Series B: Psychological Sciences and Social Sciences* 57 (2002): 501–9.

Lieberman, M. A. Adaptive processes in late life. In *Life-span developmental psychology: Normative life crises*, edited by N. Datan and L. H. Ginzberg, 135–59. New York: Academic Press, 1975.

Löckenhoff, Corinna E., Antonio Terracciano, and Paul T. Costa Jr. Five-factor model personality traits and the retirement transition: Longitudinal and cross-sectional associations. *Psychology and Aging* 24, no. 3 (September 2009): 722–28.

Moen, Phyllis. A life course perspective on retirement, gender, and well-being. *Journal of Occupational Health Psychology* 1, no. 2 (April 1996): 131–44.

Moen, P., D. Dempster-McClain, and R. W. Williams Jr. Successful aging: A life course perspective on women's multiple roles and health. *American Journal of Sociology* 97 (1992): 1612–38.

Moen, P., J. E. Kim, and H. Hofmeister. The interaction between marital relationships and retirement. *Social Psychology Quarterly* 64 (2001): 55–71.

Mutran, E. J., D. C. Reitzes, and M. E. Fernandez. Factors that influence attitudes toward retirement. *Research on Aging* 19 (1997): 251–73.

Myers, Scott M., and Alan Booth. Men's retirement and marital quality. *Journal of Family Issues* 17, no. 3 (May 1996): 336–57.

Nimrod, Galit. Retirees' leisure: Activities, benefits, and their contribution to life satisfaction. *Leisure Studies* 26, no. 1 (January 2007): 65–80.

Nimrod, Galit, Megan C. Janke, and Douglas A. Kleiber. Expanding, reducing, concentrating and diffusing: Activity patterns of recent retirees in the United States. *Leisure Sciences* 31 (2009): 37–52.

Oishi, Shigehiro, Erin Whitchurch, Felicity F. Miao, Jaime Kurtz, and Jina Park. "Would I be happier if I moved?" Retirement status and cultural variations in the anticipated and actual levels of happiness. *Journal of Positive Psychology* 4, no. 6 (November 2009): 437–46.

Payne, E. Christopher, Steven B. Robbins, and Linda Dougherty. Goal directedness and older-adult adjustment. *Journal of Counseling Psychology* 38, no. 3 (July 1991): 302–8.

Perry, G. The need for retirement planning and counseling. *Canadian Counsellor* 14 (1980): 97–98.

Pinquart, Martin, and Ines Schindler. Changes of life satisfaction in the transition to retirement: A latent-class approach. *Psychology and Aging* 22, no. 3 (September 2007): 442–55.

Quick, Heather E., and Phyllis Moen. Gender, employment and retirement quality: A life course approach to the differential experiences of men and women. *Journal of Occupational Health Psychology* 3, no. 1 (January 1998): 44–64.

Reitzes, Donald C., and Elizabeth J. Mutran. Lingering identities in retirement. *Sociological Quarterly* 2 (2006): 333–59.

Reitzes, Donald C., and Elizabeth J. Mutran. Preretirement influences on postretirement self-esteem. *Journals of Gerontology Series B: Psychological Sciences and Social Sciences* 51B, no. 5 (1996): S242–S249.

Reitzes, Donald C., and Elizabeth J. Mutran. The transition to retirement: Stages and factors that influence retirement adjustment. *International Journal of Aging and Human Development* 59, no. 1 (2004): 63–84.

Reitzes, Donald C., Elizabeth J. Mutran, and Maria E. Fernandez. The decision to retire: A career perspective. *Social Science Quarterly* 3 (1998): 607–19.

Richardson, V., and K. M. Kilty. Adjustment to retirement: Continuity vs. discontinuity. *International Journal of Aging and Human Development* 33 (1991): 151–69.

Robbins, Steven B., Richard M. Lee, and Thomas T. H. Wan. Goal continuity as a mediator of early retirement adjustment: Testing a multidimensional model. *Journal of Counseling Psychology* 41, no. 1 (January 1994):18–26.

Robbins, Steven B., E. Christopher Payne, and Judy M. Chartrand. Goal instability and later life adjustment. *Psychology and Aging* 5, no. 3 (September 1990): 447–50.

Ross, Catherine E., and Patricia Drentea. Consequences of retirement activities for distress and the sense of personal control. *Journal of Health and Social Behavior* 39, no. 4 (December 1998): 317–34.

Russell, R. V. The importance of recreation satisfaction and activity participation to the life satisfaction of age-segregated retirees. *Journal of Leisure Research* 19 (1987): 273–83.

Schlossberg, N. K. A model for analyzing human adaptation to transition. *Counseling Psychologist* 9 (1981): 2–36.

Schlossberg, Nancy K. *Revitalizing retirement: Reshaping your identity, relationships, and purpose.* Washington, DC: American Psychological Association, 2009.

Seccombe, K., and G. R. Lee. Gender differences in retirement satisfaction and its antecedents. *Research on Aging* 8 (1986): 426–40.

Shultz, K. S. Bridge employment: Work after retirement. In *Retirement: Reasons, processes, and results*, edited by G. A. Adams and T. A. Beehr, 215–41. New York: Springer, 2003.

Smith, Deborah B., and Phyllis Moen. Retirement satisfaction for retirees and their spouses: Do gender and the retirement decision-making process matter? *Journal of Family Issues* 25, no. 2 (March 2004): 262–85.

Smith, Deborah B., and Phyllis Moen. Spousal influence on retirement: His, her, and their perceptions. *Journal of Marriage and Family* 60, no. 3 (August 1998): 734–44.

Stephan, Yannick. Openness to experience and active adults' life satisfaction: A trait and facet level analysis. *Personality and Individual Differences* 47, no. 6 (October 2009): 637–41.

Streib, Gordon F. Morale of the retired. *Social Problems* 3, no. 4 (April 1956): 270–76.

Streib, Gordon F., and Clement J. Schneider. *Retirement in American society.* Ithaca, NY: Cornell University Press, 1971.

Szinovacz, Maximiliane. Couples' employment/retirement patterns and perceptions of marital quality. *Research on Aging* 18, no. 2 (June 1996): 243–68.

Szinovacz, Maximiliane E. Female retirement: Effects on spousal roles and marital adjustment. *Journal of Family Issues* 1, no. 3 (September 1980): 423–40.

Szinovacz, Maximillane E., and Stanley DeViney. Marital characteristics and retirement decisions. *Research on Aging* 22, no. 5 (September 2000): 470–98.

Szinovacz, Maximiliane E., Stanley DeViney, and Adam Davey. Influences of family obligations and relationships on retirement: Variations by gender, race, and marital status. *Journals of Gerontology Series B: Psychological Sciences and Social Sciences* 56B, no. 1 (January 2001): S20–S27.

Szinovacz, M., and P. Harpster. Employment status, gender roles and marital dependence in later life. *Journal of Marriage and Family* 55 (1993): 927–40.

Szinovacz, M., and A. M. Schaffer. Effects of retirement on marital conflict tactics. *Journal of Family Issues* 21 (2000): 367–89.

Thoits, P. A. Identity structure and psychological well-being: Gender and marital status comparisons. *Social Psychology Quarterly* 55 (1992): 236–56.

von Bonsdorff, Monika E., Kenneth S. Shultz, Esko Leskinen, and Judith Tansky. The choice between retirement and bridge employment: A continuity theory and life course perspective. *International Journal of Aging and Human Development* 69, no. 2 (2009): 79–100.

Wang, Mo. Profiling retirees in the retirement transition and adjustment process: Examining the longitudinal change patterns of retirees' psychological well-being. *Journal of Applied Psychology* 92, no. 2 (March 2007): 455–74.

Wang, Mo, Yujie Zhan, Songqi Liu, and Kenneth S. Shultz. Antecedents of bridge employment: A longitudinal investigation. *Journal of Applied Psychology* 7 (2008): 818–30.

Weiss, Robert S. The experience of retirement. *Contemporary Sociology* 35, no. 4 (July 2006): 382–83

Williamson, R. C., A. D. Rinehart, and T. O. Blank. *Early retirement: Promises and pitfalls.* New York: Insight Books Plenum, 1992.

Zhan, Yujie, Mo Wang, Songqi Liu, and Kenneth S. Shultz. Bridge employment and retirees' health: A longitudinal investigation. *Journal of Occupational Health Psychology* 14, no. 4 (October 2009): 374–89.

Index

action steps, 201–6
activities, self-esteem, 134
activities, in retirement: altruistic,
139–40; blue-collar retirees, 130;
commitment to, 138; day-to-day, 66,
183, 185; different types of, 138, 194;
early retirement, 116; experimenting,
with new, 100–103, 138, 141, 194,
200–201; grandchildren, 162, 176;
high grade, 134, 139–40, 188; home-
based, 134–36, 138, 185, 205; leisure,
69, 90, 122, 137–38; low grade, 134,
136–38; marriage and, 115–16, 119,
161, 205; meaningful, 5, 22, 80–81,
134; nonsocial, 140; non–work-
related, 179; passions pursued in, 138;
personal, 56, 78, 140–41, 160, 169,
205; for psychological issues, 133–34,
136; for retirement adjustment,
98, 116, 135–36, 138; selfish, 206;
social, 52, 74–75, 85, 111, 131, 135,
139–40, 150; solo activities, 139;
spouses sharing, 157, 205; subjective
well-being and, 134, 140–41, 195,
201; variety of, 132, 135, 140, 201;
white-collar retirees, 129–30
activity theory, 133–34
adjustment process, 4, 13, 25, 86;
activities for, 98, 116, 135–36, 138;

"big five" elements of, 197–201;
blue-collar retirees, 127–32, 137;
bridge employment for, 99, 103–4,
178–79, 203; depression in, 28–29;
early retirement, 110, 113, 117–18;
emotional support, 167, 169,
183; financial security and, 200;
improving, 114, 196; introverts, 184;
involuntary retirement, 47, 202;
levels of, 8, 196; to lifestyle, 9, 11,
21–22, 24, 30, 39, 128; marriage
and, 121–24, 155, 167; men and,
121–24; mental strategies for, 188;
nonworking, 179; personality
characteristics and, 181–92; problems,
26, 36–37, 47, 178; psychological
issues, 23, 143; self-definition and,
172–73, 176–80, 204; stages of,
3, 27–29; structure and direction
element, 197–98; summary of,
201–3; theoretical framework for,
29–35, 48; white-collar retirees, 125–
26, 129–32; women and, 121–24;
worker role and, 176
age issues, 8, 26, 37, 192, 204
alienation, 173
alternative lifestyle, 65
altruistic activities, 139–40
anonymous quotes, 21, 43

223

About the Authors

Rob Pascale was born and raised in New York City and currently resides in Garden City, New York. Dr. Pascale began his career as a market researcher, a field that utilizes polling techniques and quantitative research methodologies to assess consumer interests and needs. In 1982, having established his credentials in the field, Dr. Pascale founded Marketing Analysts, Inc. (MAi), a quantitative market research company that over the years has grown into a highly respected international research firm, building a reputation for sophisticated and creative approaches to research and for their insightful analysis of consumer attitudes and behaviors.

Dr. Pascale retired from full-time responsibilities at MAi in 2005 at the age of 51. Throughout his 25-year tenure as president of MAi, Dr. Pascale was directly involved in over 5,000 research studies for more than 50 of the largest corporations in the world and has polled well over 2 million consumers. While he continues to maintain a relationship with MAi, Dr. Pascale has mostly departed the business arena and ventured back into research psychology, prompted in part by a deep-seated attachment to the field but also as a result of having retired at a relatively young age. During his five-year hiatus from MAi, Dr. Pascale became very familiar with the difficulties that can arise in making the transition to retirement. His firsthand experiences, combined with his expertise as researcher and his intent to provide help to fellow retirees, has led him to bring this topic into the public domain.

To contact Rob, email him at robpas63@gmail.com, or contact him through the website retireesource.com.

Lou Primavera, also a native New Yorker, is a New York State licensed psychologist trained in behavior and rational emotive behavior therapies, maintaining a private practice for more than 25 years specializing in marriage counseling.

Dr. Primavera is currently the dean of the School of Health Sciences at Touro College. Previously, he was the dean of the Derner Institute of Advanced Psychological Studies at Adelphi University, held the department chair and served as associate dean of the Graduate School of Arts and Sciences at St. John's University, and has held full-time faculty positions at Hofstra University, St. Francis College, and Molloy College.

Dr. Primavera has published extensively in the social sciences, and his work has appeared in a number of prestigious professional journals in psychology. He was a consultant to the Department of Psychiatry and Behavioral Sciences at Memorial Sloan Kettering Cancer Center and has held a number of other consulting positions in medicine, business, and education. He has been a member of a number of professional organizations and has served as president of the Academic Division of the New York State Psychological Association and the New York City Metro Chapter of the American Statistical Association. Dr. Primavera is a fellow of the Division of General Psychology of the American Psychological Association, a fellow of the American Educational Research Association, and a fellow of the Eastern Psychological Association.

Rip Roach was born and raised in Hanover, New Hampshire, and currently resides in Charlotte, North Carolina. After graduating from Yale, he began his career in market research in 1979, rapidly rising through the ranks at independent research companies and manufacturers as he demonstrated his technical expertise as a researcher and analyst. He was recruited by MAi in 1989 and became a partner in 1990. With the retirement of Dr. Pascale, Roach became a senior partner in the firm and along with his other partners has led the company to continued growth and success. He continues in this role today and, having established himself as a highly respected researcher, also serves as the lead technical consultant for the MAi staff and its clients. He hopes that he, too, will be able to retire someday.

MAi was founded in 1982 and has grown to be one of the most highly respected market research firms in the industry. Its clients include more than 50 of the largest corporations in the world, and its research expertise covers the broad range of consumer and professional products and services. MAi is staffed by highly experienced research professionals and has established itself as a strategic thinking company and a leader in developing new and creative approaches to identify consumer needs. Over the years, MAi has conducted more than 6,000 research studies, interviewing well over 3 million consumers both in the United States and internationally. MAi has offices in North Carolina, South Carolina, New Jersey, New York, San Francisco, and Chicago. For more information on the company, visit their website at http://www.mairesearch.com.